Fundamentalism in America

Fundamentalism in America

Millennialism, Identity and Militant Religion

Philip Melling

FITZROY DEARBORN PUBLISHERS
CHICAGO • LONDON

For Kirsten, Thomas and Hannah

© Philip Melling, 1999

Published in the United Kingdom by
Edinburgh University Press Ltd
22 George Square, Edinburgh

Published in the United States of America by
Fitzroy Dearborn Publishers
919 North Michigan Avenue,
Chicago, Illinois 60611

Typeset in Melior
by Carnegie Publishing, Lancaster,
and printed and bound in Great Britain
by The Cromwell Press, Trowbridge

A Cataloging-in-Publication record
for this book is available from
the Library of Congress

ISBN 1-57958-261-3 Fitzroy Dearborn

Contents

Acknowledgements

I would like to thank the Department of American Studies at the University of Swansea for its support during the writing of this book and the sabbatical I enjoyed during 1996–7. I am grateful to Mike McDonald and Jon Roper for their advice and comment, to Steve McVeigh for the help he gave me with film and video material and to Dave Taylor for the articles and references he provided.

I would like to express my deep gratitude to Jim Boyd at the University of Colorado, Fort Collins, especially for the conversations we had on matters religious and for the encouragement he gave me at a crucial time in my research. Jim is both a kind man and an inspirational scholar. I am also grateful to Jim Staples, an old friend and colleague from Greenwood, Indiana, for the mass of material he sent me over a number of years. Mark Hulsether, at the University of Tennessee, was equally helpful in the texts he made available to me and the resources he provided during my period in Knoxville. Bill Ehrhart, as ever, was generous with his time. As a distinguished writer on the Vietnam war he provided me with much valuable advice during my work on the militia movment.

I am especially indebted to Peter Brooker who guided me through several versions of the manuscript. His faith in my efforts never flagged and his reading of the script was always meticulous. He is a fine editor.

Finally, thanks to Sue and Celia and their patience and support in the typing of this manuscript and for their willingness to bear with me during the rewrites.

Series Editor's Introduction

Contemporary history continues to witness a series of momentous changes, altering what was only recently familiar ideological, political and economic terrain. These changes have prompted a new awareness of subjective, sexual, ethnic, racial, religious and cultural identities and of the ways these are constructed in metropolitan centres, regions and nations at a time when these spheres are themselves undergoing a period of critical transition. Recent theory has simultaneously encouraged a scepticism towards the supposed authenticity of personal or common histories, making identity the site of textualised narrative constructions and reconstructions rather than of transparent record. In addition, new developments in communication and information technology appear to be altering our fundamental perceptions of knowledge, of time and space, of relations between the real and the virtual, and of the local and the global.

The varied discourses of literature and media culture have sought to explore these changes, presenting life as it is negotiated on the borderlines of new hybridised, performative, migrant and marginalised identities, with all the mixed potential and tension these involve. What emerge are new, sometimes contradictory, perceptions of subjectivity or of relations between individuals, social groups, ideologies and nations, as the inner and public life are rewritten in a cultural environment caught up in religious and political conflict and the networks of global consumption, control and communication.

The series *Tendencies: Identities, Texts, Cultures* follows these debates and shows how the formations of identity are being articulated in contemporary literary and cultural texts, often as significantly in their hybridised language and modes as in their manifest content.

Volumes in the series concentrate upon tendencies in contemporary writing and cultural forms, principally in the work of writers, artists and cultural producers over the last two decades. Throughout, its consistent interest lies in the making and unmaking of individual, social and national identities. Each volume draws on relevant theory and critical debate in its discussion *inter alia* of questions of gender and sexuality, race and ethnicity, class, creed and nation in the structuring of contemporary subjectivities.

The kinds of texts selected for study vary from volume to volume, but most often comprise written or visual texts available in English or widely distributed in English translation. Since identities are most often confirmed or redefined within the structures of story and narrative, the series is especially interested in the use of narrative forms, including fiction, autobiography, travel and historical writing, journalism, film and television.

Authors are encouraged to pursue intertextual relations between these forms, to examine the relations between cultural texts and relevant theoretical or political discourse, and to consider cross-generic and intermedia forms where these too bear upon the main concerns of the series.

Peter Brooker
University College, Northampton

Introduction

Ever since the work of Richard Hofstadter religious fundamentalism has been seen as the product of a paranoid style, the deadly enemy of rational debate and intellectual enquiry. As we reach the end of the twentieth century liberal critics in the humanities and social sciences devote an increasing amount of attention to Hofstadter's work and the threat that fundamentalism poses: its political status as a xenophobic faith, its new-found confidence, its catalytic power to release any number of fears and hatreds into the culture at large.

Fundamentalism, these days, is rarely thought of as a metaphysic for dunces, a psychopathology of the American small town and a provincial fascism fit only for the marginal. On the contrary, says Elaine Showalter, fundamentalism has become one of the lead agencies in the psychic propulsion of 'millennial America' from neurosis to psychosis, from Cold War ideology to revivalist religion (Showalter 1997, p. 26). Fundamentalism, write Katherine Dunn and Jim Redden, is for those who believe in the existence of 'a mind-numbingly vast conspiracy theory' (Dunn and Redden 1995, p. 11). As a revivalist movement, it occupies a place of pivotal influence in a post-ideological age. As an hysteria 'that comes out of the American crucible', it prefers the conspirational to the pursuit of 'real villains', the morally sensational to the politically pragmatic (Showalter 1997, p. 26). This link between fundamentalism and virtual truth is a 'phenomenon' that is found elsewhere at the end of the twentieth century. Andrew Gumbel refers to it as 'tabloidisation' – a condition of modernity in which 'tabloid values' and the pursuit of the salacious enters the 'mainstream' at a time of acute national anxiety (Gumbel 1999, p. 17).

In the 1990s the crisis surrounding a pervasive fundamentalism was often contextualised as an argument against the incumbent President (Clinton) and the impact which that argument was having on the nation's culture. The tabloid fears of fundamentalists, says Gumbel, came to be reported by centrist writers in the mainstream press – a point graphically revealed during the dying days of the

Clinton impeachment process when sales of tabloid newspapers, like *The National Enquirer, Hustler* and *The Star*, fell by almost 20 per cent and fundamentalist fantasies lost their appeal. While the paranoid style could still be associated with minority movements and the politics of the anti-establishment, as a source of mass entertainment it became more socially acceptable, 'deeply ingrained in the larger political culture ... [drawing] adherents from every point on the political spectrum' (Kelly 1995, pp. 62, 64).

The crisis of confidence that erupted during the Clinton presidency appeared to indicate an increased willingness in the popular and political culture to rely on conspiracy rather than common sense as a way of explaining the riddle of history. The 'readiness' on the part of the American media, says Martin Walker, 'to believe absolutely anything, takes us back to the archetypal conspiracy of the JFK assassination and the fabled second gunman on the original grassy knoll'. It is this tendency which allowed the media during the Whitewater affair – '*The Washington Post, New York Times, Time, Newsweek, ABC-TV*' – to portray President Clinton as the ruthless head 'of an Arkansas mafia' who would 'not stop at serial murder' to preserve his power (Walker 1995, p. 3). The mainstream press may have taken some of its lead from the populist film-maker Oliver Stone, who declared his hatred of the 'consensual society' and those who wish 'to be loved and approved'. For Stone, 'paranoia in moderation' is a 'healthy' conviction, 'precisely because conspiracy does not sleep' and is always helped by the complacent 'ranting' of the anti-conspiracist lobby in the press (Stone 1998, p. 4).

If those who practise the art of paranoia claim the right to censor the 'consensual', then those who report its prevalence as discourse are overly concerned with its exclusivity. Elaine Showalter describes paranoia as a vital accessory of the age we live in, a dependency that few of us can do without. Paranoia, she claims, is a pre-millennial psychic affliction, an argument that is no less extravagant or whimsical than that made by Oliver Stone when he equates paranoia with 'independent thinking' (4). The concern with paranoia implicates Showalter in a process of ingraining – the same process she complains of in others. If Americans 'lead the world', as she puts it (Showalter 1997, p. 27), in their willingness to deify the conspiratorial, then Showalter's reliance on narratives which require hysterical conclusions – in subjects as diverse as religious fundamentalism, alien abduction or Gulf War Syndrome – is no less extreme. To encase our definitions in a language which limits our understanding of life to the 'conspiratorial' and to places which act as a 'breeding ground for hysterical epidemics' (27), is to compel oneself to adopt an agenda that mimicks the neurosis of the clinically driven.[1]

Much of the terminology used by Showalter to describe the relationship between hysteria and religious mania – in particular, her
references to epidemiology, psychiatric disorder, crowd contagion and
millenarian faith as psychopathological – was introduced into the
social sciences by Michael Barkun in the 1970s. Barkun's discussion
of ecstatic behaviour as a pseudo-religious condition in *Disaster and
the Millennium* (1974) anticipates many of the same conclusions that
Elaine Showalter comes to in *Hystories* (1997). For Barkun, new
hysteria has old roots and his claim that 'all millenarian movements
are instances of the paranoid style' (Barkun 1974, p. 152) is a phrase
that Showalter could easily have written, given her interest in Puritan
revivalism and the religious epidemics of the seventeenth century
and the late twentieth century.

Barkun's influence on Showalter is explicit, though it is never
acknowledged in *Hystories*. As pre-millennial tension takes hold,
Showalter points her resolute finger at those with 'borderline
personality disorders' such as 'manic depression', 'anxiety-neurosis'
and 'dissociate identity disorder' (17). As a traumatising faith, religious
fundamentalism is, she says, one of the most 'virulent hysterias' (5)
of the 1990s, a 'contagious' form of revivalism that thrives on '*fin de
siècle*' anxiety (4) and the 'paranoias that accompany apocalyptic
moments' (5). The pursuit of Clinton was a perfect commentary on
the American 'witchhunt' at its most deranged, an idea supported by
Arthur Miller who emphasised 'the sexual elements' underlying the
whole impeachment process and the envy that Clinton's sexuality
unleashed on 'the mullahs of the religious right' (Miller 1998, p. 20). It
is a short step from the pursuit of witches to the pursuit of Jews, and
Monica Lewinsky's sexuality, so it was argued, brought to a head an
anti-Semitism that bedeviled fundamentalism throughout its history.

The association between the 'witchcraft hysteria' of Salem at the end
of the seventeenth century and the attempt to impeach Bill Clinton at
the end of the twentieth is a neat way of framing American history
through Freudian symmetries. It is also heavily contrived. To reduce
fundamentalism to a virulent hysteria is to brutalise the history of the
dispensationalist church in America and to misread the punishment
of those who offend against its doctrines.

There is yet another problem. Once we align fundamentalism
alongside Puritanism our view of anti-Semitism changes, as does the
assumption that anti-Semitism is the natural consequence of a prurient
sexuality at the heart of America's conservative culture. In the millennial church, racial encounter provides an opportunity for righteous
evangelism, not xenophobia. The Jew is a figure of embrace, a member
of a race with a unique role in the salvation of Christianity and
the creation of a new heaven and earth. For the Christian faithful,

the promised utopia is contingent upon the rescue of the Jew and without him there is no righteous future which comes to those who pursue His mission. In the dispensational churches of the Bible Belt, followers of Christ see their salvation as wholly dependent upon the unbelievers in a living Israel accepting Jesus Christ as their Lord and Messiah. The Jews, writes Charles B. Strozier, are 'instruments of fate in the minds of fundamentalists'. Without their agreement to salvation in Christ (Ezekiel 20: 40–4), Christians are unable to 'prepare for the arrival of Jesus' (Strozier 1994, p. 203). As with most apocalyptic faiths in the United States, learned optimism bases its ideas on biblical precedent: 'All Israel shall be saved' (Romans 11: 26).

In the case of President Clinton, Israel had not been saved. In the writing of the fundamentalist minister Pat Robertson, she had been left to her own devices: material excess, on the one hand, and sexual depravity (Monica Lewinsky) on the other. For Robertson, Clinton had forfeited his right to salvation not because he had indulged in sex – something for which he publicly repented – but because, as a southern Methodist, he had abandoned his obligation to evangelise the Jew – and those celebrities who claimed to be Jewish – with whom he had associated throughout his career. Clinton had thrown away a wonderful opportunity to minister to the unconverted. He had abandoned the ecstatic faith of the Bible Belt, refusing to hasten that chain of events which will lead to the fulfilment of biblical prophecy and bring about the salvation of the righteous.

The idea of converting the Jew is considered by all Protestant fundamentalists as an essential prelude to the advent of the millennium. The belief originates in the seventeenth-century millennialist church. There, it was part of a cluster of visionary ideas, some of which were taken to excess by those seeking a new spiritual experience in the colonies.

In 1633, soon after his arrival in the New England, Thomas Shepard showed his concern for a fanaticism spreading from England that glorified the apocalypse and the immediate salvation of a remnant of Jews. Shepard warned his congregation about the danger of a millennialism that threatened to wreak havoc on the covenanted churches of New England almost before their experiment in the wilderness had got off the ground. Although he was committed to the conversion of the Jews, Shepard was scared of extreme self-abandon and an enthusiasm that was liable to expropriation by extremist elements in the church. Shepard worked hard 'to dampen whatever apocalyptic expectation the people had carried with them to New England'. Compared with revolutionary Puritanism, he noted poignantly, the colonies were not yet 'in the latter part of those last days' (Delbanco 1989, p. 89).

What to do with a love affair with the last days is one of those challenges that a born-again church and an exceptionalist nation have struggled to come to terms with throughout their history. A philosophy of endings is the persistent condition of a chosen people; it refuses to go away, and it remains as much a problem for us in our century as it was for Thomas Shepard in his. The challenge today exists for the church as well as for those new religious movements which operate outside it.

In the late twentieth century the appeal of eschatology shows little sign of diminishing. Millennialist ideas regenerate themselves in new environments, while new religious movements embrace the apocalypse, if not the formal doctrine of the pre-millennial. In the last chapter of this study, I explain the transition from fundamentalist to New Age thinking as a natural development for a society that is experiencing a religious awakening in the aftermath of a period of ideological containment. I suggest that the process of religious interaction can only work, however, if we reconsider the importance of the paranoid – and the fear of syncretism – as an obligatory condition for millennialist believers. The apocalypse is not, I suggest, an end in itself and the use of 'historical pessimism', as Stephen D. O'Leary correctly argues, must be 'counterbalanced by a cosmic optimism' in order 'to satisfy audience demands' (O'Leary 1994, pp. 168, 164).

In religious revivalism the rhetoric of calamity is an interim expression in a much larger narrative of spiritual salvation. Fundamentalists might well be fixated by disaster, as I claim in Chapter 3, but they also offer us a route to the future, a meaning for life – through miraculous intervention – that lies beyond the coming catastrophe.

Virulent hysteria is not what makes religion work in a revivalist age. It is the expectation of transformation and personal change. In a period such as ours, when expressions of Rapture grip the imagination and find their way into New Age thinking, so does a belief in the spiritual journey and the thrilling retreat to a sacred location.

Fundamentalists, therefore, look outside themselves more than is recognised. So do those in the New Age church who appropriate the tenets of fundamentalism and redirect them into new religious contexts. For New Age Protestants like the Branch Davidians, the People's Temple and the Heaven's Gate cult in San Diego, terminal departure has proved attractive as a way of solving earthly dilemmas. Those who are willing to make that leap into the final frontier of eternal space have taken the fantastic hermeneutic of millennialism to a much higher level. Enthralled by a vision of the endtimes they have grasped the idea of planetary evacuation as a way of guaranteeing a rapturous future.

Notes

1. In the immediate aftermath of the Cold War the writing of history, in numerous contexts, became hysterical. Robert Block and Ryszard Kapuscinski make this complaint in their analysis of the Rwandan civil war, coverage of which they say, regularly avoids all mention of a postcolonial legacy.

In the early days of the Rwandan civil war, writes Robert Block, many observers 'tended to discuss what ... happened in Rwanda as African mayhem'. The Hutu–Tutsi conflict was regularly described as 'little more than a savage tribal freak show' even though the violence, whilst savage, 'was not exclusively tribal'. The one million people, mostly Tutsis, who 'were hacked to death, burned alive, or shot by their friends and neighbours' were 'part of a sinister political operation that had been intricately planned for years' (Block 1994, p. 3). Ryszard Kapuscinski agrees. 'It's really nothing new', says Kapuscinksi: 'But the press is reporting as if something incredible happened: "Suddenly, people start killing" ... Subconsciously, it's to show how these irrational stupid Africans start killing without any reason. You have to be careful with those Africans because you never know when they're going to kill you. It's political class conflict – they report it as ethnic conflict. It's outrageous. Really scandalous, because it's complete arrogance, and complete ignorance. It's a power struggle. It's a war for power' (Parker 1994, p. 7).

The same refusal to explore 'the psychological hinterland of those involved' in political conflict was a characteristic of war-reporting in the Balkans, writes Michael Ignatieff. In Robert Kaplan's *Balkan Ghosts*, the Balkans are described, says Ignatieff, as a dark zone haunted by the ghosts of violence and fanaticism where 'poverty and ethnic rivalry' reduce men 'to hate'. For Kaplan, 'politics has been reduced to a level of near anarchy', a doom-laden, ethnic belief that transforms the region into 'the product of some uniquely Balkan viciousness'. The more likely truth, says Ignatieff, is that 'all of the delusions that have turned neighbours into enemies have been imports of Western European origin'. In other words, 'the misery of the Balkan people does not derive from their home-grown irrationality but from the pathetic longing to be good Europeans' and to 'import the West's most murderous ideological fashions' in the form of Serbian or Croatian nationalism. Historians, like Kaplan, deluded themselves in dismissing 'the Balkans as a subrational zone of intractable fanaticism' and, in their insistence 'that local ethnic hatreds were so rooted that their explosion into violence in 1991 was inevitable' (Ignatieff 1993, pp. 3–4).

From Cromwell to the Cordilleras: America's Search for the Jew

I

In the 1990s fundamentalisms are both global in number and provincial in character. In the work of The Fundamentalism Project at the University of Chicago they are defined as cultural movements which safeguard the interests of a beleaguered race while seeking to protect the sovereign traditions and sacred character of the nation-state. Fundamentalisms enhance and unite civilisations, writes Samuel P. Huntington; they dispel cultural tensions and reaffirm the national character by retrieving a historical vision of the self. At a time of ideological uncertainty, they are said to oppose the illusion of universality – the notorious claim that what we have entered is a new world order – and those 'processes of economic modernisation' that separate 'people from longstanding local identities'. As a religious persuasion, fundamentalisms, writes Huntington, are based upon 'a reaffirmation of indigenous values' that are searched out during periods of anxiety and stress (Huntington 1993, p. 26). For this reason they are usually seen as one of the principal instruments of cultural definition at a time of cultural diffusion and loss.

In the United States such 'anxieties', suggests Charles B. Strozier, 'were quite real in the latter part of the nineteenth century ... and were grounded in the pervasive dread of a transforming modernism'. As a result of socio-economic change, patterns of regional, neighbourhood and family 'continuity' had begun to break down under the transforming impact of economic recession, mass immigration and technological change (Strozier 1994, p. 158). Protestant fundamentalism, agrees Walter Dean Burnham, reminds us of those 'conservative revitalisation movements' that appear 'at times of stress and readjustment when issues of profound economic importance are transubstantiated into symbolic or religious issues'. Anti-modernist reactions occurred in 1893–4 when William Jennings Bryan united the victims of economic collapse in the Protestant heartland and again in 1925 – a period of rapid secularism and urbanisation – when Bryan acted as the defender of creationism at the Scopes Monkey Trial (Burnham 1988, p. 3). In the United States the contest between the small town and the city was effectively over by the end of the nineteenth century, but periodically it is restaged and refought at moments of ideological or economic crisis in the struggle to preserve the sovereignty and integrity of the local community.

All fundamentalisms claim to provide a stable, internal architecture at a time when the nation-state has weakened 'as a source of identity', says Huntington, and orthodox political leaders lack the ability adequately to define the boundaries of moral and spiritual conduct in ways that allow the nation to reaffirm itself.[1] In the 1990s, he writes, religion has filled the 'gap' that 'ideological differences' have left in the structuring of international politics and it provides opportunities for cultural aspirations, which lie at 'the heart' of a nation's 'culture', to supersede the old totalitarian beliefs (Huntington 1993, pp. 26, 28). Religion, therefore, is a sensitive register of change and of the tremors that affect civilisations post-Cold War. These tremors are the product of cultural clashes which, says Huntington, have erupted along a shelf or 'fault line' that has historically divided one civilisation from another. As the history of nation-states, he argues, is based on cultural rifts or schisms, so is the history of civilisations. In the clash between civilisations religion (and fundamentalist religion, in particular) plays a crucial role in safeguarding the nation's spiritual heritage and the core beliefs of the civilisation to which the nation belongs. In all civilisations agreement on core, cultural essentials is reached through the activities of religious communities, says Huntington, a point he illustrates by referring to the chief Iranian religious leader of the 1970s and 1980s, Ayatollah Ali Khomeni, who called for a holy war against the West and who still enjoys the overwhelming support of the Iranian people (35).

The point was again demonstrated in Bosnia, says Huntington. Bosnia was 'everyone's Spain', where the new fault line wars between civilisations were visibly and definitively launched. Bosnia was not a conflict of political systems or ideology but of civilisations and religions, a conflict between Western Christians, Orthodox Christians and Muslims, in which the principal powers of Orthodoxy, Islam and the West were deeply suspicious of each other. 'The wars among the religious communities of the Balkans', says Huntington, 'may subside', but as far as the late twentieth century is concerned, they will prove, like Spain, to be a 'prelude' to something much more endemic – 'one more bloody episode in an ongoing clash of civilisations' (quoted in McNeill 1997, p. 18). This conflict, he believes, remains 'deeply rooted' in contemporary culture. The collision between Hindu and Muslim in the subcontinent of Asia 'manifests itself ... not only in the rivalry between Pakistan and India but also in intensifying religious strife within India between increasingly militant Hindu groups and India's substantial Muslim minority' (Huntington 1993, pp. 33–4). In Bombay militant Hindus use McCarthyite tactics to persecute the city's two million Muslims, while in Pakistan Islamic fundamentalists indulge their bigotries by victimising the Christian minority with witchhunts and religious discrimination. In Turkey, the Kurds are targeted; in Palestine it is Zionists; in Afghanistan the Mojahedin (and their American backers) are western infidels in the eyes of the Taliban; while in Algeria, women who wear western dress risk having their throats slashed and their genitalia mutilated.

In societies which are uncertain about their future, agrees Eric Hobsbawm, 'the easiest thing is always to blame strangers' (Hobsbawn 1993, p. 62). In Algeria and Egypt Islamic fundamentalists talk of an assault culture, 'a Caliphate', with which to resist western tourists and migrant workers, as well as the depredations of the mass market which accompany those tourists into sacred places such as Luxor (Fisk 1995, p. 107). In Algeria the 'second war of liberation' currently being fought by the Islamic Salvation Front is a 'cultural' struggle against a government that is seen as a projection of western secularism (Hirst 1994, p. 19). Tourist terrorism and the murder of foreign workers in Algeria and Egypt is little more than a symbolic attempt to target strangers and the strangeness of imported products and the secular alliances they breed. The importance of cultural struggle resonates in the campaign against a western culture of permissiveness in India and the attempt by Hindu fundamentalists in Bombay to clamp down on pornographic literature and the 'vulgar television advertising' of liquor and tampons (Bhatia 1995, p. 16).

The assumption that cultural struggle is synonymous with religious and racial militancy has a popular intellectual currency. The emergence of new political and religious fundamentalisms in the United States in the 1920s, says Loren Baritz, speaks directly to the threatened decline of the Anglo Saxon and Aryan race, to which Oswald Spengler referred his readers in *The Decline of the West* (the English translation of which appeared in 1926). In the 1920s, it is argued, America's small-town communities were faced with rapid immigration, modernist religious teaching, the enhanced political and cultural influence of the city and a liberal media which gave encouragement to the new moral codes – the acids of modernity, as Walter Lippman called them – that were eating into and transforming the entire society. In F. Scott

Fitzgerald's *The Great Gatsby* (1925) Tom Buchanan declares that
'"civilisation is going to pieces"' and talks about people '"sneering
at family life and family institutions"'. Buchanan fears that white,
middle-class America is under threat from an alien race overwhelming
America in its cities and ports. 'Flushed with his impassioned gib-
berish, he saw himself standing alone on the last barrier of civilisation',
writes Nick Carraway, a phrase which appears to capture much of
the rhetorical posturing and theatricality of the American Right in
the 1990s (Fitzgerald 1953, p. 13).

It is highly tempting to use Buchanan's complaint about civilisation
as a central metaphor for the cultural debate that is taking place in
the 1990s among the nation's fundamentalist ministers. But therein
lies a huge problem. The idea of a resonance between those who are
fearful of the impact of race and those who enunciate fundamentalist
doctrine has little long-term relevance. Religious fundamentalism
has no desire to impose an exclusion zone on alien races, nor is it
fearful of cultural contamination from the nation's cities and ports
(what Huntington calls, the 'immigration civilizations' that promote
'animosities') (Huntington 1993, p. 26).

Tom Buchanan's nightmare of a degenerate civilisation at the
nation's gates has never been feared to the same extent as theological
or 'cognitive contamination' (Hunter 1987, p. 46). Secular humanism,
liberal intellectualism and socialist atheism represent a far greater
threat to the Protestant church than racial immigration from countries
outside the western alliance. Notwithstanding Huntington's thesis,
cultural conflicts between civilisations do not provide, and have
never provided, an exact or accurate measurement of fundamentalist
attitudes in the United States. And they have not provoked anything
like the same degree of conflict as those who profess intellectual
atheism and are tainted by the philosophies of modernism. Non-
western and non-Christian races represent a crucial challenge to the
one, true church. This point is illustrated by Jerry Falwell who, as
leader of the Moral Majority movement, has often said that he is
proud to have been attacked by the Ku Klux Klan as 'an enemy of
the white race', for actively encouraging black membership of the
Thomas Road Church in Lynchburg, Virginia (Cox 1987, p. 292). In
Robert Duvalle's film *The Apostle* (1997), an evangelical preacher is
attacked physically for ministering to a black congregation and for
establishing a southern, revivalist church in a racist community.

The scriptural basis of fundamentalist theology is buttressed by a
programme of rigorous absolutes on matters theological, not racial.
Fundamentalism derives its name from 'The Fundamentals', twelve
paperback books issued between 1910 and 1915, edited by A. C. Dixon,
which received enormous circulation in the United States. Written

by conservative American and British writers, these books constituted a frontal assault upon religious modernism: the doctrines of religious liberalism that asserted an almost perfect congruence between God's will and the inevitable progress of civilisation in the United States. Fundamentalists saw liberalism as a false religion to which the Protestant churches of America had surrendered their allegiance. In his seminal work *Christianity and Liberalism* (1923), J. Gresham Machen argued that religious liberalism was not Christianity but a new religion that had replaced God with faith in humanity and historical progress. Machen insisted on six fundamental tenets of belief: the inerrancy of Scripture (the Bible contained no factual or descriptive mistakes); the virgin birth of Jesus (the Spirit of God conceived Jesus in Mary without human intervention); the substitutionary atonement of Jesus Christ (on the cross he bore the just punishment for the sins of the world); his bodily resurrection; the authenticity of the biblical miracles; and pre-millennialism. For Machen, the last condition was, arguably, the most important, and it remains so today.

Pre-millennialism focuses on the importance of Armageddon and the role of the Jews in the Second Coming of Christ. It stresses the obligatory salvation of the Jews and their return to Israel as a precondition for the establishment of the Kingdom of God on the Davidic throne of Jerusalem. These events, foretold by the prophets Daniel and Ezekiel and the last book of the Christian Scriptures, Revelation, create a rigorous framework within which all fundamentalists can understand past and future history, not as a purposeless record, but as a statement of divine will and a preparation for His eventual triumph over the forces of the Antichrist in the coming conflict known as the Tribulation.

This view of history came to be known as dispensationalism and its origins are found in the work of the early nineteenth-century theologian J. N. Darby. In Darby's theology, God has divided His activity in the world into seven dispensations, each with differing rules for obtaining salvation. Darby defined the age of Christian salvation as coinciding with the Rapture and the disappearance of the righteous into heaven and the return of the Jews to Israel. Darby placed the Jews, says Paul Boyer, 'at the heart of his dispensational system' because, as John Walvoord observed in 1989, 'God's promises to the Jews remain unalterable'. Although the Jews have rejected Christ at the coming of the Rapture, the prophetic clock has been set in motion. The Jews will return 'to center stage', establishing a nation in Palestine 'where, after terrible persecution, the surviving remnant [will] hail Christ as Messiah' (Boyer 1992, pp. 202, 183).

In *The Late Great Planet Earth* (1970), the first treatment of dispensational theology to become an international best-seller, Hal Lindsey ties the fate of humanity, as imagined by the prophets of Israel, to God's prophetic scheme for the Jews. In this scheme, says Lindsey, the re-establishment of the state of Israel is a prelude to the Last Days (the age of the seventh dispensation from Christ), when most Jews will be destroyed and the remnant will convert to Christianity. That event is precipitated by Christ's Second Coming and a cataclysmic judgement of the whole world in which Christ will separate the surviving unbelievers from the believers, casting the unbelievers off the earth directly into judgement.

Dispensationalist prophecy privileges the Jews as chosen people and expresses support for Israeli causes. Yet it also accepts that anti-Semitism is foreordained by God and that the future persecution of the Jewish people is inevitable. Hal Lindsey condemns anti-Semitism and attributes much of it to Satan's influence. He also asserts that the tragedies suffered by the Jews in history are foretold in the Bible and that the prophesied persecution of the Jews will increase in the last days. After God disappears and snatches His believers away unto Heaven, says Lindsey, He will then pour out His judgements on the world during a seven-year Tribulation period. During the second half of the Tribulation, the Antichrist will move against the Jews and all those who have accepted Christ as Saviour. At the end of the Tribulation Christ will destroy the Antichrist and his wicked followers and set up His millennial Kingdom, as prophesied in the Old Testament. After the triumph of Armageddon pre-millennialists believe that the Lord Jesus will remove the curse from nature and restore the earth to its original pre-sin condition. The believers who survive the seven-year Tribulation period will be taken as mortals into a global Theocratic Kingdom. Jesus, the Messiah, will then reign on the Davidic throne and honour the promises to the physical descendants of Abraham, Isaac and Jacob in the Abrahamic, Palestinian, Davidic and New Covenants.

For the Protestant fundamentalist, the search to evangelise the Jews is an essential prelude to millennial salvation when 'a remnant of Jews ... [will] be saved at the Second Coming' (Delbanco 1989, pp. 87, 88). The conversion of the Jews, says Charles B. Strozier, has always been central to millennial belief and Christians are obliged to revive the sacred status of the Jews through a process of conversion. Since God will never break His covenant with the people of Israel a special obligation has been imposed on Christianity. Charles B. Strozier agrees. Jews, he argues, 'are instruments of fate in the minds of fundamentalists'. Without their agreement as repentant sinners to salvation in Christ (Ezekiel 20: 40–4) Christians can not effectively 'prepare for the arrival of Jesus' (Strozier 1994, p. 203).

As the guardian of a sacred tradition fundamentalism requires an inclusive role for the Jew in the fulfilment of Christian ministry. Since 'God has sworn an oath that He will cause a national remnant from Israel to believe in the Messiah' so the believer must implement His plan and seek the conversion of the Jew 'today' (Lindsey 1990, pp. 146, 196). For all his waywardness, the Jew is a son of Abraham (whose homeland, Israel, is a sacred nation, a site chosen as the seat of His rule) and a descendant of the ancients whose election by God can never be revoked. The conversion of the Jew to Christianity is integral to the New World mission and spiritually necessary in order to meet the conditions of the Rapture and the salvation of the righteous. Since God has not rejected Israel then His 'predominant and pre-eminent servants' in the Christian church must embrace His plan. Old Testament prophecy and 'God's sovereign preservation of a believing remnant' is 'proof that there will always be a nucleus' from which a nation can rise once again. Those who evangelise to the Jew must scrupulously maintain their role as His 'prophetic teachers' and share, through their ministry, 'God's great undying love for the Jews'. While Israel might 'backslide into terrible sin', the nation's future is guaranteed in Jeremiah by an 'oath concerning Israel's future under the New Covenant' (188, 169–70, 194–5). Fundamentalists see their salvation in the period following the Rapture or First Resurrection as wholly dependent upon the unbelievers, in a living Israel, accepting Jesus Christ as their Lord and Messiah. This spiritual dependency is reflected in a cultural dependency in which those who possess evangelical aspirations are obliged to seek out and convert the Jews, wherever they are scattered, in order to accelerate their involvement with Christ. Fundamentalists regularly follow the route of the Jews to America, ministering to those whose Jewish credentials have been confirmed through patterns of emigration and settlement. 'Fundamentalists revere Jews as chosen by God', says Strozier, since 'they share a common narrative and a common God' and 'a common experience in the apocalyptic'. Not only is Jesus the Jewish Messiah, but the Book of Revelation accepted by Christians as their prophetic story, 'merely updates its Jewish analogue, the Book of Daniel' (Strozier 1994, 197–8).

From the 1960s to the present day, evangelical leaders such as Billy Graham, Oral Roberts, Hal Lindsey and Jerry Falwell have expressed their utmost support for the State of Israel in preparing the way for the Second Coming of Christ and His thousand-year reign on earth. The Six Day War in 1967, in which Israel conquered biblical territories from its neighbours, including the Old City of Jerusalem, had a profound effect on American evangelicals, whose concern for Israel bordered on the rabbinical. For pro-Zionists like Lindsey, it was proof positive that Israel had a role in God's plan for humanity, and that the messianic age was near. As 'a direct sign from God', forever linking His destiny and Israel's, the recapture of Jerusalem on 8 June 1967 appeared to confirm centuries of prophetic speculation that the return of Jesus Christ was imminent (Boyer 1992, p. 188). If some Jews outside Israel had remained spiritually deaf to His ministrations, more had accepted the compelling call of Romans 11: 26: 'All Israel shall be saved.' Since the 1960s, says the leading evangelist Pat Robertson, the process of conversion has gathered impetus and 'observant Jews are flooding into leadership roles throughout America' (Robertson 1993, p. 210).

The salvation of the Jews requires an involvement with a rich cultural tradition which a scattered and wandering remnant of Israel has accumulated. As a displaced people, Jews have had continuous contact with members of different civilisations for thousands of years and have crossed all manner of cultural divides in their search for a new Canaan. Yet, Samuel Huntington relegates the Jews to the status of a footnote in western civilisation and eliminates all reference to Jews as an influential community in modern American religious history. Huntington's thesis implies that the Jew straddles the borders of too many civilisations and has too few rights as an American claimant. Because Jews belong to a civilisation in the Middle East (and are not genetically of western stock), they have retained divided loyalties and are therefore disqualified as orthodox symbols of racial or cultural 'vitality'. The Jew's promiscuous history as a wanderer between civilisations has also made him a product of 'interactions'. These 'interactions between people of different civilisations ... intensify civilisation consciousness', and promote an awareness of difference (Huntington 1993, p. 25). This, 'in turn, invigorates ... animosities stretching ... back deep into history'.

It is these 'differences' that fundamentalist communities apparently respond to, says Huntington, by promoting religious beliefs that unite civilisations around a common core of values. Jews can never embody these values since the legacy they carry is that of a displaced people who refuse to accept cultural assimilation. For Huntington, displacement of the Jew is a distraction which takes attention away from the exceptionalist history of the New World Adam (and a society which discriminates against the allegiances with the old). This displacement, says Huntington, provides a global explanation to the phenomenon of anti-Semitism and a strain of prejudice which often arises where communities are threatened by 'people of different civilisations' (26).

Huntington's arguments echo many of the fears current in American right-wing culture about the threat (of contamination) from unauthorised entry and 'the elemental fear of trespass' (Epstein 1996, p. 31), when borders are left 'wide open' and the country overrun by an unholy alliance of 'cheap goods and desperate immigrants' (Bygrave 1994, p. 22). Throughout the 1990s the protection of America's territorial integrity was a central concern for political conservatives like Pat Buchanan who, like Huntington, believe that 'western peoples have far more in common with each other than they have with Asian, Middle Eastern or African people' (Huntington 1996, p. 3). In the 1996 Presidential election Buchanan, the Republican winner of the New Hampshire Primary (and an avid supporter of the anti-Semitic Croatian leader, Franjo Tudjman), advocated a five-year moratorium on legal immigration, the ending of financial support to illegal aliens, denying to children of illegal immigrants automatic citizenship and the construction of a security fence along a stretch of the US–Mexico border.

In making ethnic identity a central strand of racial understanding, Pat Buchanan and Samuel Huntington play to the gallery of popular superstition. Theirs is a manifesto which documents the case for 'promoting the coherence of the West' by 'preserving western culture' through exclusion zones (intellectual and legislative) and by defining its limits to those who have been subject to non-western and mestizo influences (Huntington 1996, p. 33). For Buchanan, this requires, among other things, 'controlling immigration from non-western societies ... and ensuring the assimilation into western culture of the immigrants who are admitted' (Morgenthau 1993, p. 6). Behind this argument lies the assumption that non-western immigrants (Jews included) are likely to experience the same degree of intolerance and hostility, whichever western country they enter because of their history.

The idea that prejudice is the product of civilisational discontent and that all animosities are (evenly) experienced on the basis of race and culture comes adrift in the United States, where immigrants are frequently judged and rewarded on the basis of socio-economic criteria. Racial prejudice is not a consistent feature of western society. While anti-Semitism, says Arthur Hertzberg, has 'fallen dramatically' in the United States in the 1990s, it has markedly worsened in parts of Europe, even though both continents are currently experiencing a renaissance in religious militancy. According to Hertzberg, 'the fiercest expressions of anti-Semitism' today are found in countries such as Austria and Slovakia (Hertzberg 1993, p. 51). Yet over the same period anti-Semitism has declined in the United States, except among groups who feel themselves socially and economically disadvantaged by immigrants, or Islamic élites who regard the Jews as enemies for having sold them into slavery and infecting their babies with AIDS and ebola (Davis 1994, p. 14).

The distinctive status which Protestant fundamentalists accord the

Jew rarely features in the millennial outlook of other militant religious faiths. Nor is it a characteristic of what Martin Wollacott calls the 'efflorescence' of faith in contemporary Europe (Wollacott 1995b, p. 20). In Daniel Easterman's portrayal of European anti-Semitism in *The Judas Testament* (1994), the Jew is a threat largely because of the historical baggage it is assumed he carries with him as an exile. In Russia, for example, the Jew is a menace to large sections of the Slavic community because of his genealogical heritage and reputation and tendency to graft the contents of one civilisation onto those of another. The Jew carries with him, says Easterman, a threat to the imagination. He is the intruder or cultural trespasser who violates the sanctity of national borders and provokes retaliation by his restlessness and promiscuous settlement. In Russia, physical mobility induces a fear of social mobility and political conspiracy. Anti-Semites believe in a Zhidmasonstvo, a conspiracy of 'Jews and Masons', the purpose of which is economic destabilisation and the erosion of patriotism (Easterman 1995, p. 144). Jews are also blamed for disunity among the Russian republics and are the prime suspects for the political separation and cultural disintegration of the old Soviet Union. Fear of 'dirty tricks' (149) gives way to fear of disease and pollution, and an old association between the exiled Jews of central Europe and their role in the transmission of plague and conspiracy. The Russian Jew Iosif Sharanski tries to identify the root of this neurosis:

Think carefully. The Jews who are arriving first in Europe come to France and Spain and Italy. The Spanish Jews are expelled and become Sephardim. Those who remain in northern France and Germany are Ashkenazim. Many of them, their ancestors have come from such places as Baghdad or Antioch. Years later, they are beginning to move east, and soon they settle in Poland or beyond. Also, others have travelled up the Danube Valley. These are coming from Byzantium. (130)

In *The Judas Testament*, Ur-Fascism and the 'prophecies of a right-wing ascendancy' underpin the new religious 'mood of the times' in Germany and Russia (348). A Europe that has seen its borders 'penetrated by intercontinental diasporas of diverse origins' has also experienced, says Martin Wollacott, 'the alienation, the anonymity, the anger and the attraction to covert and irregular movements that lead to acts of terror'. In contemporary Europe, he writes, 'new beliefs and religions proliferate in the vacuum left by traditional systems'. In these societies a 'culture of violence justifies the use of any means that further the expression of religious or political identity' (Wollacott 1995a, p. 22). In Easterman's *The Judas Testament*, the uncertainty over Europe's borders and the impact of ethnic migrations finds an outlet in a 'derogatory' vocabulary of race. The snatches of conversation overheard by Jack Gould in the bars of Paris about 'Coons', 'dirty Arabs', or 'shitty little Algerians' and 'hustlers', and the 'hatred and ... contempt [that] poured out like a stream of vomit', are the building materials that will 'in time erect scaffolds and the high, blind fences of internment camps' (Easterman 1995, p. 399).

The fear of being racially overrun resurrects ancient fears of epidemic and the desire to scapegoat those who are seen to assist in the spread of virus. As bubonic plague swept through Europe in 1348 popular superstition claimed that it was caused by Jews who had poisoned wells with the aid of lepers. In *The Rabbi of Bacherach*, Heinrich Heine tells of hordes of medieval Christian flagellants, who, 'chanting a mad song to the Virgin Mary', passed through the Rhineland on their way to southern Germany, murdering Jews by the thousand. He points to the source of the centuries-old lie 'that the Jews would steal the consecrated wafer, stabbing it with knives until the blood ran from it, and that they would slay Christian children at their Feast of Passover, in order to use the blood for their nocturnal rite'. Günter Grass suggests that in the persecution, expulsion and destruction of the Jews of Danzig, Heine clearly foresaw the crimes of the twentieth century against the Jews of Europe: in particular, the shift of traditional Christian hatred into organised racism and anti-Semitism and the merciless pedantry that accompanied the genocide of six million Jews (Grass 1978, p. 79). Militant Christianity, adds Arthur Hertzberg, has been the root of this curse. Anti-Semitism, he argues, 'is a kind of cultural malaria, a disease which rises occasionally like a hydra from a long existing atmosphere and ambiance which was created by Christianity' (Hertzberg 1993, p. 53).

If the pogrom against the Jews of Damascus in 1840 convinced Heine that the superstitious madness of the Middle Ages was being re-enacted in his own time, then in Daniel Easterman's *The Judas Testament*, race hatred against the immigrants and refugees of contemporary Europe, together with the rise of a 'fascist phoenix', has its roots in the mythology of the wandering Jews of Africa and Byzantium. The flight of the Jews from Baghdad and Antioch, their expulsion from Spain and the vast pogroms of Eastern Europe in the seventeenth century all created, says Easterman, a legacy of intellectual suspicion and cognitive contamination. The Jews carried with them a precious heritage of 'papyri' and 'scrolls' and 'sacred texts', the mysterious treasures that 'fathers [had] given to their sons, precious relics of the Holy Land from which they [had] been banished' – all of which appeared to confer druidic power (Easterman 1995, pp. 129, 130). In the late twentieth century the suspicion has reappeared. Europe, once again, is a violent place, its 'curse' the 'new combinations of intimacy and aggression' that afflict those communities who feel their lives have been penetrated by immigrants who live in 'close' proximity (Wollacott 1995a, p. 22).

In Europe, 'the politics of immigration will not soon subside', argues Tony Judt, because 'cross-continental and intercontinental migrations are once again a feature of European society, and local fears and prejudices will ensure that they continue to be seen as disruptive and politically exploitable'. The 'advantages of cultural and physical invisibility' which were previously available to Polish and Italian or Portuguese immigrants (whose children, 'distinguished by neither religion, nor language nor color, blended into the social landscape') are no longer there. The newer immigrants from Turkey, Africa, India or the Antilles have 'little tradition of assimilation in Europe', nor has Europe much experience of 'multiculturalism' when it comes to absorbing truly foreign communities. Either the immigrants or their children 'will join the ranks of the "losers" in the competition for Europe's resources' (Judt 1996, p. 7).

In *The Judas Testament*, fear of the Jew – and his intellectual and 'religious freedom' – is aggravated by the collapse of Communism and a generalised fear of Third World immigrants (Easterman 1995, p. 150). In Russia it forms the basis of a resurgent nationalism and an anti-Semitic security apparatus. In western Europe it attracts the attentions of Catholic fundamentalists for whom the new religious freedoms of eastern Europe are the catalyst for fascist aspirations and a resurgent Nazism, plans for which have been in hibernation since the Second World War. The novel traces a web of alliances between right-wing politicians, clandestine fascist organizations and Roman Catholic religious groups: Russian nationalists, Vatican traditionalists, Croatian priests and German industrialists. In the aftermath of the Cold War, anti-Semitism allows these groups to focus their resentment on the Hebrew faith, and the perceived link between Zionists, Freemasons, cultural imperialists and anti-nationalists.[2]

In twentieth-century American literature the migration of the Jew is synonymous not with anti-Semitism but opportunism. In Jewish-American literature economic and cultural mobility is possible in spite of cultural prejudice and the anti-Semitism generated by civilisational clash. The Jews who poured into cities like New York from 1880 to 1920, in order to escape the pogroms of eastern Europe, responded to the lure of upward social mobility by 'restaging', says Thomas J. Ferraro, their own historical 'struggle for entitlement and self-determination'. In so doing, they managed to 'discover in their alien pasts varieties of cultural transformation already tending toward modernity'. These pasts turned out to have 'American precedents and forms of self-determination' that originate 'in one or another premigratory past' (Ferraro 1993, pp. 10–11).

'We were the children and grandchildren of the last great tribal migration of our species on this planet', says the Jewish-American novelist Chaim Potok, 'the east–west wandering of the frightened, and persecuted, the hungry, the poor, the seekers after new wealth and power' (Potok 1981, p. 162). In the work of Jewish novelists from Michael Gold to Saul Bellow and from Henry Roth to Bernard Malamud, the American city is, once again, a focal point of 'wandering', a contested space of immigrant streets, diverse languages and ethnic groups, each of which competes for a foothold. In the Jewish novel the city is the very fountain of multicultural life, a place of congestion and poverty, sweat shops and laundries, stock yards and junk yards, hoodlums and politicians and a unique location in which to discover the broad sweep of twentieth-century experience. It is a place where Jews experience the struggle to break away from the world of the fathers; to construct – not always successfully – the necessary bridge between being a Jew and being an American; a place in which to acquaint oneself, as Saul Bellow's Augie March puts it, with the 'lessons and theories of power'. The journey through this border region is never easy or clear cut; it involves an experience, as Norman Mailer puts it, where 'one's emotions are forever locked in the chains of ambivalence – the expression of an emotion forever releasing its opposite ...' (quoted in Goldman 1975, p. 317).

In Jewish-American fiction the city can be loved or loathed but it cannot be avoided. 'My parents hated all this', said Michael Gold of the slums he grew up in. 'But it was America, one had to accept it' (Gold 1984, p. 30). For Chaim Potok, New York was the stuff of fiction, a place of violent confrontation between the culture of the family, the Semitic past, and the tidal energies of a turbulent city which immersed him as a youth.

The Bronx of the Thirties and Forties was my Mississippi River Valley ... And alone, on a concrete and asphalt Mississippi, I journeyed repeatedly through the crowded sidewalks and paved-over back-yards, the hallways of the brick apartment houses, the hushed public libraries, dark movie houses, candy stores, grocery stores, Chinese laundries, Italian shoe-repair shops, the neighbourhoods of Irish, Italian, Blacks, Poles – journeys impelled by eager curiosity and a hunger to discover my sense of self, my place in the tumult of the world. I was an urban sailor on the raft of my own two feet. (Potok 1981, p. 161)

Potok explains his identity as a Jew in the cultural idioms of the American interior, 'eager' to embrace the metaphors of the heartland by extending his range of reference as a Jew. Potok has a 'hunger' to discover how American civilisation is made and to embrace the 'tumult of the world' without feeling unduly threatened by its different cultural traditions. He and America are in the process of being formed, a process which involves negotiation, trial, adventure. The mutual development of self and nation sustains the youthful Potok who, in his later years, interprets the blending of experimentation with immigrant tradition as a basis for modernism. This dual enterprise reveals the emergence of a generous spirit: the exuberance of the immigrant and that of a nation which fully accepts his wandering as a Jew.

If the Jew is tolerated by America, he is also a required presence for those who subscribe to a millennial regime. In Protestant fundamentalism the Jew is necessary and his cultural ambivalence is a spiritual challenge to Christian evangelism. As a composite figure, the Jew trails history in his wake; he is a bearer of prophecies that Christian missionaries are obliged to fulfil before the apocalypse. In the 1970s Earl Rovit endorsed the point when he referred to the 'Wandering Jew' as an immigrant of 'ancient lineage' who 'might prove receptive to a religious sensibility' in American life. It is this sensibility which comes to life in the evangelical and pentecostal churches, especially those that see the Jew as a sacred 'survivor' (Bilik 1981, p. 178).

To accept the Jew as a religious 'survivor', Christian conservatives accept the Jew as a cultural 'survivor', the product of a dynamic past. By including Jews in their ministry the militant Protestant chooses to incorporate what Eric Wolf calls those 'bundles of relationships' which Jews bring with them as an emigrant race. If the notion of who can and who cannot belong to the church, on the basis of heritage, is discounted, so too is the West as 'an entity' or 'civilisation': the spiritual home of the Protestant church. This belief, more than any other, separates those whom we call pre-millennialist from other non-Protestant, fundamentalist believers. It gives them a link with a cultural 'genealogy' outside the West, an empathy with versions of the chosen, rather than ideas which celebrate the Protestant as a 'quintessential' form of American culture (Wolf 1982, pp. 3, 7).

II

The importance of an expansive outlook on race is a rarely acknowledged feature of fundamentalism and the importance of the Jew to the success of the fundamentalist enterprise is often considered a sideline event. For Richard Hofstadter, fundamentalists are 'Manichean' (Hofstadter 1964, p. 135). For Eric Mottram they are 'psychopathic' and 'single track' (Mottram 1989, p. 145), while Francis Fitzgerald accepts as sincere their desire to live in 'enclaves' (Fitzgerald 1986, p. 19). There is said to be no greater sin for the fundamentalist than that of 'ecumenism' and cultural pluralism and no greater virtue than to express one's implacable opposition to the 'secular humanism' of a liberal intelligentsia (Hunter 1987, pp. 45, 46). Fundamentalism in the United States is described as the *bête noir* of philosophical modernism and, as such, is totally enclosed by provincial history (Reichley 1987, p. 77).

Historians cling to models and formula which place fundamentalism in a localised context. They invariably see it as agoraphobic and insular, positioning it at a particular time and place in history (the late nineteenth century), its identity framed by a number of key archival debates: evolution in the 1890s, immigration fears in the 1920s, McCarthyism and anti-intellectualism in the 1950s. In academic commentary, fundamentalism is often the prisoner of its past. A product of parochialism, its philosophy is insular, leadership patriarchal, mood bucolic and backward-looking and its political agenda isolationist, nostalgic and xenophobic. It is frequently depicted in a static shorthand as a brutalised faith, evangelical yet neurotically confrontational, imprisoned by provincial suspicions and the threat posed by the enemies of Christianity and the American way: Darwinists, Bolsheviks, humanists, secularists, Wall Street capitalists, Jews and Freemasons. Fundamentalism yearns to be a law unto itself, 'terminal and Christian' as Eric Mottram describes it, a political religion that would rather have nothing to do with the rest of the world, except condemn it (Mottram 1989, p. 151).

'The Fundamentalist mind can tolerate no ambiguities', says Richard Hofstadter. It regards compromise as inconsistent with 'the realities of power which are only real in the context of power' and 'ultimate moral and spiritual values' (Hofstadter 1964, p. 135). As the quintessential expression of a paranoid style, fundamentalism is synonymous with megalomania: exuberant on the one hand, xenophobic on the other, but forever asphyxiated by ideas of history. Fundamentalists are said to select their victims on the basis of information culled from *The Chronicles of the Elders of Zion*, a racist text which, says Michael Lind, exposes 'Jews, New York and international finance' and their masters, the Illuminati, as long-time opponents of Christianity and democracy. Fundamentalists, he continues, are committed to a speculative reworking of ancient fears and prejudices, many of which originate in Catholic Europe and are subsequently projected onto French Revolutionaries, atheistic intellectuals, Jews and cosmopolitans (Lind 1995, pp. 23–4).

Fundamentalists, agrees David Brion Davis, 'have long been forced to search for subversive enemies and to construct terrifying dangers from fragmentary and highly circumstantial evidence' (Davis 1971, p. xix). Fearful of both the enemy without (ecumenism) and the enemy within (collaborationism), fundamentalism targets as its central enemies the proponents of secularism: the liberal intelligentsia and the consumer capitalist, both of whom have lost sight of the nation's history and its 'vital fundamental instincts' (Hofstadter 1964, p. 86). As a faith of the forgotten, the ill-educated and the insecure, fundamentalism articulates the fears of small-town America, those island communities whose insularity was first disturbed after the Civil War by the nationalising tendencies of an expanding, industrial economy.

There is an overwhelming temptation to see fundamentalism as a nineteenth-century phenomenon, a religion which emerges at a time of unmediated communication and moral restraint, a dinosaur lost or stranded on the other side of a great divide created by world events, technological inventions and revolutions in modes of thinking. In this scenario fundamentalism remains, without exception, a product of its origins, fixated by the threat to the independence and integrity of an older, rural and small-town America from the cosmopolitan, polyglot city.

It is this, says Richard Hofstadter, which gave rise to the reform movements of the late nineteenth century and precipitated 'the revolt against modernity' (Hofstadter 1964, pp. 117–45). Fundamentalism, he argues is a defensive reaction to the loss of social, economic and cultural autonomy in small-town America and the challenge of 'cosmo-politanism', 'scepticism' and the 'moral experimentalism of the intelligentsia'. In a rapidly secularising age the fear that an 'older America type' was passé – and that the liberal intelligentsia were 'trying to kill it' – created a new strain of anti-intellectualism in American life that has remained intact to the present day (123). The liberal intelligentsia stand accused, says Hofstadter, of having abandoned their belief in the values of the *Gemeinschaft* – perman-ence, intimacy and binding tradition – in favour of the new urbanisms of the *Gesellschaft*, of having jettisoned traditional standards in reli-gion, morality and family life. The fundamentalist flight from the new America to the familiar confines of the old may have been more symbolic than real – even those who craved a reassertion of the old moral values were still urbanites, inhabitants of the *Gesellschaft* – but, writes Hofstadter, fundamentalists were, and are, technically attuned to the cultural values from which the country is seen to have seceded.

Fundamentalists, agrees Martin Marty, believe they can live apart from the world. They draw 'dividing lines by imagining and seeking to govern a "Land of Purity" set off and secured from non believers' (Marty and Appleby 1993, p. 622). Marty is unequivocal in his assessment. All fundamentalists, whatever their nationality, he argues, identify an enemy against whom all believers should unite. Among

American Protestant fundamentalists the enemy is 'secular humanism'; in Nigeria it is 'Euro-Christianity'; in Turkey it is 'Western Christian capitalism'. In the ideology of the Muslim Brotherhood in Egypt it is called 'paganism'; in Islamist Algeria it is Francophone imperialism; for Lebanon's Hezbolah it is the Judeo-Christian, crusader culture.

'Fundamentalists are boundary settlers', says Marty; 'they excel in encircling themselves off from others by distinctive dress, customs and conduct'. In their 'enclave' culture they are 'encouraged or even empowered to spill over [their] natural boundaries and permeate the larger society' (Marty and Appleby 1993, p. 4). By 'selecting elements of tradition and modernity, fundamentalists seek to remake the world in the service' of an 'unfolding eschatological drama'. They locate and affirm the divine by neutralising a threatening 'Other'. In this schematic world 'such an endeavour often requires charismatic and authoritarian leadership ... a disciplined inner core of adherents ... and a rigorous sociomoral code for all followers'. Fundamentalism is a highly mechanistic theology in which 'boundaries are set, the enemy identified, converts sought, and institutions created and sustained in pursuit of a comprehensive reconstruction of society' (3). The renunciation of modernity is undertaken with an evangelical zeal which perfectly articulates the Manichean contest between the ecumenical and the divine. Accommodation is treachery. 'Fundamentalisms resist ambiguity and ambivalence. You have to be "this" or "that"', says Marty. 'The enemy is compromise or the compromiser' (2). Fundamentalisms, therefore, are discrete, self-contained and non-promiscuous; they shun modernisms as well as each other. 'SUBSTANTIVELY, FUNDAMENTALISTS HAVE LITTLE OR NOTHING IN COMMON WITH EACH OTHER' (17). (Their condition is one of 'singularity' (23) in the absolute.)

Pat Robertson concurs with this assessment. In his book *The Turning Tide* (1993), he claims that 'No one in the Christian Coalition (has) ... any interest in co-opting any other groups' personal or moral beliefs. The Coalition's clear mandate is to affirm and support America's historic and traditional political institutions, which happen to be founded upon ethical systems derived from (and strengthened by) Judeo-Christian values' (Robertson 1993, p. 63). In a true fundamentalism, says Robertson, ideas from one culture cannot be mixed with those from another: 'The danger we face in our culture is "syncretism", which is the sort of mindless blending of ideas about God that are neither Christian nor Jewish nor Eastern nor anything in particular, but rather a mishmash of fuzzy feelings about life and the hereafter' (156).

Those who keep the analysis of fundamentalism 'tightly within the boundaries' of a nineteenth-century debate tend to privilege 'the heated theological and doctrinal disputes' of that period and downplay the moral and evangelical fervour that fundamentalism shares with other messianic and millennialist churches (Strozier 1994, p. 182). Fundamentalism, argues Charles B. Strozier, is demonstrably greater 'than the sum of its parts'. It is not the creation of one individual but of different 'strands of thought' – inerrancy, dispensationalism, the Rapture of the righteous – each of which is exploited in order to create a 'new' religious 'mix' (183–4). The moral utopianism of 'American fundamentalism' is seen most clearly, writes James Reichley, 'in the Puritan tradition from which it is partly descended' (Reichley 1987, p. 93).

The 'Calvinist culture, which shaped much of the American religious heritage', writes George M. Marsden, was a culture shaped by the Old Testament and the Jewish Scriptures. Calvinists, more than most Protestant groups, saw their religious task as building a Christian civilisation. For this reason, 'American culture, perhaps more than that of any other modern nation', has been 'shaped by Old Testament ideals. Until the twentieth century (when they forgot most of both), most Americans knew the history of the Jewish patriarch as well or better than they knew their own history' (Marsden 1990, p. 143).

Paul Boyer agrees. The first glimmerings of the 'Rapture doctrine', he suggests, 'can be seen in Increase Mather's thinking from the seventeenth century', which Darby wove 'into a tight and cohesive system ... buttressed at every point by copious biblical proof texts' (Boyer 1992, p. 88). The Puritans of Massachusetts were not only 'imbued with a deep reverence for Hebraic culture', confirms David Eichorn, they were 'staunch premillennialists' who believed that the Jews had been 'dispersed to every part of the world' (Eichorn 1978, p. 6). Since the end was imminent, the Puritans were obliged to gather up the Jews and convert them to Christianity, thereby creating the conditions necessary for His Second Coming through the triumph of the saints. The march toward judgement in New England was often a strange and paradoxical affair involving 'an ecstatic eschatology' and a 'novel hospitality' towards the Jews, the inspiration for which came from culturally diverse sources and was rooted in a history which lay outside the traditional contexts of western theology (Heimert and Delbanco 1985, p. 9). Eschatological beliefs were an integral part of Puritan literature which regarded the settlements as 'prototypes established in anticipation of Christ's Second Coming'. The sermons of John Cotton and Increase Mather maintained that the conversion of the Jews to Christianity was a precondition of millennial rule and that members of the settlements had been elected 'to fulfil a divinely determined historical plan' in the coming apocalypse (Wojcik 1997, p. 210).

In contemporary fundamentalism the legacy of pre-millennial Puritanism is realised most clearly, says Nancy Ammerman, in the notion of a divinely appointed errand. In this regard, the Puritans were of seminal importance and their 'experiment' was 'a model to be emulated', because they saw themselves as having descended from the Children of Israel. The Puritan idea of the 'city on a hill' anticipates 'the later role of the United States as a missionary nation'. Expectant fundamentalists, she continues, interpret 'the nation's role in divine history' as 'a peculiar blending of Puritan theocracy and Jeffersonian religious liberty'. In this scenario the country is obliged to 'return to her roots' and 'restore the "Christian principles" on which she was founded'. God has 'commissioned Americans to use their religious heritage and vast natural resources to spread the gospel throughout the world. The United States [is] no less a chosen nation than was Israel' (Ammerman 1988, p. 199).

The missionary who goes into the world in order to convert an unregenerate people provides us with an unbroken link between twentieth-century fundamentalism and the Puritan experiment in New England. Ernest Sandeen was among the first to observe this when he said that 'fundamentalism ought to be understood partly, if not largely, as one aspect of the history of millenarianism', a comment which bears out the importance of the early Protestant experience in New England (quoted in Lawrence 1989, p. 166). For the colonists, the ideal recipients of Israel's gospel were Israel's children, the descendants of the Ten Lost Tribes who had gone astray in their search for a New Canaan. Just as dispensationalists believe that Christ will not arrive without the conversion of the Jews, so in the early churches of New England, the Puritans equated their own salvation with a compelling commission to minister to the fallen. In the seventeenth century the Jew provided an essential clue to the future success of His New Israel and whenever Jewish visitors arrived, says Lee Huddleston, they were treated better than 'other outsiders' (Huddleston 1967, p. 143). But there were never enough of them. Salvation could have no meaning and the millennium no relevance in a world where the Jew was conspicuous by his absence.[3]

The fear that in the New World there were too few Jews to be 'reclaimed', says John Canup, prompted a decision to substitute the Indian, who was aimless and plentiful, for the Jew who was not (Canup 1990, p. 67). The requirement of conversion as 'a necessary prelude to the climax of Christian history', resulted in 'a tendency to seize upon' the Indians as Jewish descendants and to interpret every conceivable 'resemblance between Indian and Jewish customs [as] aiding the fulfilment of prophecy' (69). If the strategy was 'indiscriminate', says Lee Huddleston, the underlying intention was to create, through biblical speculation and do-it-yourself anthropology, a dynamic plan through which a society of ancient Israelites could be readily identified. The need to confirm the Indian as a surviving member of a sacred race, an ancestral relative rather than a race apart, made theological necessity the mother of cultural invention. In an early millenarian tract (*The Planters Plea*, 1630), John White, of the Massachusetts Bay Co., claimed that Indian ideas of the Creation bore a close resemblance to the account given in Genesis, while their 'Legal Observations' seemed strangely consonant with other matters recorded in the Old Testament which speculated that the Indians may be operating on the basis of 'a tradition received from the Jewes'. He even left open the possibility that 'Some conceive, their Predecessors might have had some commerce with the Jewes in times, past, by what means I know not' (68).

White's willingness to suspend his ignorance and secure the Indian's right to the Gospel offers an early indication of the colonists' fascination with Indian genealogy and the extent to which theories of racial origin pushed back the borders of what was permissible for a chosen people in a messianic location. White's willingness to consider the Indians as a 'far-flung branch of Noah's tribe' also suggests the working of a culturally expansive imagination, together with a reluctance to identify His New Israel as an exclusively English undertaking (64). The possibility emerged that the colonists were not unique, but had been preceded, as the English geographer Nathaniel Carpenter indicated, by an original Noachian culture whose descent and 'posterity' from Noah had given them 'some form of discipline'. Although through the 'long process of time or uncertainty of tradition this had been neglected and obliterated', a realisation grew that the Indians and not the colonists were His 'first planters of America' (69). The excitement this generated was in no way dampened by the common complaint that these 'first planters' had gone to seed and fallen 'back into such waies as their own depraved nature dictated or the devil militiously suggested' (65). On the contrary, the Indians' Jewishness was a beckoning gesture from God to a community of 'silly wretches' who worshipped 'idolatrous and abominable' gods and had been 'lured' into sinful ways 'by the devil' (74, 75). Indeed, if it was the case that the Indians were Jews, awaiting 'the realisation of prophecy', it was incumbent on the Puritans to provide each other with anthropological and scriptural evidence of God's intentions. If it could be proven the Indians 'had colonized the New World long before the English', and had done this on the basis of divine intent, then the colonists might exploit their 'cultural diversity' to refute the charge that they were socially backward and 'the poorest of all the people of God' (Delbanco 1989, p. 87). Such an argument would also allow them to claim that Christian history in the New World was destined to pursue a spiritual career independently of Europe.

Hebraic theories of origin were initially devised, says William G. McLoughlin and Walter H. Conser, Jun., in order to place the Indian 'within the fold of Christian history and prophecy' and to intensify the zeal of the righteous through a millenarian eschatology (McLoughlin and Conser, Jun., 1987, p. 245). In this theology Indians were not only precious ('conversion of the Indians to Christianity', says William S. Simmons, 'was among the several reasons why English Puritans emigrated to the New World'), they were precocious (Simmons 1979, p. 200). As literal and lineal descendants of the Israelites the Indians had wilfully abandoned their 'faith', 'rejected' Christ's mission and retreated into the wilderness to consort with the devil (McLoughlin and Conser, Jun., 1987, p. 250). But if the Indians deserved to be punished for their sins they were also worthy of investigation. As old world relics who had 'lost' their way, the Indians were 'not just ... semi-human savages incapable of improvement as so many whites on the frontier believed' (253, 250). They were the bearers of a righteous history and without them the Puritan mission in New England could have no spiritual focus. 'The project of converting the Indians had long been associated', says Andrew Delbanco, 'with the doctrine of the conversions of the Jews' (an event which was 'considered by virtually all Protestants to be an essential prelude to the advent of the millennium'). Without 'the entire Jewish nation' in the New World being 'called to God' there could be no conclusion to scriptural history and no salvation for His emissaries in Canaan (Delbanco 1989, p. 109).

What is intriguing about this thesis is that while it migrated from Europe to the colonies as an idea in scriptural anthropology, it began life as a 'truly marvellous tale' in Ecuadorian folklore, where it was first discovered by two Portuguese Jews, Antonio Montesinos and Menasseh ben Israel (Huddleston 1967, p. 128). Ben Israel, in particular, says Richard H. Popkin, was a figure of 'central' importance in the history of seventeenth-century millennialism (Popkin 1980, p. 75). His book, *Hope of Israel* (1650), was 'the most important text' in the history of 'Jewish-Indian theory' and is 'still the most frequently cited' (71). A 'mixture of explorer literature, Jewish history, anthropological speculation ... and prophetic interpretation', *Hope of Israel* recounts the story of Jewish dispersal and Jewish–Indian discovery as a record of 'the progress of prophetic history towards its imminent culmination' (73) in the new world. Ben Israel had received his inspiration from Antonio Montesinos (Aahron Levi) and, in late 1644, he arrived in Amsterdam with an account of Montesinos's travels in the Cordillera Mountains of Ecuador. Montesinos claimed to have met a tribe of Indians who recited the Shema (Deuteronomy 6: 4–9), practised Jewish ceremonies and were members of the Lost Tribe of Reuben. He described in detail how he was told about the Indians by a 'cacique' called Francisco who had led him to a 'Holy People' 'hidden in the mountains' (Huddleston 1967, p. 128). This 'hidden' race of Jews explained how they had come to the Americas on an eastward journey over the Straits of Anian. Brought to the area by the providence of God, they had fought the Indians, then converted them to the Hebrew faith.

When it appeared in *Hope of Israel* Francisco's story, says Popkin, had a 'gigantic' impact on the millennialist movement in Europe (Popkin 1980, p. 72). In England, Thomas Thorowgood printed a copy of Menasseh's story in his *Jewes in America* (1650), and suggested that the Red Indians of North America were members of the Ten Lost Tribes of Israel who had migrated eastward as descendants of Shem's son Eber. Both tracts quickly found their way to the colonies, where they gained a considerable following among Protestant theologians like Daniel Gookin and Roger Williams. One version of *Jewes in America* contains a preface by the 'Apostle to the Indians', John Eliot of Roxbury, which describes the emigration and settlement of the sons of Noah after the flood. In Eliot's utopian scheme, Noah and his sons divide the world, Japheth and Ham move westward and Shem moves eastward through Asia, 'in a complex utopian dialectic of enclosure, population growth, and plantation, settling India, China, Japan and America'. These 'archetypal' pilgrims to the New World, says James Holstun, 'are both the actual ancestors of the Indians and the Old Testament types' (Holstun 1987, p. 113).

If the historiography with which the Puritans clothed their millennialist faith was given to them by Jews, it provided them with scriptural evidence for a theory of identity which guaranteed not only their spiritual future, but allowed them to participate in the millennialist enterprise sweeping through England in the 1640s and 1650s. Cromwell's decision in 1651 to repeal the laws on Jewish immigration in order to appease the millennialist fervour of the Interregnum aroused 'great interest' in Jewish conversion among the emigrating boatloads from England (Delbanco 1989, p. 111). Menasseh ben Israel, who had been instrumental in persuading Cromwell to remove the barriers against the Jews (which had held since the expulsions of 1290) was the main inspiration for Hebraic theorists in the colonies. As a result the Indian was endowed not only with a civil disposition, but with the characteristics of an ancient race of Jews whose fall from grace provided that 'missing link in scriptural history and anthropology' between the Caucasian descendants of Japheth and the aboriginal red men descended from Shem (Holstun 1987, p. 113). Roger Williams noted how, in both Indian and Jewish culture, men quarantine women with the 'monthly sickness'. John Dury and Daniel Gookin provided linguistic evidence to support the theory that the

Indians were descended from the Ten Lost Tribes. Edward Winslow referred to the Indians' 'manifold daily expressions bewailing the loss of that knowledge their ancestors had about God and the way of his worship, the general deluge, and of one man only that ever saw God ... which certainty I believe to be Moses' (112).

The Indian possessed a vestigial (if incomplete) memory of the ancient world and the Puritan's job was to reinstate it as far as possible, removing the Indian from the moral wilderness into which he had wandered. For this reason the scholar-missionaries of New England 'adapted their methods ... to native customs' and were willing to infuse 'a native element' into 'early American culture'. The attempt to create an emotional bond between the two cultures along ethnic lines countermanded the received wisdom from Europe that Christians and heathens were diametrically opposed on morality, history, spirituality, law. As a result, says Colin G. Calloway, the colonists 'no longer saw anything' that could not be redeemed in a race of people (with Semitic roots) 'who had become somewhat like them and survived' (Axtell 1997, p. 5).

The opportunity to keep pace with England during the Interregnum by discovering thousands of potential Jewish converts to the Christian church underlined the desire to connect culturally with a 'savage domain awaiting liberation' (Bercovitch 1978, p. 164). What the Puritans wanted as millennialists, was not to replicate England exactly, but to reinvent themselves as fraternal members of a chosen community who shared (however obscurely) the emigrating impulse of the Indian. 'The existence of the wilderness', says Giles Gunn, 'confronted them with a fact of "otherness" which profoundly threatened their identity as transplanted Europeans. In throwing their former identity into serious question, it thrust them into a situation where they could no longer repeat the saving formulas of the past and hope to survive' (Gunn 1979, p. 189). For James Holstun,

the New World became the appointed site for the millennial encounter of clockwise and counter-clockwise Israelites: the Indian descendants of Shem and Eber bearing themselves eastward, their civil tabula rasa more and more degenerate, but uncorrupted by gentile civility; and the Puritan Israelites bearing westward the Hebrew Scriptures, with their heretofore undiscovered model for regenerate civility. (Holstun 1987, p. 115)

In this typology the Indians were akin to emigrant visionaries, the product of an 'underground eschatology' which saw them not as 'demonic Tartars or sons of Ham', or even members of 'an intrinsically satanic race', but as refugees who shared with the Puritans a memory of life before the Flood and a common urge to travel the earth in memory of their ancestors (Japheth and Shem) (113).

The 'Jewishness' both of colonists and Indians separated them as a millennialist people from their English relatives. New England's Israel became a mythological site of encounter and reciprocity, a chosen place of interaction between the regenerate and unregenerate at a key providential moment. Here was the basis for a unique, syncretic project, an act of mission which could also be seen as a celebration of faith. While the colonies' 'origins' were overwhelmingly 'derivative', as John Butler argues, its 'most enduring religious patterns' were 'created, not merely inherited' (Butler 1990, pp. 5, 6).

The Puritans chose a 'variant' of a 'fairly widespread Renaissance theory' on 'the Hebraic origins of the Indians', in order to form a relationship with the Other that no other society could claim. They borrowed ideas to create alignments and empathies with the Indians in much the same way as they borrowed items of material culture to enhance their chances of survival in the wilderness. Conversion to Christianity justified the social proximity which the 'Praying Town' sought to create. It allowed for contact without contamination. It meant that in adapting an anthropological idea from Europe the Puritans were able to radically transform the Indian into a historical type that had come out of Asia as descendants of Eber and whose name, says James Holstun, means 'passing over (the Tigris)' (Holstun 1987, pp. 111, 113). In converting the sons of Shem and Eber 'from degenerate men to regenerate saints', the New World was not 'just a repetition of European history' but 'an accelerated epitome' of the future; 'prophesying what Europe had not yet become: a regenerate millennial community' (115). In this complex, syncretic landscape the colonists were able to embrace the millennialist spirit of Cromwellian England, yet combine it with their own multinational experience in order to create a kind of Israel that England could never be.

The millennial origins of the United States lie in a blend of spiritual imperialism and colonial multiculturalism. In the colonies the commitment to the Jews is inspired by literature and the world of the Other outside of literature; it is a millennialism of the woods and of ethnic diversity; it regards New England as an exceptional experiment but cannot ignore the native people who have brought to that region a unique portfolio of memories and manners. The millennial tradition is not that of a church which seeks to create a world unto itself, but one which cannot live with itself and is content to worship in a purified community of saints. Introversion is the route to self-annihilation; without the spiritual and intellectual challenge of those who live outside the church there is no discovery of the type of divinity that sin obscures.

The challenge of the millennial arises from liaising with a community in order to convert it to Christianity while, at the same time, creating a relationship that is favourable to persuasion, negotiation and exchange. Peter Carroll describes the Puritan 'mission' in New England as riddled with 'paradoxical' elements. The Puritans, for example, endorsed 'the subjugation of wild lands' and the 'settling of uncultivated areas', but they also created a philosophy for expansion which took them 'beyond the organic community intended by the founding fathers' (Carroll 1969, p. 3). On the one hand, they 'celebrated the process of transforming the wilderness', yet, on the other, their expansion threatened 'the collective society' they sought to create. What the Puritans attempted was to equate the Indians with the children of Israel whilst managing to avoid the degenerate baggage the Indians had collected in their uncivil state. They lived, therefore, with an enigma, a society which lacked western civility but displayed a divinity that western progress had erased from the memories of the descendents of Japheth.

Since cultural change for primitive peoples virtually stopped before the time of Christ, the Indians had retained a memory of the past long after they had crossed the Straits of Anian. As recipients of the myth of Exodus, the Indians had not been relieved, says Regina M. Schwarz, of the 'universal curse' of 'exile' and oppression. Their freedom was different from Christian freedom which had been achieved by evicting the Indian from his 'paradisal garden' ('the idealised and lost, land of Israel'), which all lost Jews sought to recover (Schwarz 1997, p. 50). The act of dispossession had been a providential sign, but had also served to stimulate, once more, 'the Exodus memory' – the legend of displacement – among the dispossessed tribes. Dispossession had given the Indians a particular pre-eminence which the Christian 'planters', in their urge to civilise, could not attain. The errand in the wilderness, in a curious way, rendered the 'planters' detached from history, whereas memory remained a condition of survival for those who were yet to be rewarded for their errand. As exiles from Israel the Indians had not been relieved of the burden of history. As a lens through which others might focus their own attention on history, the Indians had become a pressing reminder of the psalmist's cry: 'If I forget thee Jerusalem, let my right hand lose its cunning' (122).

The Indians' willingness to cling to ancient ceremonies intrigued the Puritans (and later missionaries) who worked to uncover what the Other had specifically remembered from his past. The Indians, whose progress out of Israel was spiritually unfinished, appeared to carry with them a more complete evolutionary record of their journey. They were able to reveal an imprint of divinity that the sons of Japheth had lost or buried beyond all recognition. To become acquainted with the Indians – to study their language, custom, religion and anthropology – was to get to know not just the Other but the Other that the self may once have been: the self as it was in an original form, the self with its virtues in spite of its sins. The wilderness may well be tarnished, but it was also a beckoning mirror in which it was possible to see the mystery of Israel and the splendour of its vagabond children.

III

Andrew Delbanco has argued that 'the idea of the Indians' Jewish origin, was ... a short-lived and tentative element in New England's search for purpose' and that it 'flourished only briefly, under the pressure to find something with which to match revolutionary events at home' (Delbanco 1989, p. 10). Yet while the conversion of the Indian was never as successful as ministers and missionaries, like John Eliot and Daniel Gookin, hoped it would be, Semitic theories of origin did not peter out in the seventeenth century. On the contrary, they persisted and evolved into an occasional and dynamic plan for understanding the mind and manners of migrating tribes and wilderness individuals in 'hidden' locations. The belief that Amerindian people were members of a Jewish diaspora was more than 'a crackpot theory', and for the next three centuries it made a vigorous contribution to the millennialist debate. In the outreach communities of Latin America and Southeast Asia, for example, it gave the evangelical church an opportunity to retrieve that 'sacred tradition' which, says R. Scott Appleby, fundamentalists 'claim' as central 'to their faith'. It also gave expression to a less formal spiritualism, which, in the case of a writer like Mary McCarthy in the 1960s, yearns to 'reach back to retrieve elements' of 'things unseen' and thereby exhume the vital features of a forgotten race (Appleby 1993, p. 217).

This point has been convincingly argued by Mcloughlin and Conser, Jun., in a paper which shows how the persistence of Semitic theories of descent created 'a pluralistic concept of ethnicity' in American religious life for over three hundred years. From the colonial period to the late nineteenth century, they write, generations of Christians, missionaries and scholars were prepared to investigate the Indian tribes in order to bring them 'within the fold of Christian history and prophecy' (McLoughlin and Conser, Jun., 1987, p. 243). John White's claim, for example, that the Indian name for New England 'proves to be perfect Hebrew, being called Nahum Keike, by interpretation, The bosome of consolation', gave way to an extended 'inventory of traits' built up by clerics, scientists, linguists and anthropologists to support a theory of Jewish descent (246). While Hector St Jean de Crèvecoeur's Andrew the Hebridean was located at the epicentre

of American cultural and mythic experience as 'an individual emancipated from history', other observers in the eighteenth and nineteenth
centuries were concerned to establish that the 'first' American, as
Daniel S. Butrick (a missionary to the Cherokees) put it in 1864, was
not white but 'red', and permeated not with heathenism, but the
manners of Asia (254).

After the Civil War the disappearance of a self-enclosed, Semitic wilderness was less able to provide Old World clues to the identity of the
Indian than had been the case two hundred years earlier. Furthermore,
the appearance of large numbers of Jewish immigrants in the nations
cities appeared to eliminate the need to seek out a wilderness liaison
between Indian and Jew, while urbanisation and the emergence of a
mass industrial economy further violated the rural lifestyle on which
that liaison had come to depend. In the late nineteenth century the
emerging fundamentalist church, and those sympathetic to it, regarded
the urban Jew less as an object of scholarship and more as a subject
for evangelical renewal. In 1894 the American Board of Missions to
the Jews (formerly known as the Brownsville Mission) was established
by Leopold Cohn in Brooklyn, New York, in response to the arrival of
hundreds of thousands of Jews, most of them young men and women
thought to be in need of a new moral identity. The American Board
of Missions to the Jews, and the 'Jews for Jesus' movement which it
led to, represent the modern origins of the movement to install the
Jew, especially in the nation's most heavily populated areas, as a figure
of essential importance in God's Christian plan.

Yet, in another sense, the legacy which nineteenth-century missionaries like Daniel S. Butrick inherited – that 'hidden' descendants of
the Ten Lost Tribes could still be found in the nation's hinterland
– did not disappear from the Protestant church. At the turn of the
century, Christian missionaries who belonged to the American Board
of Commissioners of Foreign Missions were sent to Asia 'to win the
hearts and minds of Asians' for Christ. Many of these missionaries
pursued the same theories as Edward Brerewood, who, in 1614, in
Enquiries Touching the Diversity of Languages, had proposed that
the American Indian, in terms of custom and language, originated
in Asia. Benjamin Smith Barton also followed Brerewood's lead in
the seventeenth century and investigated language as a path to
proving the Asiatic origin of the American Indian, while Thomas
Morton's *New Canaan* (1637) and John Josselyn's *An Account of
Two Voyages to New England* (1674) used similar approaches to
demonstrate the Indian's Asiatic origins. The belief that the Indians
came from Northeast Asia 'is the one theme', says Lee Huddleston,
'running throughout the writing of the seventeenth century', but, as
an evangelical and theological conviction, it came of age in the work

of Methodist and Baptist missionaries to China in the early years of the twentieth century. Missionaries and evangelicals who belonged to the China Inland Mission, says Alvyn J. Austin, were predisposed to interpret China not as it was, but as though it were the Holy Land in biblical times, a place of Jewish heritage and faith (Austin 1990, p. 66 n. 53).[4]

It is not only Protestant missionaries who have explained the common cultural traits of Indians and Asians through an Hebraic theory of origin. It also features, surprisingly enough, in the work of those who have been vigorously opposed to ideas of mission, religious and political. In the 1960s and 1970s Mary McCarthy was a disobedient witness to America's role in Southeast Asia but found it necessary, nevertheless, to support her writing with a Semitic theory of Vietnamese descent. While condemning her nation's Calvinist errand McCarthy shared many of the same maverick tendencies as those who wandered among the Indians in New England and noticed a link between Asia and the Orient. While remaining totally opposed to the idea of ministering to the Jewish fallen, she was aware that Vietnam's spiritual and philosophical heritage had been shaped, for a millennium, by Chinese rule.

McCarthy's interest in Vietnamese culture makes her, in the words of Benjamin DeMott, one of the 'most original and readable Puritans this country has produced' (quoted in Gelderman 1989, p. 350). She sees the Vietnamese (as Roger Williams saw the native Americans) as a people who have fulfilled the legacy of Israel and are able to avoid, by their openness, the mistaken offerings of the Puritan mission. For McCarthy, the North Vietnamese are destined for an errand in sacred history because they are openly committed to accepting the conversion of the unregenerate and the redemption of the disobedient. The landscape of the North is a spiritual garden; it satisfies her 'dream of a New Jerusalem', a land that repudiates America's belief in a divine appointment and a singular mission (McCarthy 1968, pp. 102–5, 130). Here she reminds us of Roger Williams, who, in his *Key to the Language of America*, regarded the Indians as descendants of the Jews, the Lost Tribes of Israel whom the Puritan colonists were dispossessing in the Canaan of New England. For McCarthy, the act of dispossession in the Canaan of Hanoi is manifested in the saturation bombing of the North and the offences committed against those who put their trust in nature.

McCarthy's decision 'to look clearly into the eyes of the wild and see our self-hood, our family, there' is both sensuous and nostalgic (Oelschlaeger 1991, pp. 275, 276). McCarthy replicates a seventeenth-century fascination with spiritual ecology as well as a yearning for intimate encounter with an archaic Jewishness. Her vigorous testimony cannot disguise a girlish infatuation with a disobedient Puritanism, one which bears the hallmark of a rush to embrace the revolutionary bucolic. Crossing the Red River in North Vietnam, McCarthy sees herself in the company of Indians. The ethnic tribes of Meos, Muongs and Thais remind her of the Indians she encountered in her Minnesota childhood. The flashback forces a deeper introspection on the nature of her own dispersal. She is 'aware of a psychic upheaval, a sort of identity crisis, as when a bomb lays bare the medieval foundations of a house thought to be modern' (203–4). The idea that the first American was not white but red tends to haunt McCarthy, as does the feeling that the Lost Tribes of Israel came through Asia on an eastward journey to the woods and fields of the country she lives in (203–4).

In *Hanoi*, McCarthy understands culture as 'a mosaic of ever-changing and yet recoverable parts that can be reintegrated into the present'. She tells us that 'by clearing away the undergrowth that obscures our connection with the archaic' she can recognise her 'many affinities with the ... past' and thereby 'discover vital relations between wilderness and human benigness [*sic*]' (Oelschlaeger 1991, p. 7). McCarthy's sense of the beautiful journey of Israel and its people has its origins in seventeenth-century scholarship. It is rooted not only in English colonial historiography but also, perhaps, in the work of hispanic theologians like Father Gregario Garcia, the Latin American historian who was arguing a case for the Asian origin of America's Indians as early as 1607.

As a displaced people, the Jews were long known to have had continuous contact with members of different civilisations – with the Tartar, Teutonic and Caucasian communities of Europe, Eurasia and the Orient. Gregario Garcia was particularly interested in the relationship between the Jews and the Chinese (Tartars, Schythians and Mongols) and other related Asian races. In *Origien de los indios de el Nuevo Mundo* (1607), Garcia identified the sons of Shem with those Asian races who had crossed the Straits of Anian when it was frozen and carried with them the ancient ceremonies of circumcision and the festival of the Passover. The proximity of the Chinese homeland to America had allowed this migration to take place, he believed. This was evidenced by the cultural and biological similarities of Indians and Asians: facial features, physique, colour, lack of beard. Garcia also noted the way in which both Chinese and Indians worshipped the sun as a god, practised idolatry, used lunar months and allowed nephews rather than sons to inherit property. Through his research Garcia did much to install the idea of the Indian Jew as a beautiful degenerate: an ancient Israelite of tawny complexion and copper-coloured tan whose memory and ancestry were multicultural.

Such theories were intermittently popular in the New England colonies and assumed an increasing importance in the studies of nineteenth-century anthropologists and novelists like Elias Boudinot (*The Star in the West*, 1816).

In the long-running controversy over Jewish identity in the Americas, says Lee Huddleston, the possibility that the sons of Shem had derived their features, as well as their ideas, from a diverse community of civilisations and nationalities – and had deposited their own ideas among these communities – made America the unique recipient of a divine knowledge and a diverse folklore. The Jews, who had wandered widely, had not only violated boundaries, they had traversed the very fault lines of civilisation, ignoring the threat of ancient conflict and cultural rift. New England theologians like John Eliot and Daniel Gookin recognised this when they subscribed to a Jewish theory of tribal origin and extended their enquiries to consider the possibility that the Indians were descendants of 'the tawny Moors of Africa' (Canup 1990, p. 261).

The prominence given in colonial writing to the dark-featured Jew, the sexual beauty of the forest, is a recurrent fascination for travellers among the Indians, says James Axtell. Colonial writers were intrigued by the importance which Indian women attached to painting their faces '"with a shining black"' and the status which black had as 'the color of beauty' was frequently commented upon (Axtell 1981, pp. 153, 182). For those who proposed Semitic descent, the Indians were distinctive because of their willingness to bring to the Americas the tropes and trophies of other civilisations unearthed during a long history of cultural adventure. What they offered was not only divine knowledge but the erotic promise of an experiential wisdom which their physical beauty seemed to reaffirm. The Indians not only appeared precocious and sexually advanced, they inspired fantasies of vicarious sexual adventure at all levels of society. John Josselyn describes the 'dark beauty' of Indian women who are 'wild, passionate and alluring', while, in the late eighteenth century, the Philadelphia naturalist William Bartram, on his travels in the Carolinas, refers to promiscuous Indian maidens 'disclosing their beauties to the fluttering breeze' (Kornfeld 1995, p. 302).

Hebraic theories helped to install the Indian in 'the collective memories, imaginations, and even subconscious of the colonists', writes Axtell, creating 'a deep but blurred intaglio' of intrigue (Axtell 1981, pp. 308–9). Not only were the Indians mysteriously immune to the restorative power of scripture, their lifestyle appeared to contradict the need for the ascetic withdrawal that Christ's example in the wilderness inspired. In New England those whom the pulpit condemned as ugly appeared the most physically attractive, their beauty an affront to a religion that emphasised the 'heathenish ignorance and barbarism' of the Indian (154, 276).

What the colonists and missionaries 'admired' in their 'hosts', says Axtell, was not just their 'physique' but their strength of character and generosity of spirit. In their pre-civil state the Indians reversed the process of purification, empowering themselves and acquiring in the process, a 'seductive mien' which ignored the virtue of self-denial. Those colonists who were attracted to the 'sensuality' of the Indian, recognised the power of beauty in nature and found it lacking, unnaturally, in themselves (153).

The ease with which New England's settlers were 'charmed' by 'the power of beauty in a savage' created enormous confusion among ministers of the church. As Nathaniel Hawthorne shows us in *The Minister's Black Veil*, ministers who proclaimed their vigorous opposition to the 'shadowed corners of the land' invariably harboured a secret desire to enter into it, while those in authority who condemned the wilderness as a place of sin were invariably drawn to replicate its features (159). Secret sin as an alternative to intimacy was equally appealing to ministers and parishioners and functioned as an adjunct to remonstration and paranoia. Cotton Mather's 'obsessive self-flagellation' has been well documented as have his 'autoerotic temptations and sexual fantasies'. Other preachers struggled with 'psychosexual disorders' like the Reverend Michael Wigglesworth, who, as a young tutor at Harvard, 'suffered fearful anxieties over wet dreams and sexual discharges' (Thompson 1989, p. 39).

The presence of sexually attractive and 'alluring' Indian women in the midst of an environment condemned for its rankness and savagery created insecurities that were not easily resolved (Delbanco 1989, p. 108). More often than not the visible saints suppressed their feelings or, like Hawthorne's Reverend Hooper, translated them into a sado-masochistic fantasy of sin.[5] The physical beauty of the native American became a cause of both wonder and concern, their dark complexion – '"more swarthy than *Spaniards*"' – a vivid reminder of a rich and varied history of adventure (quoted in Axtell 1981, p. 154). If missionaries among the Indians were attracted by the 'living light' of 'Hebrew fountains' and the 'gleam of Palestine' in the New England woods, others interpreted the Indian's uninhibited appearance as a sign of sexual prowess (Hayden 1981, pp. 650–1). Their 'tawny' dye and 'merry ... complexion' was seen as the imprint of a promiscuous nature which had taken them on an alternative journey to the Americas, a journey of colour through cultural climates outside the West (Axtell 1981, pp. 153, 157). For the sons of Japheth, however, the Puritan journey, as Charles L. Sanford tells us, had been a 'journey toward light', a journey within the West towards spiritual illumination and the bright beam of God symbolised by the life-giving sun (Sanford 1955, p. 302). The organic texture of Indian society symbolised the rich and sensuous deposit of the past. Those who were attracted by it were always in danger of setting in motion, says John Canup, a 'subversive strategy', a seduction that 'could easily shadow forth the colonists' own descent into barbarism and apostasy' (Canup 1990, pp. 69, 65).

What James Axtell calls the 'extraordinary drawing power of Indian culture' is a feature of both the early pre-millennial experience in New England and the Protestant church on more recent missions (Axtell 1981, p. 180). Semitic theories of Indian origin continue to excite the imagination of missionaries and travellers and create considerable confusion. The Indian appears 'not only terrible or inferior but also alluring', says Eve Kornfeld. From the seventeenth century onwards he can attract as well as repel and is 'dangerous precisely because of this duality'. The 'danger in facing' the Indian is 'not just external', since he 'threatens the integrity of the self by offering alternative, unrealised and suppressed possibilities'. The threat can be repressed or faced down by affirming ones 'belief in a stable, fixed, essential identity'. The alternative and 'deeper challenge' is 'to confront' the 'repressed alternatives' to one's own culture that the exotic 'Other' represents (Kornfeld 1995, pp. 289–90).

Those who locate the 'hidden' places in which the Jews are deposited – and may still remain – accept the challenge of encounter first outlined by Antonio Montesinos and Menasseh ben Israel. But the dangers are considerable. A missionary whose exclusive task is to evangelise the heathen can easily be distracted by other enquiries, the purpose of which is not conversion but fraternisation. 'Criolian Degeneracy', as Cotton Mather called it (Axtell 19891, p. 160), is always possible in missions which require 'close and frequent contact with prospective converts' (Canup 1990, p. 156).

In the fiction of Peter Matthiessen the temptation to seek out the Jew as an object of beauty and a challenge to faith is to separate an aesthetic of wilderness from a theology of errand. In his novel *At Play in the Fields of the Lord* (1965), Matthiessen returns us to Ecuador and the very location where Antonio Montesinos first encountered a 'holy' remnant of the Lost Tribes of Reuben. The novel opens with an aerial view of the Cordilleras but is set in one of the 'last wild terrains' of South America, the Ecuadorian Amazon, a place whose 'dark beauty' and savage tendencies contain many of the contradictions of history that have long challenged American missionaries (Matthiessen 1965, p. 3). These missionaries view the Ecuadorian jungle as rank and degenerate and its native inhabitants as corrupt and heathen. In the novel the Huben and Quarrier families, none the less, are sustained by the memory of a divine link between the Lost Tribes of Israel and the Indian enclaves in the wilderness. Driven by a desire for the conversion of the Jew they find themselves driven apart by a 'gleam of Palestine' in the tribal settlements, the complex beauty that illuminates the jungle and threatens to obliterate the light of God.

The mission that drives the Hubens and Quarriers comes from a belief in the direct descent of the Indian from an original Noachian culture. This belief denies the Indian a right to worship alternative gods and to continue living in a country where 'one was never asked about a past or future but could live as freely as an animal, close to the gut'. The missionaries enter the jungle with a spiritual imagination instructed by Calvinist prejudice. Since the 'great allure' (2) of the wilderness has caused social dispersal, they support an imperialism that subjugates, what Cotton Mather called, 'the dismal thickets', in order to create habitable settlements (Caroll 1969, p. 125). Matthiessen shows us the extent to which this errand in the wilderness of the Amazon remains a static encounter imprisoned by the referents of seventeenth-century historical experience: 'tools and plants and shotguns' (Matthiessen 1965, p. 146), 'presents for the savages' and a government militia which protects the missionaries as long as they cultivate the 'pleasant gardens of Christ' (132).

The Huben and Quarrier families arrive like colonial New Englanders and construct a network of defensive fortifications to exclude the native contaminants of 'cruelty and filth'. The idea of a sanctuary proves impossible to maintain and in the 'moral battlefield' (132) of Remate the search for refuge deteriorates into an obsession with cleanliness. Hazel Quarrier's perspective on faith is shaped by the memory of 'clean kitchens and church suppers' and of a Christian duty performed on 'the green bright plains of North Dakota where Satan, as her father said, "had been run clean across the country"' (4). For the messianic Hazel the absence of Satan is treeless space, while the presence of vegetation, when the 'jungle walls ... crowded in' (156), generates the same fear of covert action and infiltration that regularly undermined colonial confidence in the settlements of New England. As Increase Mather puts it at the conclusion of King Philip's war in 1675: 'when the summer was come on, and the bushes and leaves come forth, the enemy would do ten times more mischief than in the winter season' (Caroll 1969, p. 208). In the pungent Amazonian interior, with its 'dark enormous greens' (5) and 'drastic odours' (11), the assault on the senses is violent and intrusive. Hazel, who is 'obsessed with shorts and dresses' – the clothes she wore when she worked in the Sioux mission schools of the Dakotas – recoils in horror at its sensuality (148) and 'oppression'. She is equally despairing of the rancid moral abandon of the native people who take an 'erotic' delight in the 'spectacle' of 'dirt' (149).

In the Protestant orthodoxy of Hazel Quarrier and Leslie Huben, the jungle is 'a cathedral of Satan' which has 'pinned' its ministers 'in' and built around them a 'savage' church of sound and 'sombre' enclosures (295). In *At Play in the Fields of the Lord*, the Christian church is a vigorous opponent of open space. The enlargement of habitable settlements and the prejudice against dark forces receives its cultural inspiration from the Calvinist theology of William Hubbard and Cotton Mather. In *Magnali Christi Americana* (1702) Mather lauded the subjugation of the New England wilderness and praised the transformation of His New Commonwealth from a refugee outpost to a settled land. When Leslie Huben refers to the need to speed His word 'into those dark rivers where the souls of the lost cry out to us' (18) he is directly echoing Mather's complaint against the devil who has 'decoyed those miserable savages hither' in the 'hopes' they would not become acquainted with the Gospel. Hazel Quarrier's belief in spiritual illumination – '"That's why the Lord has sent us here, to rescue these poor heathens form such darkness"' (4) – restates Mather's fear of a degenerate darkness that troubled him from the outset of his career. In Madre de Dios Hazel feels she is 'surely entering the realm of Satan' and 'must prepare every defense' (9). Her husband Martin, who has begun to doubt the wisdom of exclusion, can no longer tolerate her 'deranged mind' (64). He senses a growing antipathy in their relationship, especially after Billy, their son, dies of blackwater fever.

In the Sioux mission school were he worked for ten years Martin Quarrier has experienced a loss of 'evangelical zeal', together with a growing 'respect' for the beauty of Indian culture. Quarrier's awakening interest in ethnography (partly the result of his father's influence as a missionary in China) signals his immersion in the 'beautiful' religion of 'tribal sacraments'. Hazel, who is disappointed by his openness, believes 'that his fascination' has 'not only impeded the harvest of souls' but is 'downright disrespectful to the Lord' (26). Hazel's zeal, which depends on a 'stable internal architecture and external boundaries' comes rapidly undone in the jungle. Martin witnesses an 'ordinarily immaculate' body going to seed and a mind, overwhelmed by the menace of filth, embracing the very blasphemy she finds abhorrent ('"Oh Jesus, make love to me, screw me, cruel Jesus, damn you Jesus"', 312).

Quarrier is slowly taken with the physical beauty of the wilderness through which he can escape his own fear of 'ugliness' and the 'pattern' of religion that has granted him a safe and uneventful mission in his work with the Indians. In Oriente state 'the pattern flies apart'

(335). In a plane ride over the snow-covered Andes the jungle inverts his expectation of mission and he finds himself 'entering Heaven from above'. The jungle possesses a Wordsworthian 'gleam' of divine beauty, an aesthetic promise that is tempered by the memory of His sacrificial 'pain'. Religious reference constrains his imagination but gives way to aesthetic revery as he feathers himself to earth along a flight path of 'celestial light' that 'signals ... sane harmonies' beyond the 'wild demonic gleams of the landscape' (3).

Those 'gleams' appear less demonic the further he enters into the jungle, the darkness lightened by the illuminating presence of Leslie Huben's wife, Andy, whose 'communion' with 'darkness' (27) follows a similarly inquisitive route to that of Martin's. As Martin is sexually attracted by Andy so she, like him, is 'excited' (155) by the jungle, and its Indians, for whom she develops an emotional yearning. Under the influence of an exiled American Indian, Lewis Moon, she remembers the Indians she knew as a child in the mission schools of the Northwest, where her father preached a 'soul-crippling' religion (229). Like Martin Quarrier she realises that 'Ours isn't the only religion in the world' and begins to see the jungle as an earthly 'paradise' whose 'beautiful' savagery offers the release she has 'wanted' all her life. In her desire to commit sin with an Indian she craves immersion in a sexuality whose mind and body has a natural resonance with that of the jungle. '"Because"' Moon '"belonged there where he was"' she wants to feel 'assaulted', physically purged of the contrived emotionalism of her marriage to Leslie and of a religion which lacks spiritual spontaneity (259).

Andy Huben's 'Criolian degeneracy' parallels that of Lewis Moon and his partner, Wolfie, a pair of itinerant mercenaries who stand condemned, by Leslie Huben, as '"no better than those who nailed Our Lord upon His cross"' (22). Moon and Wolfie are not heathens but Jews (or types of Jews) whom the New Fields Mission church in America has failed to convert. Moon is a native American, a quasi-Jew who has escaped the best efforts of the Christian mission on the midwestern reservation where he lived. Like Wolfie, the urban Jew from the eastern seaboard, he is living out a fantasy of sin as one of Satan's '"lost souls"' (53). As wandering Jews, Moon and Wolfie are equally alienated from the spiritual values the Protestant church claims to offer. They may be 'fugitives, perhaps, or criminals' but, like the Niaruna Indians, they 'are still not pacified' (35).

The failure to civilise Moon and Wolfie as errant members of a chosen race undermines the likelihood of social reform or Christian salvation with the Niaruna. Neither type of Jew – indigenous or immigrant – appears to have a future outside the jungle. When Moon tells Wolfie: '"You're a born loser"', Wolfie acknowledges the fact of exclusion with ... '"Ain't we all"' (63). Moon and Wolfie are embittered by a memory of anti-Semitism and their exploitation by an imperialist church and an imperialist state. As a member of a Cheyenne mission school Moon was a 'Christian' and a Vietnam veteran with 'a fine war record'. Yet he was thrown out of college for stealing money and abandoned by a country whose interests he served with distinction. His partnership with Wolfie is an act of retaliation against a state that discarded him and a religion that fed him on a diet of depravity. For the missionary Hazel Quarrier, he is a remnant of Israel lured into the jungle where Satan has reserved a wilderness for the Indian. Like Wolfie, his partner, he is a Jew in exile, denied a home in a country that lacks any social 'justice' (31).

In the States Wolfie played the role of urban, immigrant Jew to Lewis Moon's Plains Indian. In New York, Wolfie was '"the best kid on the block"' who took his bar mitzvah and '"never ate goy dreck"'. But then he abandoned the idea of being '"a Talmudic scholar"' and ended up, like the classic picaresque hero, '"the Man without a country"' (31). As a picaresque saint, Wolfie plays with the prejudice of others in order to gain an advantage over them. When the commandante of Oriente State, Rufino Guzman, asks him to carry out a bombing raid on the Niaruna, Wolfie agrees (in order to get himself an exit visa) but uses dud bombs. His threats against the Indians (with whom he shares the same fate as a remnant in exile) are a way of explaining his discontent at the loss of a home. But the threats are a pretence. Wolfie accepts the Niaruna as '"a bunch of Jews ... the Lost Tribe of Israel"', who have responded to the call of the wild and been persecuted for it (80). They are the enemies of the state and of missionaries like Leslie Huben who want to make '"beggars out of them, not to mention all the booze and slavery and syphilis"'. For this reason, they '"are better being run back into the jungle where they got a little human dignity"' (54). Wolfie drops his bombs '"in the river"' (76), since he '"got no lousy death wish"' desire to see the Indians evicted from their land (84).

Sensitive to the importance of the jungle as a 'Christly' place to which the Niaruna have trekked, Wolfie appreciates the search for a garden. His awareness of the link between race and ethnicity shows up in his relationship with the spiritually inquisitive Lewis Moon, whom he meets in Israel. On his travels, Moon renounces the teaching of the New Fields Mission and its view of the 'wilderness' as 'malevolent ... poisonous and stagnated, miasmal' (191). Moon condemns the cultural denigration of the reservation Indian, 'reduced to the white man's denims and ... grateful for rolled cigarettes and sweet canned foods' (78), and an ecclesiastical mission which places him within a declinist, tradition of sin. Damned for his history – 'You are the Lost Tribe of Israel, and therefore you must pray especially hard, for the Lost Tribe of Israel is under God's everlasting curse' (89) – Moon turns his back on a Jeremiah church.

Moon's search for the divine brings him into contact with the Niaruna who have managed to overcome their exile out of Israel and preserve what Moon and his people have lost to the white man: 'the true dignity of the Old Ways' which 'he had heard about but never seen' (270). In the jungle he feels himself 'one of them', able to resist the menace of evangelism and 'proud' to discover the exuberance and passion of his own lost past. In response to a question from Father Xantes: 'And who are you, Mr Moon? Are you anybody?', Moon chooses a ceremonial riposte. In an inspirational moment during a plane reconnoitre with Wolfie he sees the way forward:

A naked man appeared at the edge of the clearing, and stamping violently on the ground, raised a black bow. Moon did not see the arrow until it hung suspended for an instant at the top of its arc: a gleam of blue-and-yellow feathering, like a small bird, a turn of dull light on the cane shaft. (77)

As guerrilla theatre, the Davidic attack inspires Moon. He decides that instead of 'pissing' his life 'away' and looking 'like some Hollywood Geronimo trying to kick a ninety-dollar habit' (38), he must recover what little is left of life and a rapidly vanishing heritage.

The bright shimmer of the arrow, the lone naked figure howling at the sky – it had been years since he had grinned like that, with all his lungs and heart; he actually yipped in sheer delight. Now he had sensed something unnameable and always known, something glimpsed, hinted at, withheld by sun and wind, by the enormous sky. (79)

His re-entry into the playful defiance of tribal life occurs when he steals Wolfie's plane and, travelling in an easterly direction in 'dawnlight', parachutes into the jungle. His descent into unconfined space, tangled in the lines and silk of the parachute, is that of an Indian who is born again in a ceremony of innocence and umbilical play.

The wind tore at his face, and his arms ached. Short of the clearing, a mile and a half above the trees, he kicked himself backward and away. Shoving his free arm among the straps, then clasping both arms tight to his chest, he closed his eyes against the gut-sucking suspense, and the blow of the silk snapped open; he fell the length of a long howl before the impact all but wrenched his arms out of their sockets. He blinked, in tears; he was alive again, laughing idiotically in the clean sunlight of the upper air, legs dangling and swaying like the legs of a rag doll, drifting, drifting down through the great morning, in a wild silence like the wake of bells. (126)

Moon surrenders to instinct, says Eileen McClay, and tries to 'recapture not only his own innocence but that of his race before they
had knowledge of the white man' (McClay 1989, p. 64). In part, he
does. But although Moon is alienated from the church, the journey
he makes is that of a Jew. Moon undertakes a figurative flight of his
own and his presence in the jungle announces the arrival of a promised
messiah for the children of Reuben. Although he laughs 'idiotically',
his euphoric descent is not that of a fool who eschews history, but
a wandering Jew who has flown like a God out of ancient Israel and
is pleased with the manner of his intervention. For a time Moon is
worshipped as Kisu-Mu, the Great Spirit of the Rain, 'the bringer
of flood', a post-Noachian angel who evokes 'the benevolent Great
Ancestor' (318). As a sky god Moon is also an astrological messenger.
He re-enacts an ancient ceremony of visitation and performs for the
Niaruna a function similar to those extraterrestrial travellers, who,
according to Barry H. Downing, intercepted the ancient Israelites on
their flight out of Egypt.

Moon is a 'phenomenon' (67). He has retained his connection with
Israel and a spiritual desire to find a home in the paradisical wilderness. Carrying the memory of displacement with him, Moon has felt
the 'outrage of Jehovah' (62). He is the Jew you '"run inta ... all over
the world"', says Wolfie. He is '"the guy on the road, he's always
on the road"', the '"halfbreed"' Jew whose blood is mixed and who
'"learned long ago to travel light"' and is '"condemned to it"' (66).
Moon embodies the history of exile. He has even spent time searching
the mountain regions of South America for the 'wild Indians' of
Patagonia where Mennasseh ben Israel claimed the descendants of
Israel were driven (Huddleston 1967, p. 131). Disappointed by their
tameness Moon has kept travelling, as if obliged to undergo a period
of wandering, 'not as nomadism, but as purging ... punishment and ...
cleansing' (Schwartz 1997, p. 52).

In the Amazon Moon finds the Jew he is looking for, not the praying
Indian who 'spoke American and raised the American flag at school'
and 'wore blue jeans and looked at magazines in stories' (Matthiessen
1987, p. 89), but the invigorated 'utopian' full of violence and 'play'.
The remoteness of the Amazon basin qualifies as the type of settlement
the Children of Israel would have made for themselves. Moon's new
life, like theirs, is based on sacrifice, physical hardship, cultural
immersion: the learning of new disciplines, fluency in language, skills
in battle, the honing of a naked body in the rivers and forests. '"When
there's a jungle waiting"', says Moon, '"you go through it and come
out clean on the far side"' (122). In the world where he comes to
earth, 'the aura of the supernatural' (164) awaits him and the 'rude
broken clearings' (165) make him feel 'omnipotent' (166). Although

Moon is confronted by the rivalry of the warrior Aeore, he is imbued with 'the talent of a God'. The life that awaits 'was like being born all over again ... He had never envied anything so much as the identity of these people with their surroundings, not realised quite so painfully how displaced he had always been' (186).

The 'single flesh' Moon shares with the Niaruna, says Father Xantes, is that of a sojourner who feels himself as 'light as the air' and whose '"being"' has been swept across continents, '"a mere particle of the universe"', like '"a leaf or wing of dragonfly or wisp of cloud"'. Moon's origins, like those of the first American who crossed the Straits of Anian, are red not white. His is a civilisation whose people do not '"seek"' a '"meaning"' for life in a 'Fundamentalist Lord of hellfire and damnation'. The Indians eschew '"abrogation"' and '"self-sacrifice"' for '"joyous self-expression"'. They accept who '"they are"'. They have '"come out of Asia"' and belong to '"essentially an Eastern culture"'. They regard themselves as '"eternal"', unlike those in their missions who seek to fulfil a bargain with God in order to satisfy the terms of the Rapture (309).

Moon's journey reaffirms the 'quintessential' (Wolf 1982, p. 7) importance of the American as easterner, a traveller whose past precedes that of the West and whose behaviour dissolves the 'leaking categories' of ethnicity in the Americas (Kornfeld 1995, p. 290). If 'the first man on earth' is red, then what Francis Fukuyama terms 'the last man' owes his origins to those born East of him. His descendant is Moon, who lies 'naked' under 'the sun' and has 'drifted eastward in celebration of the only man beneath the eye of Heaven' (Matthiessen 1987, p. 3).

Notes

1. For a consideration of the impact of leadership skills on political and religious sensibilities in the 1990s, see: Barber (1995, p. 19) and Samuel (1995, p. 27).
2. In *The Judas Testament* the motive for violence is the appearance of a number of ancient documents and manuscripts in the libraries of eastern Europe. At a time of *perestroika* and *glasnost*, says Easterman, rabbinical literature is associated with anti-Christian, Zionist propaganda. In Russia the archives reveal the existence of a papyrus scroll containing Aramaic writing, reputedly in the hand of Christ. It is discovered in Moscow among a collection of Jewish artefacts, 'a huge library of Judaica' (Easterman 1995, p. 128) collected by the Germans during the Second World

War. This library was part of 'the library of the Reichsingitut for the
History of the New Germany' (27) and housed a vast quantity of anti-
Jewish material which the Germans used to provide 'evidence for their
racial theories'. Much of this collection of antiquarian objects – 'Torah
scrolls, tefillin, chanuka, menorahs, plates for seder, challah cloths' (128)
– was acquired by the Germans from rabbinical libraries in occupied
Poland and Lithuania, from storehouses and synagogues and yeshivas,
Tarbut and Yavneh schools, the homes of rabbis and tsaddikim, Jewish
clubs and religious libraries. The plunder is of great historical significance and includes manuscripts and papyri dating back to the first
Christian century. Initially, it was sent back to Germany and then transported, along with books and paintings, to the Soviet Union by
Communist troops who occupied eastern Europe at the end of the Second
World War.

The novel tells the story of Jack Gould, a student of Middle-Eastern
history and linguistics, who is introduced to this priceless storehouse
of Jewish manuscripts at the Moscow State Library by an old Russian
colleague, Iosif Sharanski. The Aramaic manuscript written on parchment
is authenticated as the work of Christ by carbon dating and spectographic
analysis. It takes the form of a letter written to Joseph Caiphus, a
representative of the Jewish establishment in Jerusalem, and reveals Jesus
to be the son of a Rabbi. It also shows him to be a militant Jewish
'fundamentalist' (142), a believer in the Law of Moses and a non-pacifist
violently opposed to compromise with Rome. Sharanski fears the political
implications if the scroll falls into the wrong hands. If the Vatican
acquires the scroll it will be destroyed and Christ's life as 'a Jewish
teacher, a Galilean rabbi, a political extremist' (426) will be buried
without trace. To counter the threat of a resurgent Zionism and the
'wicked use' of 'scandalous theories' (160) which the scroll might inflame,
powerful elements within the church intervene to counter the threat of
revisionist history. In order 'to step into the vacuum ... left behind'
(433) by Communism they activate fascist links of their own (German
and Croatian), formed in the 1930s. The infrastructure of a new clandestine fascism (Crux Orientalis) provides the political muscle with
which the Catholic church can counter 'the twin threats of modernism
and secular liberalism' (432).

3. On the place of the Jews in pre-millennialist thought see Ariel 1991. At
the end of the colonial period there were 2,300 Jews, a great majority
of them Spanish or Portuguese origin. The first Jews settled in New
Amsterdam and encountered some opposition from the Dutch Governor
Stuyvesant which ended with the intervention of the Dutch West India
Company. Jews were granted freedom of worship in 1683 although a
synagogue was not built until 1728. Other early Jewish communities
existed in Newport, Rhode Island (sixty families at the time of the
Revolution) and in Philadelphia and Charleston. Jewish peddlers were
familiar figures throughout the colonies. See Lebeson 1931.

4. Research by American Sinologists still continues. Most of it centres
on China's Jewish communities in the city of Kaifeng where Semitic
traditions can be traced to the Northern Song Dynasty (Poole 1998, p. 17).
For further discussion of the physical similarities between Amerindians
and Eastern Asians, see Kohn 1997, p. 45. For an analysis of the scientific
evidence of ancient Hebrew remains in the Americas see Wavell 1998,
p. 7.

5. The Reverend Hooper provides us with an example of how the fantasies of true believers serve as strong sado-masochistic outlets for wilderness voyeurs. Hooper wears a black veil to demonstrate the secret sin of his parishioners. He is obsessed with concealment and the frequency with which sin is committed and unacknowledged. He conceals his facial identity in order to illustrate what is visible in others and the moral profligacy which makes him a martyr to his parishioners sin. Hooper claims to be full of 'sorrows' and the mythological wilderness on which his imagination feeds is the basis of his penance, a world he must enter but can only do so by shielding behind a 'mysterious emblem' of black crepe. Hooper is unmarried and while the 'Spruce bachelors' at Sunday Sabbath cast 'sidelong' glances 'at the pretty maidens' who come alive in the 'sunshine' and appear 'prettier than on week-days' Hooper prefers a more 'meditative' style. If there is something 'ghost-like' (Hawthorne 1987, p. 189), his withdrawal behind the veil is also voyeuristic, an impression that is confirmed when he begins to smile at those whose curiosity is aroused by his bizarre appearance. Hooper denies himself the pleasures of the flesh and a life of companionship with 'his plighted wife' Elizabeth (192) but the smile that continues to flash across his face suggests that the 'awful power' he exerts 'over souls that were in agony for sin' is an 'efficient' ministry. The enjoyment he takes from living in a world of darkness is Hooper's own secret, and gives him the chance to appear an 'efficient clergyman' without the public need to acknowledge his desire for the darkened world his voyeurism yearns for. The unpardonable sin is the transparency of his martyrdom which a traumatised congregation is unwilling to expose. His camouflage which barely conceals the desire to emulate a world of 'dark beauty' is literally accepted as a symbol of his shame at the world's adultery. Hooper's pretence is that he must darken his face in defence of society in order to locate the threat which it faces from the dark or coloured races without. What lies within is the hinterland of the country, the 'Criolian degeneracy' of that 'new, strange, and even dangerous' land (Axtell 1981, p. 284) that tempts Hooper to abandon his identity and acquire the dark regalia of the 'Other'.

Hooper's mask signifies devil's work as well as martyrdom. In wearing it, Hooper is able to fabricate a vision of the sacrificial priest as well as the Indian as ceremonial Black Man who lives in the veiled and secret world of the forest. By appealing to the power of blackness within – and the body of the other that can not be seen – Hooper attempts to dramatise the horror of 'contamination' (Stanniard 1992, p. 232) that awaits those who embrace the hinterland. Hooper's occult costume is not only a contaminant in itself, it also anticipates the activities of the Ku Klux Klan. It provides us with an early version of the way masks, robes and hoods were later used to articulate a fascination with the 'Other' as a contaminating presence.

2

Race and Promiscuity:
Millennial Ministry and the Legacy
of Ham

I

The 'very essence' of a culture, says Lionel Trilling, resides in its central conflicts or contradictions, and its religious spokesmen as well as its writers are likely to be those who contain a large part of the dialectic within themselves, 'their meaning and power lying in their contradictions' (Trilling 1951, p. 9). In the 1990s fundamentalism is a vital repository of these contradictions and however much it might claim to have escaped them it can no longer protect the pious 'from information that might call their beliefs into question' (Fitzgerald 1986, p. 158). Fundamentalism, therefore, is not something that stands apart from the world. On the contrary, all fundamentalisms are fully implicated in the stresses and strains of world history and embody in their very existence a sense of the world's struggle, its debates and dialectics.

Fundamentalism, as Malise Ruthven has argued, 'is a modern word that eludes easy definitions'. While it may have begun 'its semantic career around the turn of the century' as a way of defending 'Protestant orthodoxy against the encroachments of modernism and the teaching of evolution', by the 1970s it had 'expanded to include the activity of anti-western religious radicals in the Muslim world who sought to overthrow predominantly secular governments'. In subsequent decades 'it attached itself both to ultra-orthodox Jewish groups and to militant Israeli settlers (like Gush Emunim), who refused to accept any compromise with Arab Palestinians on the grounds that all of the Land of Israel had been given to them by god'. In the 1990s funda-mentalism 'has strayed far beyond the umbrella of "Abrahamic" monotheism' and is used to describe a whole range of religious political activists: from the Sikhs at Armritsar, to the Hindus at Ayodyha, to the Buddhist monks in Sri Lanka who have taken up arms against Tamil separatists. Fundamentalism 'now encompasses many types of activity' and to some extent has surrendered its autonomy by opening itself to a process of 'copy' and 'duplication'. Although it is not possible to empty the term 'of its culture-specific' or 'tradition-specific' contents, fundamentalism is more 'accessible' than ever before and does not seek to withhold itself from the outside world (Ruthven 1993a, p. 31).

Fundamentalist groups in different countries have tended to converge intellectually over the last ten years and share each other's anxieties and concerns on an informal basis. On issues such as the sovereignty of borders, the state of public morality, the role of women, sexual promiscuity and the failure of liberalism, fundamentalists are willing to seek reassurance in each other's company. On occasion, they might copy from or conspire with each other, borrowing from sources they probably should not, while refusing to acknowledge their cultural dependence on political regimes they claim to oppose. In the post-Cold War, religious fundamentalists – and their political allies – claim to operate in the absence of borders in order to police the territories that elected governments appear to have abandoned. Yet fundamentalism is itself vulnerable to the styles and sensibilities to which the erosion of borders inevitably leads: penetration by forces of diverse origin, each of which engenders new affinities and the promise of new, exploratory relationships.

In an age of trans-nationalism, fundamentalism ought to be seen in the context of a widening of alliances and resemblances between extremists in general and a cultural osmosis that is taking place between people of different political and religious convictions. In Islamic countries, writes Timur Kuran, Islamic radicals believe that Islamic economics should be categorised as a 'fundamentalist doctrine' based on a set of immutable principles drawn from the traditional sources of Islam and Koranic law. Islamic banking practices in countries like Pakistan, Turkey and Iran are designed to reassert the primacy of Islam and to eliminate the western love of money by eliminating the 'desire to accumulate wealth for its own sake' through interest-based loans (Kuran 1993, p. 308).

Yet while 'the rhetoric of Islamic economics', says Kuran, 'conveys the impression that it seeks to rediscover and restore the economy' of 'the Golden Age' of Islam, as it was implemented 'a millennium and a half ago', it also 'draws heavily on modern concepts and methods' of western banking, 'including many that originated outside the Islamic world'. Islamic economics, says Kuran, exhibits 'more willingness to accept economic realities than it does in theory'. All 'doctrines labelled "fundamentalist" claim to rest on fundamentals set in stone, yet in application these prove remarkably malleable'. Formal Islamic opposition to interest-bearing loans is enshrined in the principle of 'murabaha' which replaces the principle of customer risk with a policy of risk-sharing between banker and lender. In their application of murabaha, however, Islamic banks generate an equivalent amount of interest by substituting a 'service charge' or 'markup' on loans to clients. This is also accompanied by 'an ingenious method for penalizing accounts past due' with charges 'in advance for late payment'. As a result of these policies, writes Kuran, the advent of Islamic banking has altered only the cosmetics of banking and finance and has nowhere led to a perceptive reduction in poverty or inequality – the curse of the West – or the elimination of western capitalist practices (305).

Islamic militants in the United States fare no better. The same split-minded approach to economics is evidenced by Louis Farrakhan's Nation of Islam, which, on the one hand, affiliates with international socialists like Momar Gadafi while adopting, says Manning Marable, 'a conservative programme not all that different from the white Conservative Christian Coalition'. The Nation of Islam 'favours petty capitalism as its basic economic strategy, opposes gay and lesbian rights, criticises black feminist demands for full equality, social empowerment and reproductive rights'. As a neo-fundamentalist movement 'it is authoritarian, patriarchal, and has no pretence of participatory democracy' (Marable 1995, p. 13). As proof of his opportunism Farrakhan takes his cue from the capitalist system and has entered the farming and restaurant business as part of an ambitious programme to build an economic empire in the United States that will promote self-help among African Americans. Like a black Jeremiah who orates from his pulpit in a remythologised New England, Farrakhan asks his congregation to 'atone' for their wicked ways and to blame themselves for their own oppression (13).

The 'bizarre and eclectic theology' of the Nation of Islam which 'Farrakhan has revived and enriched', writes Malise Ruthven, glorifies 'the approach of Armageddon when the black Nation will be redeemed and Babylon utterly destroyed'. In the endtimes God will supervise the destruction of the white race from an artificial planet known as the 'Mother Ship' or 'Mother Wheel'. UFOs or 'baby planes' from the planet will be sent to earth with heavenly instructions. In a providential meeting, Farrakhan meets the Honourable Elijah Muhammad, the occulted Messiah, who confirms his authority as leader. A scroll containing the sacred Scriptures is placed in the back of Farrakhan's brain to be revealed properly in the new millennium. While awaiting deliverance, the faithful must purify themselves, avoiding meat, junk food, alcohol, drugs and sexual promiscuity – the devil's weapons aimed specifically at enslaving African Americans. In so doing the Nation of Islam, writes Ruthven, 'recycles themes' from a variety of conservative traditions 'already widely present in American religious culture'. These include 'pre-millennial dispensationalist eschatology, gnosticism, kabbalism, Zionism, identity Christianity, Scientology, Arminianism, the deification of man as taught by the Mormons, the positive thinking of Normal Vincent Peale and the science-fantasy theology of L. Ron Hubbard'. Each belief is 'packaged in colourful mythological wrapping adapted from Jewish, Christian and Islamic traditions' in a bizarre expression of 'religious heterodoxy' (Ruthven 1997, p. 5).

As 'national boundaries become more permeable', says Joseph Nye, those who defend them 'around the globe' become 'more aware of each other' (Nye 1992, p. 85). Conservative religion can sometimes resemble a collaborative venture, a faith made up of certain preoccupations and fantasies common to people from different backgrounds. Religious leaders may claim autonomy while readily accepting the requirements of a culture of exchange and negotiation, a trading community where leaders of faiths can occasionally abandon their old insularities in order to embrace a new collegiality.

In countries where 'the people active in fundamentalist movements are young, college-educated, middle-class technicians, professionals and business persons', religion lacks the insularity and cultural baggage we normally associate with an older generation (Huntington 1993, p. 26). A new, entrepreneurial élite 'provides a basis for identity and commitment that transcends national boundaries' and searches out correspondences, if not affinities, between leaders and their constituencies (Hirst 1994, p. 13). Fundamentalists who tune in to the world on CNN (like Iran's Ayatollah Rasfanjani) share its collective sense of fear and anxiety at the breakdown of borders and long-standing local identities, as do the Protestant conservatives who voted for Pat Buchanan in the 1996 Presidential elections, or the supporters of Louis Farrakhan fearful of ethnic displacement by Asian and Hispanic immigrants. As these new collaborative clusters emerge and disparate groups are riven by the same discontents, history loses its traditional shape and cultural fault lines begin to blur.

In a period of rapid change and uncertainty there appears to be no escaping these patterns of convergence; what Adam Krzeminski refers to as the 'osmotic processes' that transcend national boundaries and displace the governing frameworks of race and class with new intellectual and religious alliances (Krzeminski 1994, p. 41). Malise Ruthven captures something of the change. 'The fundamentalist impulse' transcends the idea of regional congregation, she argues, and 'is a reaction to changing circumstances by selecting and recycling parts of a received repertoire of texts and symbols in novel ways.' Recently, fundamentalism has become 'an aspect of post modernity'. It seeks to remake the world by 'eclectic combinations of modernity and tradition, presenting old motifs in new, unexpected guises' (Ruthven 1993, p. 66).

In some respects fundamentalism is experiencing the same problem as radicalism in general: that is, of what happens to belief in a world which prefers opportunism to doctrine. In the United States right-wing patriots like the Freemen of Montana fall victim to a similar condition. Led by John Trochmann, the Freemen declare themselves 'resident aliens of the foreign country of Montana' and fear the onset of consensus politics and the European influence of a one-world government. But they also base their separatist philosophy, says Jonathan Freedland, on the Magna Carta and English Common Law and dress it up in 'a hokey Latinate legalese' (Freedland 1996c, p. 3). Declaring themselves to be outside world history, the Freemen of Montana are caught in a classic, postmodern dilemma. Unavoidably compromised by the messages of the past, their attitude to history is both critical of and complicitous with that which precedes their own existence. In their guerrilla campaign to rid America of Russian bombers, tanks and troop carriers, history is reclaimed yet also renounced. Ideas reverberate and styles of life become entangled in contexts which have little in common with one another. The Freemen fall victim to populist sentiment and the fear of being portrayed as narrow, between their love of the backwoods and their hatred of those who see them as backward.

Religious fundamentalists share something of the dilemma of the Freemen of Montana and are often, says Malise Ruthven, too 'utopian' or too indifferent to the goal of creating 'decent and prosperous lives for [their] citizens' (Ruthven 1993, p. 31). What they rarely lack is what Kenneth Tynan has called 'high-definition performance', the ability to translate archaic agendas into modernist contexts with charismatic effect. Opportunism is the key and a willingness to create in a postmodern age hybrid structures where texts interact with new technology and oral performance is accentuated heavily as a media event. All successful fundamentalist leaders create exhilaration by appearing priestly and theatrically compelling but they do so by utilising in novel ways the styles and strategies of postmodernity, modernity and tradition.

The forms of modern fundamentalism may very greatly from country to country but the social and religious contexts of fundamentalism share certain 'family resemblances': a 'raw bid for power' that characterises the aspirations of those who stimulate – like Ayatollah Khomeni

– traditional belief in 'societies that are threatened with political and economic change' (31).

Fundamentalism exploits what Malcolm Bradbury calls the 'consciousness of uncertainty' (Bradbury 1990, p. 21). It represents, in the modern age, a curious amalgam of exhilaration and gloom, a fantasy for the traditional which expresses itself in eclectic arrangements and novel forms. Fundamentalism, therefore, has a schizophrenic character. It establishes a dictatorship of the virtuous but is underpinned by a mood of apprehension, if not loss and disappointment, about the absence of the past. It offers its adherents the fuel of the future, a political religion which is so intense and emotionally compelling that one's sense of history as an amalgam of competing interests and ideas is easily obscured.

Millennialist and fundamentalist theatres, says Malise Ruthven, are appealing because they are able to combine rigour and charismatic fervour, utopian idealism about the future and an opportunity for priestliness in obtaining it. The appeal of fundamentalism rests on the promise of 'supernatural intervention' and the immediate liberation of individual power through the grace or permission of a shaman, mystic or ethnic ideologue. In the high-octane world of fundamentalism, hostility towards the 'rationalistic' is matched by an emphasis on 'divine imperative', the folklore of providence, signs from God, nature or the afterlife:

a restored patriarchy under a charismatic leader who draws his (or occasionally her) legitimacy from God or some other 'transcendent reference' ... intransigence born of millennial expectations ... a tendency to 'fight back' against the current of the times, while appropriating those aspects of contemporary culture that seemed necessary or desirable. (Ruthven 1993, 31)

Fundamentalism plays to the gallery of popular superstition but exhibits an awareness of intellectual life far beyond the borders of its own domestic constituency. It has evolved as a hybrid enterprise crossing the borders of nation-states, trafficking at will in all directions with host cultures, a promiscuous agent transmitting itself along viral lines. Fundamentalists who claim their work is divinely inspired can no longer claim divine originality when many of their ideas are shared by their opponents. Fundamentalists are not only members of a dynamic, interactive global culture, they also belong to a culture of piracy, in which ideas promoted in one community are frequently borrowed and plagiarised by members of another. In a postmodern age styles of life art are entangled. Ideas echo and reverberate between one country and another and are offered for popular consumption to constituencies which, racially and culturally, have little in common.

In the ongoing search for new presentations, larger audiences and more devout congregations, patriarchal leaders resemble one another. The tele-evangalist in the United States brings to mind the mullah with a microphone who sits outside the mosque in Tehran after Friday prayers. Fundamentalism allows us to see how technology can work its magic on dissimilar constituencies through audiovisual aids and how charismatic preachers exploit the power of orality in post-literate societies through tape, television and sophisticated sound systems. 'In spite of its claims to be based on the Book or the Word of God', says Martin Wollacott, modern fundamentalism 'is based much more on image and oratory transmitted by modern electronic means. This is not the fundamentalism of the Monkey Trial or of nineteenth-century mullahs, but the fundamentalism of the sound-bite' (Wollacott 1995a, p. 22).

Fundamentalist communities are no longer free of outside influence nor can they prevent the ideas they cherish from being coveted by others outside their faith. Fundamentalism is part of a culture of 'copy' and we find slivers of it in places we should not and bits of it borrowed by those to whom fundamentalists are implacably opposed (Julius 1996, p. 5). Where knowledge is derived from synthesis rather than supernatural sources and texts are 'a tissue of quotations drawn from the innumerable centers of culture', fundamentalism reveals 'the increasing unavailability of the personal style'. In such a culture the author's 'only power is to mix writings ... in such a way as never to rest on any one of them'. The fundamentalist may pride himself on the avoidance of replica, and on his status as a semi-divine seer, 'the magical creator of works ex nihilo', but he cannot avoid behaving like an apothecary, forever mixing and remixing elements into different compounds as the basis for his remedies (5).

The degree of correspondence that now exists among those who oppose western popular culture and the products of the mass market makes it difficult to attribute ideas with dual or multiple nationalities to the work of a single author. In the United States fundamentalists are unable to claim copyright for the sermons they write in a way that certifies their texts as the sole intellectual property of an author. Pat Robertson's attack on the forces of secular humanism in *The Turning Tide* and a popular culture that turns out 'filth in the name of "art"' (Robertson 1993, p. 151) replicates any number of fundamentalist texts and projects, especially those that are currently popular with radical Islam.

In countries with strong Islamic faiths such as Algeria, Egypt, Turkey and Afghanistan, the opposition to western texts and products by fundamentalists and 'warriors of god' reminds us, says Jonathan Steele, of America's 'evangelical Bible-bashers', who fear the influence those products will have on women, children and family life. The student fundamentalists of Asia and the Middle East have a particularly strong sense of patriarchal responsibility. They remind us of 'Islamic protestants' on a mission of purity, 'stirring up the faithful against the wayward prophets of the establishment', such as the mojahedin in Afghanistan and the agents of western cultural imperialism who betrayed 'the people's hopes'. In Islamic countries, liberalism and 'the forces of globalisation backed by the electronic media' (which all fundamentalists are beneficiaries of, incidentally) are said to have brought about the destruction of 'local cultures' and introduced 'the values of the city ... into the remotest rural areas' (Steele 1996, pp. 2, 3, 17).

This complaint finds its echo in the argument of Pat Robertson, leader of America's Christian Coalition, that global technologies directly assist in the transmission of a culture of permissiveness. In both communities the liberal mass media is seen as the vehicle of 'secular humanists [who] are atheists with a well-defined and dangerous agenda' and whose 'core ... philosophy is a hatred of God and religion'. Where the Taliban in Afghanistan denounce other Islamic cultures as being too lax in their interpretation of traditional Sharia law, so the Christian Coalition in the United States targets the work of the anti-Christian, soft-left intellectual, for 'attempting to dismantle the historic cultural values' of America and for 'moving' the country 'toward a homogenised world' in which there is no 'Christianity and Bible-based religion' (Robertson 1993, pp. 144–5). In *End of Millennium* (1997), Manuel Castells argues that 'fundamentalist movements ... take up the Koran, the Bible, or any holy text' to denounce liberalism 'and use it, as a banner of their despair and a weapon of their rage'. As a result, 'fundamentalisms of different kinds and from different sources ... represent the most daring uncompromising challenge to [the] one-sided domination of informational global capitalism' (Castells 1997, p. 1).

The Protestant crusades of organisations like the Moral Majority and Christian Coalition provide us with a mirror-image of that link between scholarship and faith in the Islamic church, a faith which is underpinned in both religions by the inerrancy of sacred texts (the Koran and the Bible). According to Harold Bloom, 'something of the rocky strength of Southern Baptist Fundamentalism is interestingly similar to Islamic Fundamentalism', especially in countries like Egypt where faith and revelation are at the top of a new anti-secular intellectual agenda (Bloom 1992, p. 221). In the Middle East, a young generation of Islamic scholars, says Richard Gott, is concerned not so much with the western military threat as with western models of modernisation and development. For many in the Islamic world, agrees the philosopher Hassan Hanafi, the idea of the West summons up a number of antagonisms in the minds of the Islamic faithful: 'atheism, materialism, anarchism, hegemony, exploitation, racism, capitalism and anti Islam'. Hanafi envisages an end to the influence of the West, characterised by its 'absurdity, nihilism, scepticism, relativism, agnosticism, deconstructionism, and post-modernism'. These values, he argues, express 'the end of a culture, a failure of nerve and a death in the soul' and are wholly anathema to Islam (Gott 1996, p. 31).

Pat Robertson shares a similar fear of western liberal secularism and deals repeatedly with the moral and spiritual wound which religious society has sustained from this 'evil system that so deeply damages people's lives'. For Robertson, the wreckage of 'informational global capitalism' emanates from a liberal press and a mass media which is largely responsible for the secularisation of Christian communities. In America, he says, 'virtually every effort of people of faith – whether Evangelical, Roman Catholic, or Orthodox Jew – to restore the moral climate of our nation has been ridiculed, denigrated, and opposed by the liberal press' (Robertson 1993, p. 131). Robertson objects to those who equate the 'fundamentalist' with the 'extremist', 'intolerant' and 'narrow-minded', when the very people who dominate the media and promote these ideas are responsible for an 'epidemic of violence' in the United States and the 'dumbing down' of culture through an 'infusion' of trivia and an 'illicit sexuality' (134, 153). [1]

Although he would vehemently deny it, Robertson could just as easily be speaking to an Islamic audience as to a Christian one. Indeed, says Nancy Ammerman, fundamentalists have 'come to claim for themselves the role of prophet, calling the nation back to morality' in the endtimes (Ammerman 1988, p. 200). Spiritual retrieval has a cross-cultural dimension. Islamic societies, and fundamentalist scholars like Hassan Hanafi in Egypt, are currently 'sustained by a revival of popular religion comparable with the protestant Reformation' and see the Islamic faith as belonging 'squarely in the Judaeo-Christian tradition'. Indeed, says Richard Gott, 'What has been happening in the Islamic world since 1979, and virtually unacknowledged outside it, is very close to what the West might recognise as a Renaissance – of scholarship, study, discussion and political activity' (Gott 1996, p. 31).

David Hirst agrees. Just as radical Islamists in countries like Algeria are engaged in a war of liberation, a '"cultural" struggle … against western power, western secularism, and forms of corruption "that are western as well as indigenous"' (Hirst 1994, p. 21) – so religious fundamentalists in the United States use 'their political power to force morality on otherwise unrepentant sinners' who 'would take the United States away from a "godly" way of life'.

Political action, claims Pat Robertson, is necessary on issues such as abortion, gay rights or the Equal Rights Amendment, in order to counter the 'dominating theory' of liberalism that has overwhelmed the nation's schools and universities. In the American educational system, writes Robertson, 'traditional values' are seen as 'old-fashioned and meaningless' and 'the minds of our children have been vacuumed and sanitized, leaving them open to anyone capable of exploiting their trained biases, their materialistic desires and their programatic gullibility' (Robertson 1991, p. 218). Religion is a serious absence from the nation's schools and fundamentalists, writes Nancy Ammerman, 'do not accept', 'that public places must be kept free of religious activities and ideas'. Prayer in the classroom is a prerequisite 'of a godly state affirming its godliness and offering its citizens the free opportunity to participate'. Since 'fundamentalists believe that honoring God should not be an embarrassment in a "Christian nation"' their 'strategy for change differs from that of liberal or secular political reformers' and 'begins with seeking spiritual change in individuals'. As in Islamic societies, 'spiritual change will produce changes in social institutions' and the saving of individuals is a prerequisite of the saving of society (Ammerman 1987, pp. 201, 200).

II

'Few activities', says Eve Kornfeld, 'reveal as much about a developing culture as its construction and representation of the Other.' 'In periods of uncertainty or crisis', or in periods which require the articulation of an 'imperial discourse', the identities of popular and élite cultures as well as the belief of dominant individuals and social groups 'are constructed in opposition to a culturally different Other'. In militant political and religious faiths cultural identities are often constructed out of deference to the Other, not simply through arguments which confirm the Other as a repository of deviant values.

In the 1990s fundamentalism exploits 'uncertainty' by treating the Other as an adversary of the church while sharing the convictions it claims to condemn. In a world of rival faiths, ideas are the product of 'contrapuntal ensembles' and the transactions that take place between adversaries. Militant belief is a fugue composed of replication and copy, much of which is covered up by the rhetorical performance and single-mindedness of the evangelist (Kornfeld 1995, pp. 289–91).

The paradox that makes militant Protestantism an opponent of, and a collaborator with, other non-western religious communities originates in the colonial experience of race in New England. The millennialist church that emerges out of the seventeenth century does not create a world unto itself but one that embraces the legacy of Israel through the ages. As a transnational faith, the church looks outside the immediate locality for signs of Jewish emigration and encounter. It recognises that the settlements of Israel are so widely dispersed throughout the world that those who pursue them are obliged to follow an emigrant trail, one that extends from the Americas to the Orient.

In his third novel, *In an Antique Land* (1994), Amitav Ghosh shows us why America's fundamentalists attach so much importance to the pursuit of Jews across national frontiers. Ghosh returns to the twelfth century when Jews held slaves but gained a much wider access to nations and national cultures. Ghosh investigates the life of Bomma, a twelfth-century Indian slave and his Arabic-speaking Jewish master in Tunisia. Bomma is from the south Indian coast but grows to be the business agent of his slave-owning merchant, Ben Yiju, and a respected member of the household. By counterpointing his own travels and his decision to learn the Arabic dialectic spoken by medieval Jews, Ghosh sheds light on the medieval past in which the Jews were active as travellers and merchants. Ghosh discovers a world of accommodations between different races and civilisations in which the histories of Indian and Egyptian, Muslim and Jew, Hindu and Muslim are intertwined. For Ghosh, Jews and Arabs contribute to the cultural enrichment of Asia and Africa on the basis of a willingness to interact with people of different civilisations. He shows how the fluency of travel between Africa and Asia in the Middle Ages persists as a legacy of transience which drives Egyptians to work in Libya, the Gulf States and Iraq and the cross-cultural links and inter-religious ties which continue to override political borders.

The legacy of Jewish dispersal has had a compelling effect on missionary activity in the evangelical Protestant church and has also led to a widespread interest in the traits and traditions of other communities (whom the Jews may have visited). The search for Semitic resemblance requires, in part, an admission that we do not know who the Jews really are. Since the Jews can be anyone, fundamentalists are sometimes tempted to fulfil, through copy and collaboration, an obligation to contact those whom the Jews may have influenced.

The eclectic tendencies within fundamentalism can only be held in check so long as there is a formal acknowledgement of the dangers involved. In the work of Pat Robertson, such an acknowledgement is not forthcoming and the extent to which militant faiths coalesce and correspond is deliberately disguised. Much of Robertson's writing involves a cover-up of one sort or another and the moment we begin to investigate the spiritual originality of his thinking, many of his ideas look tired and second-hand. Rather than come clean on the extent to which he borrows ideas from non-Christian sources, Robertson projects

himself as a devout iconoclast, an anti-ecumenical who subscribes to
a system of demarcation in religious philosophy and a textual theology
that sanctions the autonomy of cultural borders. Robertson claims to
certify the authenticity of the Protestant faith through the 'singularity'
of the Christian Coalition. Yet on closer inspection, much of what
he says plays to the gallery of popular superstition. This is accomplished by cultural hijacking. In *The Turning Tide* (1993) and *The
New World Order* (1991) many of the political and religious leaders
whose ideas Robertson uses are opposed to the church whose cause
he professes. Robertson is shameless in enlisting the support of
unlikely bedfellows: from Pope Pious XI, 'a true believer in the
Christian social order' (Robertson 1991, p. 2), to Robert Kennedy,
whose 'vision' for America gave 'a secure moral foundation for those
who desire a better world for themselves' (Robertson 1993, p. 245)
to Julius Nyerere of Tanzania, whom Robertson sees as a socialist
opponent of the global racism that an ecumenical order tolerates.

Fundamentalists may occasionally share the beliefs of those who
worship outside the Judeo-Christian tradition, but they are also liable
to vilify them as purveyors of 'misery', corruption and class subjugation. 'Hindus let people starve', says Pat Robertson, 'rather than kill
rats who breed disease and eat the people's food, because they believe
rats are reincarnated people' (Robertson 1991, p. 219). Robertson
endorses Samuel Huntington's argument that we are now (more than
ever) gripped by a 'clash of civilizations' which pits 'the West' against
'the rest'. Robertson refuses to concede an alliance with other non-
western religions. The fear of being damned as 'syncretistic' drives
him to make extraordinary claims about the dissimilarity of the
Protestant, Hindu and Islamic traditions. He condemns Hinduism, for
example, as a corrupt partner in a dubious alliance of humanistic and
New World adventurers, a 'syncretistic religion based on the "New
Age"' worship of 'the universal spirit' (214). In contrast, Protestant
evangelism is the one true faith, the enduring meta-narrative blessed
by God and singularly appointed to play a divine role in the moral
leadership of the world. Described by one journalist as sharing the
same beliefs on abortion as Muslim and Hindu fundamentalists,
Robertson reaffirms the evil of ecumenism and complains about a
media penchant for 'prejudice masquerading as news' (142).

Robertson's blustering is an attempt to disguise his fascination
with race and his search for liaisons that are liable to plumb the
depths of 'Criolian degeneracy'. Throughout the 1980s and 1990s
Robertson's overseas ministries, from Guatemala to Zaire, brought
him into contact with political leaders who were corrupt and
repressive, and whose notoriety appears to have had a corrosive
effect on his moral standards. Like a promiscuous Puritan, Robertson

proclaims his vigorous opposition to the 'shadowed corners of the land' but harbours a powerful desire to enter into it, as if he is compelled to negotiate deals and exchange intimacies with those whose morality belongs in the gutter.

Secrecy was paramount in Robertson's relationship with Mobutu Sese Seko, President of Zaire until 1977 when he was deposed in a people's revolution. From 1992 until it was exposed in 1995, the Robertson-owned African Development Company ran diamond-mining and forestry operations in Zaire. Robertson's involvement began with Operation Blessing which first landed in Zaire to head up an unsuccessful relief effort on a corn farm outside Kinshasa. A later Operation Blessing in Goma was 'strongly criticised', says Alec Foege, by American aid groups 'for wasting too much money on transport costs and spending too much time proselytizing while more people died'. Robertson subsequently became Mobutu's most vocal supporter, arguing that the Clinton administration's refusal to grant him a visa was 'outrageous' even though Mobutu was relying 'on a hefty take' from the country's 'largely unregulated $300 million-a-year diamond trade'. To the bitter end, Robertson stood alongside 'Washington conservatives and lobbyists' in claiming that Mobutu was 'heading toward democracy', in spite of his appalling record on human rights and his growing reputation as a money-launderer (Foege 1996, pp. 217–18).

Pat Robertson's work in Latin America offers another example of a promiscuous love affair with political dictatorship. Throughout the 1980s Robertson was a strong supporter of the right-wing agenda of the Central Intelligence Agency (CIA), multinational business interests and the anti-revolutionary strategies of politically repressive leaders. The politicisation of the evangelical church and its alignment with dictatorships can be seen in the church's opposition to working-class, revolutionary movements and the willingness of the religious right, as David Stoll has argued, 'to turn missionary work into an instrument for US militarism' (Stoll 1990, p. 308). W. E. Biernatzki develops the point:

When General Efraim Rios Montt, a convert to the Pentecostalist church, became president of Guatemala in 1982, he was hailed by the more politically-oriented North American tele-evangelists, particularly the '700 Club' of Pat Robertson. Guatemala was by no means unacquainted with militarism and repression prior to Rios Montt's presidency, but a new element of zeal was added by his Pentecostalist identity which may have contributed to the slaughter of thousands of Indians during his campaign to repress a leftist rebellion allegedly inspired by Catholic liberation theology but labeled 'communist' by the army. (Quoted in Tehranian 1993, p. 329)

In his book *The New World Order*, Robertson talks about 'the enlightened leadership' shown by Rios Montt 'who insisted on honesty in government' and then had every official sign a pledge that read, 'I will not steal; I will not lie; I will not abuse!' Robertson describes how he was in 'Guatemala City three days after Rios Montt overthrew the corrupt Lopez Garcia government. The people had been dancing in the street for joy, literally fulfilling the words of Solomon who said, '"When the righteous are in authority, the people rejoice"' (Robertson 1991, p. 228).

In the case of the Pentecostalist preacher Jimmy Swaggart, a righteous ministry in Latin America was a profitable one. In the 1970s and 1980s Jimmy Swaggart Ministries dedicated itself to the cause of world evangelisation, enabling the Swaggart organisation to expand its influence to new countries to combat the Antichrist. Since Christ's Second Coming 'depended on viewer contributions', says Quentin J. Schultze, Swaggart regularly announced to his congregation that 'the Saviour would not return until, as predicted in the Book of Revelation, Christ was preached to all people'. In this way Swaggart yoked his 'own financial condition to the earthly return of Jesus Christ'. This allowed him to build up the highest-rated weekly syndicated broadcast in the United States. and to become its 'most successful fund-raiser, generating nearly a half-million dollars weekly in contributions' (Schultze 1991, p. 111).

In his Gospel crusades in Central and South America, 'Swaggart used satellites and syndicated tapes to become the closest thing to a Protestant pope in Central America'. According to Rose and Schultze, 'his popularity in Guatemala in the mid-to-late 1980s far exceeded his television appeal in the United States, even though he was the highest-rated tele-evangelist. During his heyday, before the sex-and-money scandals ... Swaggart's show was seen regularly by at least one-half of the nation' (Rose and Schultze 1993, p. 435). In Latin America, Swaggart played the role of charismatic showman and corporate emissary while his extreme political views gave him access to right-wing dictators like Chile's Augusto Pinochet, a man whom Swaggart congratulated, writes Susan Diamond, 'for having expelled the devil in the 1973 CIA-sponsored coup' (Diamond 1989, p. 34).

Swaggart's involvement with political reactionaries like Pinochet was not only promiscuous in name but promiscuous in nature. As both tele-evangelist and regular visitor to Latin America, Swaggart offered his congregation salvation through ecstasy, a religion which was both theatrical and sexual. Like the early evangelist Aimee Semple McPherson, Jimmy Swaggart made sexuality an integral feature of fundamentalism and his extravagance and 'dramatic flair ... seemed to resonate' with the orality and braggadocio of Latin American life

(Brouwer, Gifford and Rose 1996, p. 60). Swaggart's religious broadcasts on Guatemalan television were a way of making Christ the saviour physically and emotionally accessible to Latin American audiences. As a media event his broadcasts emphasised libidinous performance; they spoke to the poor, the oppressed and the disempowered, by offering instant gratification. According to Rose and Schultze, Swaggart was popular because he 'communicated in a powerful aural and visual style that conveyed ... the illusion of being live, unrehearsed, unplanned' (Rose and Schultze 1993, p. 435). This helped to generate an immediate rapport, a 'communicative affinity between the oral cultures of Pentecostal Guatemala and the Pentecostan southern United States' (436). The basis of that affinity was emotional and sexual. Swaggart managed 'to program his message' so that it built 'to an authentic sense of frenzy'. His was a performance of 'libidinal high wire voltage', writes Ray Browne, 'the closest you can come to simulating explicit sexuality on camera' (Browne 1987, p. 67).

Jimmy Swaggart was the role model for Gore Vidal's Saint Paul, the inventor of Christianity in *Live From Golgotha* (1992) who is swept through Palestine and Asia Minor on a tide of emotion and promiscuous conversion in the aftermath of Christ's crucifixion. Under the pretext of evangelical conversion Saint becomes sexually obsessed with the beauty of different races and faiths – especially the Jews – and the economic opportunities that accrue to the church from a policy of mass conversion. Saint embodies – 'as most saints do' – a contradiction at the heart of Christianity, 'a fantastic double standard' (Vidal 1992, p. 45). As the first great Christian evangelical he will 'do anything to sell himself – and his Message' (120). But as an ex-Mossad secret agent he can never renounce his Jewish affiliations: love of personality and sense of the theatrical. Saint's decision to stress the sensuous beauty of Christ, his 'mega' manner (32), is calculated to raise expectations among his congregation. In Asia Minor, Saint is adept at 'putting on a great show'. The revenue he generates goes straight into the pocket of James at the Temple in Jerusalem who invests the proceeds in 'mutual caravans' (107) for the Zionist church. In return, Saint is allowed to indulge his passion for young boys, none of whom can resist his advances if they want 'to be saved' (108). Christianity offers Saint the opportunities that Zionism cannot: sex and money, both of which he trades in at an inflationary level. His is a deeply acquisitive religion, sexual conquests and increased profits are the targets he aims for in order to satisfy his lust for capitalism and alternative audiences. Saint never teaches 'the real cause for the Crucifixion ... only the cover story' (119), and he promotes personality at the expense of doctrine. His Jesus is a charismatic who falls on hard times, dies for his beliefs and stages a comeback via the Resurrection.

In Saint's philosophy 'appearances are everything'. As a balding dyslexic, evangelism is his route to the top. With nothing 'going for him', only his voice, he works 'the circuit like there was no tomorrow, preaching, collecting money, and putting together what was, frankly, the greatest mailing list ever assembled by anyone in the Roman world'. As a capitalist and a 'conman' (7), 'show business' is 'his life' (76), a way of accumulating converts and financial capital at the 'bottom' end of the scale. 'Thanks to our wonderful Message', says Timothy, his boyfriend, 'we really do make your average creep feel pretty happy with himself' (78).

The discipline of preaching provides Saint with a chance to compensate himself at the crowd's expense. Ministering to a crowd allows him to speak 'in tongues' in order to disguise his epilepsy (73). He revs it up 'like a drunk spider spinning a wild web' (36), while Timothy, his assistant, accepts 'donations' with a 'faraway smile'. Saint's weighty and histrionic manner makes him 'a martyr to flatulence' (39); like Christ, his role model, 'the one thing he can not live without' is 'a live audience'. Crowds are 'all he cared about', says Timothy; they are the ultimate mechanism through which casual appetites are stimulated and capital transactions and accumulations generated (27). Failure with crowds makes Saint 'more insatiable' (44). Although he tells his audience that he 'hated all sex inside and outside of wedlock on the grounds that it made you unclean in the eyes of God' he 'never stopped fooling around' with his trophies, like his boyfriend, Timothy (45).

Jews who become Christians, says Timothy, the narrator, are always inclined towards sexual promiscuity and are disinclined to eliminate the word 'lust' from their vocabulary (80). In their urge to become acquainted with an ever-increasing congregation, Christians suffer from attention deficit disorder, an affliction brought on by the search for new audiences and dynamic partnerships in Christ. Believing themselves born-again, Christians imagine a world made in their own image and are constantly in search of utopian schemes through which to expand their empire.

In switching his attention compulsively from one synagogue to another Saint is fixated by the possibility of conquest: the Jew who is yet to become a Christian and the Christian, like Timothy, who can never forget he was once a Jew. In a world of ever-expanding horizons the Children of Israel with their 'flashy cornflower-blue eyes and hyacinth golden curls', are irresistible to Saint (24). For a balding paedophile in search of 'youthful flesh', the beauty of religion lies in the knowledge that '"you never know when or where you'll make a convert"' (25). As a Christian, Saint can 'not really relate to anything non-Jewish' (79), just as later generations of Christians can not conceive of their own salvation without a saving remnant to guide them. The culture of dependency is that of the voyeur, says Vidal. Wherever they go, Christians can never forget the youthful promise of 'every red-blooded Asia Minor boy': the lust of a lad like Timothy who dreams of 'a horny, melony-soft eunuch' to 'pitch' him 'a slow ball' (75).

For Vidal the promiscuity of the ex-Jew (Saint) in pursuit of the unredeemed Jew of Palestine and Asia Minor typifies the sexual and economic fixations of the church in pursuit of the profit of godliness. With the early disciples like Saint, that search is cleverly concealed by Christ's heroic leadership of the people and Saint's presentation of him as a Keynesian visionary and liberal reformer. Christ's cruci-fixion is heroic because Saint transforms him into a corpulent dwarf with a 'serious hormonal problem' (29), a fixer who cheats death in the interests of full employment. Saint's particular spin allows Christ to overcome his disability by appealing to the crowd as an economic reformer. Described by Timothy as a 'politician with a lot of demagogic funny-money schemes' (126), Jesus drives the fiscally orthodox, rabbinical Jews out of the Temple in Jerusalem for using it to imple-ment anti-inflationary banking policies and for pursuing high interest rates and low inflation. Jesus, a 'full-employment, supply-side econ-omist' threatens the economic viability of the treasury in Rome by undermining its banking system in Jerusalem. As an anti-monetarist, Christ's execution sets up 'the messiah myth' (118) which Saint exploits to create a cult following. As a philosophy based on perse-cution and reform Judaism, Christianity allows Saint to follow in Christ's footsteps and launch himself on an evangelical crusade for conversion. Like Jesus, Saint remains a 'Jew' (109) at heart and, according to his lover, Timothy, 'even more serious than the Big Fella in the sky had made him in the first place' (7). Throughout his ministry, Saint demonstrates his lingering love-affair with Jewishness by 'paying a lot of money into the Temple treasury', now controlled by Jesus's brother James, one of the old 'Temple rabbinate' and a committed anti-inflationist (119).

The economic opportunism of the right-wing church, together with its free-trade philosophies and indiscriminate political relationships, has been reflected throughout the 1980s and 1990s in its evangelical approach to mission. For the converted Christians of Latin America, says Richard Gott, the evangelical church is an extension of the market economy selling itself in dynamic displays of media marketing. The marketing mission of Protestant pentecostalism, writes Gott, does not 'hark back to the old', but encourages its converts to 'make sense of – or at the very least adjust to the dramatic new world of consumer capitalism in which they find themselves' (Gott 1995, p. 18).

In countries like Chile, Argentina and Brazil the new Protestant, evangelical 'hegemony' claims to be about 'helping people adjust to the new economic order' by demonstrating the virtues of a liberal bourgeois ideology. In reality, this same ideology undergirds the consolidation of consumer capitalism and 'conspicuous plenty' and reinforces its own imperial expansion at the expense of native customs and indigenous values (18). This is particularly true in the Oriente region of Ecuador, says Gott, where 'the Quechua Indians have turned to the evangelical church in droves' (14).

The economic and spiritual damage that Protestant fundamentalism has been willing to inflict on the Ecuadorian Amazon is discussed by Peter Matthiessen in his novel *At Play in the Fields of the Lord* (1965). Here, Matthiessen shows us how evangelical religion has had the same pernicious and corrupting influence on tribal civilisation as oil development, and that both activities have brought about the disintegration of tribal culture and 'homeland'.[2] For the Protestant missionary Leslie Huben, the commercial exploitation of the wilderness is beneficial to his mission in the Oriente, allowing him greater access to the Niaruna Indians in the jungle settlements of Remate and Madre de Dios. Huben understands the benefits of allying with the corrupt prefect of Oriente State, El Commandante Rufino Guzman, who has lost patience with the Niaruna's resistance to the commercial development of their ancestral lands. Huben realises the Niaruna will be far more receptive to the Gospel should Guzman's plan to make 'this great land ... safe for progress' be successful. Huben's support for Guzman is based on the knowledge that Guzman is an agent for a government that wants the 'lands developed' and that development will make the Niaruna vulnerable to his Christian ministry. Since '"Nobody"' gets in Guzman's way Huben supports his plan for resettlement (Matthiessen 1987, p. 22). He would rather the Niaruna were '"cowed a little"' and '"softened up for an outreach of the Word"' (24).

In Mattheissen's novel, the commodification of native culture encourages the church to support the efforts of a genocidal government. While the ministers of the Bible Belt regard the Indians of the Oriente as the Children of Israel they are less than scrupulous in respecting their environment as a sacred wilderness. The New Fields Mission endorse the urbanisation and resettlement policies of the government in order to implement a righteous plan of conversion. Christ's message is conveyed through a programme which twins intimidation with evangelism and reclaims the worshipper through ecological imperialism and the introduction of a consumer culture. The tribal 'Legend of the Deluge' (190) convinces Huben that his anthropological analysis of the Niaruna makes them a genuine remnant of Israel, a post-Noachuian culture worthy of Christian education and settlement, a marketable asset he can advertise in his church journal, *Mission Fields*.

Huben expects to be successful providing he can wean the Niaruna away from Roman Catholicism – a rival product – with 'a good old-fashioned' threat of 'hell'. If he does nothing the Niaruna will fall to the Catholic mission of Padre Xantes, which is '"lying in wait to see us lose the advantage I have won in Jesus' name"' (24). In preparation for Guzman's attack Huben intends that when 'the wild bands' of Indians are 'contacted', he will 'infect them with a need for cloth and beads, mirrors and axe heads'. Once this 'need' has been 'established, their exposure to the Gospel [will] be assured, and conversion [will] simply be a matter of time' (154).

This 'basic method used by missionaries across the world' (154) is coterminous with the pacification programmes of the American military in Vietnam, whose wilderness mission Huben shares. Huben has the mind of a 1960s resettlement officer stressing the benefits of the Strategic Hamlet to Montagnard tribesmen. His religious inclinations are those of a developer prepared to violate the rural and cultural traditions of the country in order to eliminate tribal opposition. During periods of colonial conquest, says the novelist William Eastlake in *The Bamboo Bed* (1969), fear of the unseen is the dominant psychosis: 'Americans love the open. Americans do not trust the jungle. The first thing Americans did in Vietnam was clear a forest and plant the cities' (Eastlake 1969, pp. 24–5).

III

The colonial ambition of Leslie Huben is one of the principal reasons why religious fundamentalism has become discredited in other millennialist communities. Over the last two decades, says Madeleine Bunting, millennialism has broken away from right-wing Christianity and has undergone a 'fragmentation of belief' (Bunting 1996, p. 2). The erosion of loyalty to church-based doctrine is evident in the 'breaking down of boundaries between denominations, between faiths and between all spiritual beliefs' (2). Fundamentalism now finds itself in direct competition with a millennialism of the new, a religion that is prepared to mix ideas from the old prophecy movement with those which offer 'a kinder and gentler apocalypse' – theosophy, spiritualism, eastern religion – yet has strong misgivings about the ethical standing of the church as a guardian of spiritual values. In New Age religion those who are embarking on a search for the sacred in their lives – especially the generation that came of age in the 1960s – accelerate the tempo of the millenarian drama through biblically unscripted and direct initiatives (3).

'Cross-cultural' faiths, argues Sharon Begley, consciously avoid the discredited opportunism of the Bible Belt and prefer openly to synthesise religion from 'different traditions' – Zen, meditation, Gregorian chant, eco-fundamentalism, Buddhist rap – in order to 'find a path' that is 'more spiritually profound' (Begley 1994, p. 41). This blending of discrete ritual is a way of escaping from the bogus prescriptions of an 'hierarchical faith' whose 'moral authority', says Deepak Lal, has been 'undermined' (Lal 1995, p. 526) by political scandal and the questionable morality of the church. New religious movements distance themselves from the corporate policies of fundamentalism but remain intrigued by spiritual eschatologies: the imminence of the apocalypse, the promise of salvation through rapturous experience, the presence of a sacred, cosmic presence in rural and 'hidden' locations. In New Age religion the search for a saving remnant of Jews is remythologised in order to accommodate a new supernaturalism: actors and characters are assigned new roles, leading protagonists are redeployed, the field of action relocated to messianic locations.

The reinstatement of the sacred within the mystery of space is echoed in the 'eco-fundamentalist' attempt to invest the wilderness with the status it enjoyed in the seventeenth century. Deepak Lal, for example, describes the 'sense of loss felt' in the face of modernity's treatment of the environment, which comes from the 'fear of losing' a cherished lifestyle. Eco-fundamentalists, writes Anna Bramwell, not only see 'the earth as man's unique domain', they also 'believe in an absolute responsibility' for their 'action and for the world in general'. Where 'there is no God the Shepherd', then 'man (himself) becomes the shepherd', acting responsibly in order to stimulate His eventual return. Spiritual ecology is 'apocalyptical' but remains distrustful of those who have 'caused the impending apocalypse by [their] actions' (quoted in Lal 1995, p. 522). Apocalypse may or may not be averted. We await salvation in the new millennium, or redeem the planet through cultural and political intervention. Since 'the moral authority of the centre ... has been undermined', responsibility for implementing religious belief has passed 'outside the hierarchical structure' of the church, and is now assumed by 'non-governmental organisations' (526): Amnesty International, environmental bodies, aid agencies. Environmentalists search for a mysterious divinity by escaping the society of crowds and power. Lal quotes from the work of Mary Douglas:

The sacred places of the world are crowded with pilgrims and worshippers. Mecca is crowded, Jerusalem is crowded. In most religions, people occupy the foreground of the thinking. The Sierra Nevadas are vacant places, loved explicitly because they are vacant. (530)

In seventeenth-century millennialism, the mountainous regions were also 'loved' because they were vacant of all but the hidden races, a saving remnant who required the protection of a vigilant 'Shepherd', respectful of their Israel. Some notion of how this love has reappeared in contemporary cultural studies is conveyed by Quentin Tarantino in the film *Pulp Fiction* (1994). At the conclusion of the film Jules, a contract killer, removes his shades (the filter through which the world is darkened by sin and retribution) and acknowledges 'God's touch' (Tarantino 1994, p. 173). Jules has prefaced his earlier killings for the warlord Marsellus Wallace (and conceivably, the United States government for whom he has fought in Vietnam), with a passage memorised from Ezekiel. The moment he renounces violence Jules also abandons his punitive involvement with the Old Testament. He announces, to his colleague Vincent Vega, a new-found desire to 'walk the earth' (173) and become a 'shepherd' (99) in atonement for his sins. Missions of such singular and hierarchical importance – in pursuit of 'the tyranny of evil men' (186) – no longer concern him. He loses interest in the cult of war and the 'cold-blooded ... shit' of Ezekiel (186–7). Although he remains 'uncertain' about the future, he imagines for himself a life on the road from where he will await the '"moment of clarity"' that comes to a 'bum' (174–5).

As an avatar of the 1990s Jules connects with the spiritual fervour of American society and the 'religious renaissance' that, according to John Gliona in the *Los Angeles Times*, is spreading through the gangster fraternity of southern California (Gliona 1995, p. 7). Although Jules is unlikely to find the hidden wilderness he is looking for in Los Angeles, his desire to become the 'righteous' man who 'shepherds the weak through the valley of the darkness', is partly fulfilled (Tarantino 1994, p. 186). The appearance of two hoodlums, Pumpkin and Honey Bunny, gives Jules the opportunity to interrupt his stylised violence with a line in pastoral care and suggests something of a transformation from 'cold-blooded' killer to benevolent interventionist. This is a mission that lies outside the church but accepts the need for a devout evangelism.

The hoodlum's bullet that misses Jules in the apartment, and brings about his spiritual conversion, is an example of what *The Celestine Prophecy* (1995) refers to as, the 'phenomenon' of 'synchronicity'. It is one of life's 'coincidences' from which Jules learns the language of 'the nine insights' (Redfield and Adrienne 1995, pp. 4–5). Jules sees this as 'divine intervention, a spiritual message that came down from heaven and stopped the bullets ... a fuckin' miracle!' (139). The bullet that misses Jules clearly speaks to him. As a merciful agent of providence it inspires him to become a New Age 'shepherd'. Through his own salvation – and the salvation he proposes for others – Jules discovers, in the words of *The Celestine Prophecy*, 'an underlying principle of order' which will bring 'insecurity and violence' to an end. The miracle he has witnessed allows him to 'experience an inner connection with the divine energy within', an opportunity to discover his own 'spiritual mission' and a personal way in which he can 'contribute to the world' (Redfield and Adrienne 1995, pp. 5–6).

In spite of its message of hope and redemption, *Pulp Fiction* concludes with a note of caution, one that is hauntingly familiar to students of cults and 1990s messiahs. For Jules's partner, Vincent Vega, gangsters who fancy their chances as saviours, invariably end up as 'bums' (Tarantino 1994, p. 174), deluded charlatans in search of a remnant on which to impose their own special tyranny. Jules aspires to the pastoral but could easily wind-up trapped, in what Malise Ruthven describes as, 'a penumbra of semi-occultisms', a 'reconstituted' pre-millennialism with him as the 'mystery' Californian guru playing the part of a demented Jesus (Ruthven 1989, p. 184). His desire to walk the earth like Caine in Kung Fu does not exactly inspire confidence. It may involve his retreat into the kind of activity described by Janet Turner Hospital in the novel *Oyster* (1996), in which 'people who want to gain power tend to go for frontier spaces where they can wall themselves off from society' (Neustatter 1996, p. 6). While fringe religions and New Age cults in the 1990s, says Pat Kane, centre on 'the empowerment and enrichment of individuality' they often encourage those who believe in them to 'head for areas that have the right climate for a fervent faith' (Kane 1995, p. 13). For David Koresh it is Waco, and for Turner Hospital's Oyster, a lean, elegant figure who appears out of the dust with a promise of salvation, it is the tiny community of Outer Maroo in western Queensland.

The power of personality is a dangerous addiction for those whose 'modern mysticism', says Pat Kane, is 'borne out of the extreme incoherence of contemporary western lifestyles' (Kane 1995, p. 13). In novels like *Oyster* the experimentalism of the New Age messiah is doomed to failure by the intensity and extravagance of his endtimes vision. The attempt to enter uncharted wilderness – to release the spiritual energies implicit within it – moves away from the playful theatre of 'Utopian amusement' (William Wood's phrase for the Christianising of the Indians (Axtell 1981, p. 268)) and becomes a ministry whose consequences are terminal and disabling.

New Age gurus like David Koresh and Jim Jones embody the megalomania of the mainstream church. Maverick separatists and rebellious saints are no more immune from the temptations of authority than the fallen ministers of fundamentalism like Jim Bakker or Jimmy Swaggart. Fixations with the apocalypse are as popular as ever, while myths of salvation and rescue manifest themselves in deluded schemes of suicidal worship and wilderness escape. Gurus and cult leaders are inclined to take responsibility for the Rapture away from God and put it in the hands of an earthly messiah. In the Heaven's Gate community, God's procrastination is overcome through the righteous action of Marshall H. Applewhite and the Rapture is reconfigured as an earthly mechanism of evacuation in the endtimes. While not a formally religious sect the Heaven's Gate cult were pro-Zionist. Their mass suicide in San Diego in 1997 anticipated a more righteous encounter with the Jews in the cosmos, the extraterrestrials who were already saved and installed in heaven.

If the cosmic pursuit of the Jew can lead to the grand delusion of suicide in California – the embracing of the Jew in heavenly death – the terrestrial pursuit of a damaged remnant in Thom Jones's *Cold Snap* (1995) raises the spectre of 'Criolian degeneracy' in Africa. The doctors and aid workers in Jones's stories live outside the church but continue to share the Semitic prophecies of Daniel 11: 36–45, that the tribes of Ham migrated to 'the land of Cush' (Ethiopia) from where they spread out across the whole of Africa. The signs of promiscuity, says John Canup, which Daniel attributes to the descendants of Ham (as 'rebellious outcasts from the Ur family'), are evident throughout Jones's work (Canup 1990, p. 66). In the jungles of Rwanda, Somalia and Zaire, the filth and contamination of Africa lives on in the tribal settlements where the doctors and aid workers have volunteered their efforts. While the settlements are a victim of famine and disease, much of the sickness with which they are afflicted is not endemic. It is an imported sickness and one that is made worse by those who are there to care for the country, to 'shepherd' the sick and needy 'in the name of charity and good will'. The aid workers who we find caught up in the biblical racism of Daniel share his reverence for the degeneracy of Ham: the kind of promiscuity we see in the ministry of Pat Robertson in Zaire.

On the surface, the aid workers in *Cold Snap* – doctors, nurses, fundraisers, missionaries – appear to have given short shrift to Old Testament racism and the 'foreboding failure of political will' that western leaders have been guilty of in Africa (Soyinka 1994, p. 20). By devoting their lives to the sick and injured, these volunteers signal their willingness to intervene in a continent whose people have been blighted by disease, genocide and the arms trade. Like Dr Koestler, the aid worker is a 'loner' (Jones 1995, p. 48) who has gone to Africa to rid the region of its western heart of darkness tag. As a 'righteous man [he] nerves himself for ceaseless activity', only to end up in 'quicksand' (110), a victim of what Cotton Mather described as 'Indianization' (Axtell 1981, pp. 274–81) and those 'psychosexual disorders' that afflicted the early Christians in New England. Like

New England, Africa is a 'savage domain awaiting liberation', where 'Satan terribly makes a prey of you and leads you captive to do his will' (307). Seduced by the sickness he is attempting to cure, the aid worker becomes an implicated man, psychically extended by the challenge he is set, drawn to the heart of the very disaster that western imperialism has created in Africa.

The stories in *Cold Snap* all have a touch of disaster in them, a sense of the high emotional cost of human involvement in the times and the psychic over-extension among those committed to a ministry of healing. Jones's expatriates are deeply immersed in their adventures. Like Scott Fitzgerald's Dick Diver, they feel compelled to risk their sanity by plunging into the melée of advanced social experience, as if the claims of consciousness and the responsibilities of the human condition demand this. The belief that the aid worker must know his times and serve in the places where the times are acted out most fully has both a creative and humanitarian dimension. In penetrating the interior space of those who are malnourished and disease-ridden the aid worker sees himself as the first generation of a new condition of modernity; a person who has come from the world of the prejudicial past in order to live in the experiential future, an experimental landscape on the other side of some essential line drawn across human experience. Those who survive that experience and come to maturity because of it are the bearers of a special kind of knowledge that an older generation – and, especially, a church generation in the Bible Belt – does not possess.

The principal qualification for understanding Africa in the lives of these aid workers is not book-learned knowledge but, as Hamlin Garland once said, knowledge that comes from a direct contact with life. The problem with their Africa is that it does not always generate knowledge, or a desire for knowledge, that is wholly consistent with moral enlightenment. Soon after he arrives at the mission compound in 'Way Down Deep in the Jungle', the young doctor, Indiana, begins to sense the basis of the dilemma: '"I came to serve humanity, and already I'm filled with a sense of the incompatible"' (66). Indiana's 'sense of the incompatible' – the lure of the bestial as well as the beautiful – brings to mind the menace of contradiction that proved such a bewildering feature of the wilderness in colonial New England.

The African jungle in Jones's stories is redolent with the ambivalent power of the early American wilderness. It is an authentic place in which the Jews have been scattered, but its rare, archival beauty is also its curse. As a saving remnant the children of Ham are a sacred race. But their biblical divinity is also degenerate. They cannot escape the curse of Ham who was sexually compromised after the flood, spied on his naked father, and told his brothers what he had seen.

If the visitor to Africa must cure the country he must also overcome the legacy of the curse, a process that requires the aid worker to jeopardise his own survival in the quest for truth. Those who try to cure Africa must come to terms with the nature of the curse or, at least, accumulate, in their clinics and surgeries, a mass of evidence to expose (or validate) the myth of promiscuity.

The task proves impossible. At a time when AIDS and the ebola virus and other sexually transmitted diseases, have been described as 'African in origin', the liberal missionary transforms his surgery into a laboratory (Horton 1995, p. 24). In his search for an authentic Africa the aid worker falls back on 'intensive fantasies' (Jones 1995, p. 71) and associates the sickness of the host with the imagined promiscuity of an 'alluring' remnant, with all its underground derangement and filth.[3] Aid workers like Moses Galen, in 'Ooh Baby Baby', are so indiscriminate in their sexual conduct, they appear to want to infect themselves with full-blown disease: AIDS, ebola, Hepatitis B, the Marbury virus. By imagining Africa as a place over-run with disease and infection, they reaffirm the myth that has made the country, as Ryszard Kapuscinski and Robert Block have suggested (Block 1994; Kapuscinski 1994), the modern-day equivalent of medieval Europe (when Jews were held responsible for the spread of Bubonic plague and cholera). Africa becomes a lived experience, not simply a treatable one, and, as such, it offers proof of a continuing degeneracy.

In 'Way Down Deep in the Jungle', Dr Koestler wants to cure, as 'cautiously' (Jones 1995, p. 5) as he can, the 'Old Testament' (60) lepers of the mission compound and the sick children bitten by cobras. But something gets in the way. The 'regal' (51) quality of his patients confirms his belief in Hamitic descent, a theory first popularised as 'race science' by German and Belgian colonialists in the late nineteenth century (Gourevitch 1996, p. 58). In attempting to discover what it is like to have been cursed by Noah for illicit sex, Koestler uses the jungle as a theatre of operations in which to practise quasi-scientific investigations and plumb its degeneracy. He becomes fixated by a divine depravity in his quest to uncover whatever is lodged within the psychic depths of a Hamitic race. 'The altruism of most volunteers, Koestler thought, was pretty thin. Those who stayed seemed to do so for reasons that were buried deep in the soul' (Jones 1995, p. 94). In his work for the Global Aid mission Koestler reaches in to the 'hidden' interior of the 'bush'. He uses as his project a pet baboon, George Babbitt, which he trains to appear 'uncannily human' (48–9). Koestler wants Babbitt to reveal the personality of a Hamitic Africa and for this reason he makes the baboon display the promiscuity he imagines is part of the larger

society. The baboon is 'not an ordinary baboon' (50) but one with
'a flair for the dramatic' (49), given to climbing trees and putting
on a show for the audience beneath. As one of 'God's creatures',
Babbitt blows the cover on the spiritual 'unreason' and corruption
of Africa which, Koestler believes, chooses the wisdom of 'megalo-
maniacs' and 'Antichrists' in preference to the moral decency which
he represents. Babbitt is an avatar of Ham and his children: he
drinks alcohol, masturbates, steals drugs, smokes, gets drunk on
whisky and smokes grass with a 'look of sheer ecstasy' on his face
as if he were 'undergoing something Holy' (47).

Koestler's Babbitt is closer to Africa than the icons venerated by
the Christian church. The 'artificial structure' denuded of 'tribalism',
which the Christian mission imposes, makes little sense to Koestler
and 'never seemed to take very well in the bush'. Koestler prefers
'resourcefulness, individualism, and self reliance' and is willing to
carry 'self-containment to a high art' (48). With 'baboons to tame and
tropical diseases to vanquish in the here and now of Zaire', Koestler
has a lust 'for the rough-and-tumble', preferring 'the hardships of
Africa to the pleasant climate and easygoing customs of his homeland'
(48). As a consequence, he parodies the church's evangelical ambition
to convert the natives into respectable Christians. As a '"long-term
experiment"' (58) Babbit is a more realistic presence through which
Koestler can ridicule the church and its icons.

Although Koestler is lonely he has not 'lost heart' (54) and while
Africa might laugh 'derisively' (55), he observes a curious divinity in
his experiments. In a world where '"God looks after drunks"' (54),
Babbit acts like 'the prodigal son' (55). A sick descendent cursed by
Noah, Babbit is a Jew whose chosenness cannot be revoked. Koestler
trains him to exhibit the filth and degeneracy of Africa. He also cares
for him as a specimen of the wilderness into which the biblical
Israelites retreated, an animal whose phenomenally retentive memory
reveals an essentially Jewish nature.

Koestler devotes himself to this once wandering Jew of the forest
with a cervical collar and amphetamine sulphate. In contrast, he rides
the local Africans 'hard' (56), not only because they see his work as
'folly' (55), but because they are whimsically ignorant of the errant
sexuality that Babbitt has confessed to. Scared of admitting their
descent out of Israel, Koestler turns against them with the deranged
intensity of a fascist. Lured by the experiments Hitler conducted on
the Jews, Koestler demands 'heel-clicking service' (50) from the
Africans in the mission. In his search for 'absolute power' he walks
around the compound with a 'Gestapo stroll', 'barking orders' (56)
and demands a submissive response from his patients. They, in turn,
refer to him as 'the big boss'. The compound becomes 'as quiet as

a ghost town' and is run like a labour-camp with 'over forty-five procedures by four-thirty' (56).

Koestler, thus, remythologises Africa. He mimics the Germanic manner and uses the terminology of colonial racists on recalcitrant Africans. He sees himself as healer, protector and fascist thug, an experimentalist who transforms the villagers' lives and cures those who are useful to him. In a society that is unresponsive and far from ideal, baboons are the next best thing to human beings and have learned a lot from the company they have kept throughout history. '"Incredible animals really"', he says. '"Very smart. Did you know they can see in colour?"' (58).

Babbitt might also be useful for other, colour-coded projects. Koestler's goal, as he tells Indiana, is to turn Babbitt into '"a full Cleveland"' in '"a polyester leisure suit"' with '"white-on-white tie, white belt, [and] white patent-leather shoes"' (58). If Sinclair Lewis's Babbitt is a 'facsimile' of an adult, Koestler's Babbitt is a facsimile of an ape, 'a clown beating a bass drum' (Lewis 1926, p. 390) who allows his owner to amuse himself and while away the hours before he goes home. 'Feelings of shame' at what he is doing to the baboon are suppressed by the drugs on which he is dependent: the Demerol, antivenin and B12 injections, 'the magic bullet he used on himself to relieve hangovers' (51). Koestler struggles to see through the fog of an imposed mythology, as he does the consumerism of a drug-addicted lifestyle. Overwhelmed by affected weariness, the 'old-hand in Africa' (57) struggles to connect with a sacred tradition, while moments of insight are rare.

Koestler never specifies his dependency on the fictional philosophy of the Belgian and German colonialists who introduced the idea of a Hamitic hypothesis to Africa. From the end of the nineteenth century to the First World War, says Philip Gourevitch, Hamitic theories were used, in countries like Burundi and Rwanda, to explain that Tutsis were the lost tribes of Ham – a tall beautiful master race – and that Hutus were a slavish Negroid subspecies. The political motive underlying this thesis was to factionalise opposition to colonialism and disempower the tribal structure by creating divisions within the territories administered. The resultant tribal division created a long-standing system of racial privilege among Hutus and Tutsis. Hamitic theories provided the script for the politicisation and violence of the late twentieth century and were an underlying reason for the genocidal bloodshed of the 1990s.

Koestler's Africa is a twentieth-century western invention, underwritten by colonial theory and biblical exegesis. In his equally discredited search for the Hamitic, Koestler attempts to ruin it, to make Africa behave in accordance with his plans as a coloniser. An

Africa that is worthy of rehabilitation and personal rescue must first of all be rendered corrupt. It must become a Hamitic wasteland of post-colonial disease and famine, a place of war and refugeeism devastated by the arms trade and a new exploitative 'gun culture' (Brittain 1991, p. 21). Koestler's Africa is what others before him have made of it, a place of corporate wreckage, a dumping ground for 'international icons' (95) and the signs and billboards that are fast becoming the ecological instruments for a new imperialism.

The idea of Africa as an invention of the West, says Robert Block, is easily forgotten by those who interpret the recent civil war of the sub-Saharan regions as an 'exclusively tribal' expression of violence. In the 1990s the tragedy of Rwanda and Burundi, Block argues, is that the violence is not 'random', 'spontaneous' or 'irrational', an expression of psychic derangement and post-modern 'mayhem' (Block 1994, p. 3). Ryszard Kapuscinski agrees. Those who see the African continent haunted by the ghost of violence and ethnic rivalry, he writes, ignore the 'background story' of class conflict and the struggle for political (rather than tribal) power between the Hutus and Tutsis that was part of the original colonial legacy (Parker 1994, p. 7).

In 'Quicksand', the psychological hinterland of Africa is not its primeval degeneracy but that mythopoetic heart of darkness which allows both junkies and warlords to flourish. As a fund raiser for Global Aid Hunger, Ad Magic, the pseudonymous central character, is a paranoid saviour who learns about the devil by sharing some of his bodily toxins. As Jones puts it: 'The heart of darkness Conrad wrote about so vividly was available in modern-day Arusha just as much as in some ghastly trip upriver on the Zaire. It seemed that he (Magic) had fallen into an eternal vortex of hell' (Jones 1995, pp. 77–8). For Magic, Africa's sinfulness is confirmed through visions, a Hamitic curse which comes to life in the 'horrible hypnogogic dreams, or wide-awake bouts of visceral evacuation' (77) that torment his life. Magic's 'dark night of the soul' is the obligatory experience of his profession. The malarial sweat and 'bilious' fetid atmosphere of the Hotel Arusha is a way of invoking the presence of the dead, the 'delirious ... paranoia' (77) which a divine curse has left behind.

Magic eschews the need for immunity in order to re-enact the exposure of the continent to the curse of degeneracy which Noah placed on the descendants of Ham. 'The squalid scene' (80) of his diarrhetic crisis, with which the story begins, is brought on by 'colossal' self indulgence (81). The body's exposure to malaria and diarrhetic sickness – 'picked up' (71) or put down almost at will – transforms it into a site of conflict and spontaneous violence. This craving to know the sickness of Africa, the body outside, is shared by Dr Erika Lars, Magic's lover, who, during intercourse in 'the missionary position', sticks her 'wet' finger into Magic's 'raw' anus (89). Magic is inspired to 'fuck her to death' but accepts that Lars is complicit in his search for contamination. Through anal sex he makes her body into something of a war zone. Lars's orgasms give way to 'her greatest cry', a tribal shout which generates 'the furnace heat' (89) of sexual explosion and the possibility of an early death.

If sex is a way of immersing oneself in the sickness and savagery of Africa it is also a way of connecting with the portents of the last days: the famines, wars, plagues and environmental disasters which God visits upon the earth in readiness for His millennial paradise. Magic's inability to fully escape the dispensationalist position is signalled by his belief that the 'ubiquitous signs of doomsday are a cause for rejoicing' (Wojcik 1997, p. 58). The presence of sickness is an important marker in 'God's predetermined timetable'. For this reason, Magic seeks to familiarise himself with a world where God has become a traumatic influence on the sinful, punishing the Africans as he did the Indians with plague and pestilence. Now that slavery has ended, God's continued punishment of Africa signifies His watchful presence in a world where the curse of Noah has yet to be lifted.

Magic's tormented quest for Africanisation is driven by a desire to encounter God through the catastrophe of a sickness that may be interpreted as a form of redemption. Magic tries to focus his life on God's providential ministry. In his direct-mail advertisements for Global Aid, he describes the hunger and disease of Africa as a scene from the Old Testament and says that his letters are written by 'The Holy Spirit' (Jones 1995, p. 82). He refers to his style as 'biblical' (84) and acquaints his readers with the '"living waters"' (85) of Israel in order to engage their sympathy and financial support. 'Buzzed on morphine' (98) he relates how he has 'heard voices' and how '"God talked"' to him the time he '"was nearly killed in Rwanda"' (98).

Ad is driven to desperate measures to explain his spiritual awakening in Africa to an aid organisation which belittles his efforts as insufficiently commercial. Magic's disillusion with the corporate rhetoric of his employers plunges him deeper into the dark night of the African soul, prompting a search for spiritual immersion way beyond the terms of his appointment as corporate fundraiser. When Lars asks him: '"Did you ever imagine yourself to be Christlike?"', he replies that Christ was a '"paranoid schizophrenic"' (105–6) who understood the beauty of sacrifice as well as salvation.

Unlike Koestler, the supernatural promise of Africa makes him sceptical of the sanitised culture that Global Aid is determined to create. Global Aid compromises his spirituality, based as it is on the veneration of '"air conditioners, Land Cruisers, a river launch, a pharmacy, slit lamp ophthalmology, clean water, three square meals a day, HIV prevention and treatment, an immunization program, Hausen's disease eradication – the whole deal"' (99). Since 'immuniza- tion' obviates a genuine encounter with the curse of Ham those who seek an experience of the divine – as both sinful race and saving remnant – find the society of ancient Africa dangerously threatened. Science and pharmacy will cure the curse and terminate biblical history. Since drug companies are now at the forefront in the search for new consumer markets in Third World countries, aid workers like Magic are Trojan horses forced to adopt a missionary position on behalf of a pharmaceutical industry that uses them to dispense its products. Only by contaminating himself with the magic of 'juju' (Jew Jew) and witnessing the ancient filth of the witch doctor with 'crusted eczema patches' on his arms, can Magic free himself of the sanitised modernism of his '"enemies in America"' (102).

Since the work Magic does inhibits the very sickness he wishes to savour, his knowledge of Africa is self-defeating. The weakness of his need is underlined by a dependency on the 'hallucinating' (84) power of drugs, which his search for 'juju' is a repudiation of. Magic cannot do without drugs to create within himself a '"stoned"' (102) disregard for the biblical advertisements of the phoney messiah he has made himself into. Just as Africa is in danger of making itself well by irreligious means, so Magic's only resort is to experience the drugs that Africa is prescribed. He does this not to gain an immunity from sickness, but to share the trauma of addiction and withdrawal, the psyche of the casualty who finds himself having to deal with the side-effects of 'a once-in-a-lifetime score' (97). As his mind is tranquil- lised and his body made safe as a site of conflict so his delusions are less problematical and easier to manage. When he steals a vast quantity of morphine and Dexedrine from the Methodist medical clinic in Makongoro he can pretend to empathise with what Hartman in 'Way Down Deep ...' calls: the African love affair with 'needles' (61). In reality, Magic is just another bum on the scrounge whose vision of redemption has gone terribly wrong. 'Jamming pills into his deep bush pockets' (97), he resembles Dr Koestler's baboon as it heads off into the jungle with the Canadian Mist.

In stories such as 'Ooh Baby Baby' Africa is not only the twentieth century's new drug culture but a place that enacts its own terrible revenge on those who abandon its divine promise. The terrible curse of the jungle follows Moses Galen back to California after an early career on a burns unit in Somalia. Galen is 'something of an Africa buff' (124), but has swapped his life as a physician with the Peace Corps for private practice in cosmetic surgery in downtown Los Angeles. Instead of burned skin and wounds 'teeming with flies and maggots' he performs liposuction and breast implants and develops a repertoire of sexual ploys with Hollywood starlets and 'full-fledged movie stars' (136).

In Africa Galen was 'big, strong, and good-looking in his youth' and 'believed he could make a difference to the lives of his patients' (122). But he got bored and 'dropped' his friends and instead of staying on, said 'Fuck Somalia!' (123). As a Jew in California, the only 'Red Sea' that parts for him now is the one he comes across in a traffic jam. Yet in southern California there is nowhere to 'move' (132), no community of exiled Jews for Moses to lead out of their misery the way he did on the burns unit. In California he has swapped skin transplants on war victims for cosmetic surgery on burned-out narcissists who yearn to 'suck' his expertise 'dry' (137). Galen's California is a 'junkie' culture whose body, like the stage sets of Hollywood, perpetuates a quest for novelty and reproductive framework. Here, Galen is in flight from a past he seeks to erase through 'classic plastic surgery' (129), even though the past has given him the very skills he has chosen to transplant. Preoccupied with sex instead of sickness he cannot escape his past refusal 'to look at death' (144). Even his own sickness – 'the hell that was going on inside his own skin' (123) – is no distraction for '"the blood bath in Rwanda and ... Somalia"' (121).

Galen is punished with a virus incubating inside his body and a girlfriend, Linda Foley, who threatens to drain him of what limited energy he has managed to retain. Linda reminds us of Erika Lars in 'Quicksand', the casualty of a war zone she will never encounter, a make-believe African who wishes to experience, through plastic surgery, the meaning of the 'Hamitic hypothesis', the notion of a beautiful master race with the capacity to inflict genocidal violence. Linda is in love with the promise of violence and its sudden release through 'state-of-the-art liposuction technique' (129). Her implants and transplants and surgical reconstructions have made her more sexually demanding but are likely to accelerate her body metabolism and lead to an early death.

Like Erika Lars, Linda is a mercenary looking for a war zone. Violence is chic. When Galen, who has learnt his skills in the war zones of Africa, reconstructs her body, she reminds him of the 'writhing human' (124) skeletons in agonising pain on the operating tables in Mogadishu. From being 'a bad case of burnout' her reinvented body releases 'a whole flood of sexual imperatives' (130), including the requirement to experience 'absolute' pain and to indulge 'insatiable and varied appetites'. In her quest for virtual trauma Linda has 'fallen into a window of time' (130) through which her illusions of eternal health and strength are kept alive by medical science. Her body becomes a casualty-station, simulating the suffering of Africa as well as her nation's love affair with beauty as an act of mutilation and repro-war surgery. Her damaged and damaging promiscuity is a constant reminder of the punitive wilderness which lives within Galen's body, the eight hundred and thirty-five women he has slept with and the 'fast viruses' he can never escape 'that turned you into goo and had you bleeding from every orifice three days after incubation' (123).

In *Cold Snap* Africa has become, like the New England wilderness, a seductive place with a capacity to inflict 'psychosexual' and spiritual damage. After a period of immersion the wilderness becomes 'too much to ponder' (124). Liberal reformers and millennialist visionaries like Magic, are unable to distinguish between what Richard Slotkin calls 'intimacy with the Indians' (Slotkin 1973, p. 126) and Cotton Mather, 'Criolian degeneracy'. Mather, who was always suspicious of the difference, was certainly aware of the personal torment and insecurity which afflicted those who sought to reform the heathen. The wilderness in Africa remains, as ever, an unsafe place in which to venture for missionaries who risk being 'tainted' (27) through casual sex and random dispersal. In Rwanda and Somalia, America's errand fails of discipline and the threat of degeneracy. The lure of sexual primitivism is reintroduced, while the drugs that facilitate sexual release are as 'ubiquitous' as 'Coke signs' (95).

In *Cold Snap* the search for both a damaged humanity and a divine encounter turns catastrophic. The emissary of post-millennialism finds himself in a wasteland of his own making yet without the spiritual protection of the church. In a place that was once His sacred domain – His place of triumph over temptation – Christ is classed as a 'paranoid schizophrenic' (105) who cannot control the spread of disease and the rise to prominence of 'corporate mammon' (95). Little wonder that Dr Koestler should reject what Nathaniel Rogers referred to as the 'Christianizing of the Indians', and should turn his attention, instead, to 'Utopian amusement' with Babbitt the baboon (Axtell 1981, p. 268). Koestler performs his miracles in the wilderness with a drunken animal, unable to approve the lesson of Matthew 4: 1–11 when Jesus resists the temptations of the devil after he is led by the Holy Spirit into the desert. What Steve Russo describes as, 'a prime example' of Christ's resistance which inspires us with 'confidence' in his 'victory' (Russo 1994, p. 130) over Satan, has little appeal in the African bush. It is here that Koestler feeds his pet baboon on whisky and bananas and teaches it to masturbate.

The ritualised escapism of Dr Koestler, Ad Magic and Moses Galen parodies the ascetic Christ who undergoes a time of testing and trial prior to revelation. In *Cold Snap* the jungle is an inversion of the Biblical wilderness and conveys little sense of repentance or sanctuary.

In Christian mythology, the wilderness is the preserve of dangerous and lurking beasts, 'the location of refuge, trial, temptation, and ultimate victory over Satan' (Stanniard 1992, p. 174). In 'Ooh Baby Baby', Moses Galen turns his back on the wilderness – the one that challenges him spiritually and emotionally in Rwanda and Somalia and the memorial wilderness of Palestine – on which His ministry among the sick was founded. The reform Jew gives in to temptation and demonstrates his powers of miraculous ministry among the aimless and ageing in southern California. Galen's actions raise questions about the relevance of Christ's original mission in places that are now overrun with disease and violence. It also raises questions about the value of an errand in which human beings through concerted effort struggle to engage with the legacy of Israel but find themselves overwhelmed by the challenge.

Notes

1. Robertson's views are shared not only by Islamic leaders but also by right-wing groups in western and post-Communist communities throughout Europe. In France the National Front, the extreme right-wing party of Jean-Marie Le Pen, argues that secular values in American cultural imperialism create the 'Trojan horse of globalisation' (Dejevsky, 1996, p. 21). The American media, says Bruno Megret, wants to 'impose its global and degenerate ideology' on societies with high standards of aesthetic and cultural achievement and so reduce them to a dependency on trivia. In France, music and film, says Megret, are unhealthily dominated by Hollywood, which 'is degenerate, depraved and negative' and saps 'the national morale'. Just as the National Front strives 'to defend French language and culture' from the 'onslaught of the English-speaking world' and 'the cult of all things virtual', so, in Russia, right-wing nationalists like Alexander Lebed and Gennady Zyuganov fear the loss of Russian culture as one of the cornerstones of our national security and attack the sexual trash and violence of soap operas that have flooded the country (Reeves 1996, p. 14). Similar complaints have surfaced among nationalist communities in the Baltic Republics of Lithuania and Estonia where the influence of western culture on the religious and aesthetic life of the region is seen as corrosively anti-national. Where Alexander Lebed identifies the enemy of Russian culture as the soap opera, Estonia's Jaan Kaplinski attributes the erosion of Baltic culture to 'Barbification' and cultural imports such as dolls, comic strips and cable TV (Lieven, 1993, pp. 129–30).
2. For a discussion of the links between religious and commercial exploitation on the Amazon basin see Kane 1993, p. 56.

3. Note Gore Vidal's suggestion that Saint Paul 'hated cleanliness' (Vidal 1992, p. 27).

Prophecy and the Literary Imagination

All millennialists, whatever their beliefs, are united in their opposition to the enlightened rationalism of the New World Order. In the early years of the 1990s this novel philosophy exerted an overwhelming influence on the political and intellectual life of the United States. As the Cold War receded liberal determinism looked to have 'removed a potent form of religious politics from the world stage'. It also looked to have replaced the Marxist 'kingdom of humanity' (Campion 1994, p. 493) with a new prophetic community of saints, one composed of free-market capitalists, secular intellectuals, economic globalists and corporate industrialists. In his book *The New World Order*, Pat Robertson condemns the idea that human perfectibility can be achieved through global economic development and that spiritual growth can be attained through a Hegelian vision of enlightened progress. Robertson is particularly annoyed with 'the silly so-called intellectuals of academia' (Robertson 1991, p. 239), who accepted the triumph of capitalism over the Communist Antichrist, even though the Russian Gog clearly remained an enemy of Christianity and a continuing threat to Israel's security in the Middle East (Wojcik 1997, p. 203).

Robertson's argument with liberalism is directed at books like Tom Englehardt's *The End of Victory Culture* (1995). Launched amid considerable acclaim, Englehardt's analysis of Cold War culture provided fundamentalism with a classic demonstration of liberal silliness, as seen by its willingness to consign imperial Communism to the dustbin of history. Englehardt's thesis that the United States must learn how to live 'without external enemies' confirms the suspicion that academic liberalism is hooked on the novelty of a transient postmodernism. This is evident when Englehardt asks the reader to consider if there can still be 'an imaginable America' in a world 'without enemies and without the story of their slaughter and our triumph?' Englehardt ponders the need for 'a new story' that Americans might decide to 'tell about ... themselves', one that can 'sustain them as citizens of the twenty first century' (Englehardt 1995, p. 15). This flirtation with the 'new' is a punishable offence for Pat Robertson. Liberal academics will soon 'find themselves', he says, 'irrelevant and then expendable when the real power begins to operate' (Robertson 1991, p. 253). Robertson's antipathy to new narratives reminds us of Will Hay's sceptical one-liner in the film *Steamboat Round the Bend.* In 1931 New York Rabbis were predicting the arrival of a messiah who would soon be along to end the depression. When asked if he had seen the new Jesus, Hay snapped back: 'I ain't seen the old one yet, mister'.

In *When Time Shall Be No More* (1992), Paul Boyer shows us how an interest in prophetic religion and the doctrine of Armageddon quickly displaced the consensus agendas of the post Cold War. Liberal determinism failed to satisfy the spiritual needs of the American people. The Cold War and its aftermath was neither a time of spiritual resolution nor a defining eschatological moment in American history, says Boyer. It did nothing at all to lift the veil of historical interpretation that had framed the imagination and intelligence of the American people since the colonial period, nor did it invalidate the millennialist errand they had agreed to undertake. The proliferation of prophecy publications in the last decades of the twentieth century is another indication that the Cold War has yet to draw a line under history nor has it precipitated a collapse in the nation's favourite mythologies. The phenomenal success of prophecy paperbacks in feeding 'an apparently insatiable market' (Boyer 1992, p. 11) is reflected in the best-seller list for nonfiction paperbacks. By 1990 Hal Lindsey's *Late Great Planet Earth* (1970) had sold 28 million copies while Salem Kirban's *Guide to Survival* (1968) had gone through sixteen editions by 1988 selling half a million copies. Paul Billheimer's *Destined for the Throne* (1975) reported sales of over 650,000 by 1988 and continued to sell in the years following the Cold War. John Walvoord's *Armageddon, Oil and the Middle East Crisis* (1974) was updated and reprinted in 1990 and immediately sold over 600,000 copies from December 1990 to 1991. Here and elsewhere the need for 'the literature of last things' (8) was reconfirmed (not disconfirmed) by the collapse of Communism, while the triumph of a free-market philosophy did nothing to satisfy the voracious demand for apocalyptic narratives.

If, as Boyer argues, 'prophecy belief' has 'loomed large in the twentieth century's waning decades' (8), millennial speculations – many of which utilise dispensational themes – have become 'America's favourite pastime' (Wojcik 1997, p. 6). The massive outpouring of eschatological and apocalyptic literature and the continuing cultural preoccupation with the endtimes (at a time when, ideologically at least, the end is apparently no longer in sight) demonstrate, says Boyer, the power of the 'Protestant imagination' to influence apocalyptic thinking. This is true, even though many of those who embrace the more 'imaginative end-time scenarios' (Boyer 1992, p. 3) do not formally read the Bible or subscribe to the dispensational teachings of the church. In the victory years of post-Communism, says Malcolm Bradbury, the return of history as an eschatological system of belief has proved a much more persuasive notion than the end of history. Although the 'monsters' changed 'from nuclear threat to ozone depletion and global warming, the consciousness of uncertainty' still remains 'with us' (Bradbury 1990, p. 21).

The idea of a millennium without an eschatology was attacked as unchristian almost as soon as it appeared. The arrival of a New World Order may have inspired George Bush in 1992 to announce that 'changes' had occurred of 'almost biblical proportions' (Bush 1992, pp. 1–2) in the political landscape, but for conservatives like Pat Robertson, these 'changes' threatened to bring to an end the country's unique status under God and its compelling commission to Christianise the Jews. In the aftermath of Communism religious fundamentalists continued to live, as Michael Sherry has phrased it, 'in the shadow of war' (Sherry 1995). For conservatives, the impending apocalypse was born of an insidious one-worldism and the threat posed by the agents of the Antichrist at the highest levels of government and education.

In *The Turning Tide* Robertson describes the New World Order as a post-millennialist confidence trick whose sole purpose is to disguise the rigours of the Tribulation period (which none of us can avoid) and discredit Armageddon. In his jeremiad, *The New World Order*, Robertson also targets the new, global dynamic of mass culture as the brainchild of the Illuminati, a secret fraternity of Communists, Jews, Freemasons and international financiers, whose mission is to generate allegiances to corporate products and new multinational corporate logos. Industrialisation, the growth of the city, technological advance and the presence of new ecumenical loyalties threaten to separate the righteous from their old religious dependencies, he argues. The consequence of secular freedom is spiritual crisis: social control by a monied 'order' and the elimination of Christian faith by 'the inner circle of a secret society ... under the domination of Lucifer and his followers' (Robertson 1993, p. 37).

The errand to secularise America through the peaceful practice of liberalism is described by Hal Lindsey, in *The Late Great Planet Earth*, as one of the great 'counterfeit' missions of the Antichrist

(Lindsey 1981, p. 5). In order to achieve this goal, the Antichrist is assisted by a number of false prophets, of whom the most notorious is the liberal intellectual Francis Fukuyama. In the 1989 issue of *The National Interest* Fukuyama proposed a notion of post-history in which he claimed that America and western Europe were able to produce, independently of Christ, a new, conquering, messianic ideology.

In this and other faddishly influential essays, and in his book *The End of History and The Last Man* (1991), Fukuyama dismissed the idea of Christian theocracy as the ultimate arbiter of human aspiration. Instead, he proposed that consumer capitalism and western liberalism had spawned a new beginning in global history. As a result, we were all living in a world beyond history and had entered the society of the 'last man'. In this society the absence of ideology, or any significant religious faith, was concurrent with the absence of prejudice and the release of a new consumer idealism. This was an age of redemption through capitalism, said Fukuyama, an age in which we had all been granted the Adamic opportunity to begin our lives again. The link between 'industrialisation', 'liberal democracy' and the power of increased consumption firmly established the American experiment in liberal democracy as 'the only legitimate ideology left in the world' (Fukuyama 1990, p. 23). What the American model of historical progress held out to Third World nations, wrote Fukuyama, was a morality of enlightened rationalism infused with the dynamic of free-market economics. This ideology had been successfully exported by the United States, especially to Southeast Asia and Latin America, where the need for economic reconstruction had been heavily reliant on free-market capital. East Asia and Latin America, said Fukuyama, 'demonstrate that latecomers to the process of economic development are in no way disadvantaged, and in fact can achieve the highest levels of technology and consumption, provided they remain connected to world markets and permit free competition at home' (23).

In our post-historical landscape, said Fukuyama, it was abundantly clear that market forces would determine 'the strength of a nation's domestic base, and its ability to create decent and prosperous lives for its citizens'. What we were seeing was not a world bifurcated 'along East–West lines, but ... a post-historical and an historical part. Each part will play by a completely different set of rules: economics will dominate the former while military power will reign in the latter' (23). In the democratic desire to appreciate the benefits of mass culture, Marxism had suffered a terminal decline. The products of the marketplace and the benefits of mass culture offered the consumer, in the words of C. W. E. Bigsby, 'a model not merely of balance and completion but also of confident assurance – an assurance contained in the product itself and therefore projected on to those exposed to it' (Bigsby 1975, p. 15). Richard Gott put it more vigorously: it was 'the headlong rush towards capitalism', he argued, that toppled and transformed most of the hard-line socialist regimes throughout the world (Gott 1989, p. 23).

The idea of being born again as a consumer in the redemptive fire of American capitalism accords well with the thesis that modernity is a thing of American definition. And if, by modernity, we mean, more specifically, the rationalisation of culture through commodity – a process for imposing hegemonic control through corporate management – the market economy had become, for Fukuyama, a convenient way of re-articulating a born-again myth. A myth, that is, of advanced capitalism rather than advanced Christianity, yet one, nevertheless, which referred its origins to the business metaphor that John Winthrop employed on board the Arbella when he exhorted his congregation to build a metropolis for the rest of the world to admire. In 1989 fortune seemed to favour the secular. The modernisation of Christ's ministry in the New World Order had been accomplished by co-opting His message to the colonists of New England. If the world had been born again through its economic rather than its spiritual convictions the process of redemption had, none the less, been accompanied by a physical journey (what the Puritans referred to as an 'ocean crossing'). In East Germany the act of self-transformation that accompanied the journey from one ideological state to another involved a tearing down of walls and a symbolic act of physical passage from East to West through the Bradenburg Gate. The lure of American consumer capitalism, writes George Steiner, seemed to have become the ultimate arbiter of democratic desire.

American standards of dress, nourishment, locomotion, entertainment, housing, are today the concrete utopian revolutions. Video cassettes, porno-cassettes, American style cosmetics and fast foods, not editions of Mill, De Tocqueville or Solzhenitsyn, were the prizes snatched from every West Berlin shelf by the liberated. The new temples to liberty (the 1979 dream) will be McDonalds and Kentucky Fried Chicken. (Steiner 1990, p. 47)

For the Communist classes of Eastern Europe the idea of revolution was no longer an expression of political or spiritual will, but a yearning for material release. After 1989 history had become a thing of 'surface and superficiality', a bourgeois process, an occasion for nations willingly to surrender their ideals and allegiances to the products of the marketplace; to a world where, as Karl Jaspers predicted, there is no continuity only past time.

Revivalist capitalism threatened to terminate the fundamentalist search for a saving remnant of Jews just as it threatened the memory of Israel among the old Scythian and Oriental races of Russia and China. The end of Marxism, as defined by 'counterfeit' prophets like Francis Fukuyama, brought with it the end of Christian obligation to the unconverted: the elimination, that is, of a divine plan of ministry to the Lost Tribes of Israel. The evangelism of mass consumption gave the Antichrist and his agents a new disguise with which to utilise their 'humanistic-occultic' powers (Robertson 1991, p. 258). The false prophet, Fukuyama, ignored the dispensational challenge of Israel and, unilaterally, brought to an end the conversion of the Jews as a precondition of Christian salvation. Economic imperatives had overridden spiritual agendas and even though God had yet to decide on a suitably propitious moment to intervene, the biblical programme designed by Him and revealed to us in the prophecies of the Old Testament had been waved aside by a parvenu priest.

In Fukuyama's programme, history occurred independently of Christ nor did it require a period of conflict between arch protagonists to secure His throne in a new Jerusalem. The battle for Armageddon had been avoided; the conflict between the Russian hordes and the forces of Christianity had been postponed by 'the unilateral acts of the Soviet Union' (Cummings 1992, p. 91). Fukuyama's ending to history not only pre-empted divine intervention, it abandoned Israel to the winds of fate and disqualified the Jews from acting out their chosen role as a saving remnant 'in the climactic endtimes' (Lind 1995, p. 21). As an agent of Lucifer, Fukuyama had co-opted a millennial philosophy for the purposes of creating an Hegelian state. In the imagined post-dispensational age of the New World Order, the need for spiritual regeneration through violence had been withdrawn and the rational piety of the liberal capitalist as free marketeer threatened to undercut the terrible revelations of Ezekiel and Zachariah.

Western liberalism may have overturned 'the Marxist Millennium' of a workers' paradise, says Nicholas Campion, but it did little to satisfy 'the religious imperatives and mythological assumptions' which remained such a potent force in a messianic society like the United States. Fukuyama's argument that history had come to an end (and that postmodernism had triumphed) betrayed a 'profound lack of awareness' of the role 'that eschatology and millenarianism' have played in the prophecy movement. The 'new dawn' promised by democratic liberalism also betrayed 'a deep absence of historical knowledge' and, at the time of the Gulf War, was unable to make much political sense of the nation's moral fervour and the enthusiastic way the American people responded to Operation Desert Storm (Campion 1994, pp. 493–5).

Americans venerate piety under pressure and never more so than in periods of apparent security. For many conservatives the Gulf War was 'a cause for rejoicing', an important marker in 'God's predetermined timetable' (Wojcik 1997, p. 58). Saddam provided the United States with an opportunity to rededicate itself to the historical narrative of millennialism, to reaffirm a biblical pursuit which began in New England. The nation's spiritual need to finish what it had started was reflected in its willingness to portray Saddam as the coming Antichrist, a descendent of Babylon who threatened the safety of Israel in his quest to create 'the greatest and richest commercial center in the world' (Henry 1990, p. 16). For Fred Henry, in *The Middle East – Destined*, biblical 'prophecy [was] being fulfilled at a rapid pace and our redemption draweth near' (17). Saddam Hussein had taken a vow to 'attack Israel first' and should he carry out his threat he would 'ensure a victory, not only for Israel, but for the United States as well' (21). Henry interprets the war with Saddam as confirmation of Revelation 18. This foretells the destruction of Babylon, 'the city ... which Saddam Hussein is desperately trying to rebuild' (16) to serve as the 'headquarters' of the Antichrist for 'the first three and a half years of the Tribulation Period' (15). As 'the second Nebuchadnezzar' (14), Saddam's fate would come to mirror that of his ancestor and involve the destruction of the huge palaces he had built on the ruins of the ancient city of Babylon, where Nebuchadnezzar had taken many of his Jewish captives.

During the Gulf War the importance of endtime prophecy was reflected in the huge sales of prophecy books, prophecy sermons and telephone hotlines providing daily updates on the endtimes significance of events in the Gulf. John Walvoord's *Armageddon, Oil and the Middle East Crisis*, originally published in 1974, sold more copies in ten weeks in 1991 – 600,000 – than it had in the first ten years of its publication. These book sales were the sign of an expectant people, not one whose victory was already assured by its triumph over Communism or one whose religious beliefs were no longer relevant in a secular age. They were not the sign of a race willing to ignore millennialist teaching in order to realise its destiny under God.

Historical endings that dispensed with the Jews dispensed, in a sense, with America itself. As a Christian nation America could not be granted an end to history without acknowledging its obligations at birth, the divine pursuit to save the Lost Tribes that had taken the Puritans on their errand in the wilderness. What was happening in the Gulf, preached Billy Graham, was 'happening in that part of the world where history began' (Boyer 1992, p. 328). Like The Six-Day War of 1967, Saddam's manoeuvre appeared to confirm centuries of prophetic speculation about the Middle East. In a pre-millennial religion, where 'All prophetic truth revolves around the Jews' and 'The Jew is

God's time clock', Saddam's invasion was final confirmation of 'a grand narrative that refused to die'.

The Gulf War 'swelled eschatological interest across America' (329), says Paul Boyer, and 'demonstrated ... how readily, in moments of crisis', the old belief systems 'could move from the periphery to the centre of American consciousness' (331). Even more remarkable was the way these belief systems adapted themselves in order to accommodate political change. As the war came to an end, 'it became apparent', says Daniel Wojcik, 'that predictions of a global conflict initiated in the Middle East would not be fulfilled' (Wojcik 1997, p. 158). Best-seller writers like Charles Dyer may have seen the Gulf as a defining moment in world history but the cathartic energy that was to 'ignite the events of the endtimes' lost its spark (158). The prophecy movement became a casualty of its own extravagance, unable to satisfy the expectations of spiritual deliverance which doomsday scenarios in the Gulf had raised. Saddam may have set fire to the oil wells (blanketing the region in the 'grievous sore' of Revelation 16), but as the decade wore on the prospect of Armageddon receeded. Kuwait was liberated but the multinational task force, dependent for its legitimacy on a United Nations mandate, refused to launch an all-out war on Baghdad. As Saddam turned his back on Israel, the threat from Iraq faded like a mirage. For a time, it was replaced by a political diplomacy which emphasised the virtue of compromise and the need to maintain a balance of power throughout the Middle East.

If 'wars and rumours of war', in Matthew 24, precede the end (Boyer 1992, p. 328), then the Persian Gulf was a false dawn. As the tension of the endtimes metamorphosed into an uneasy stand-off, prophecy writers moved on to other subjects – the threat of homosexuality, the AIDS virus, radical feminism – leaving their readers in some frustration that war with Saddam had failed to escalate into a global conflict. Millennial idealism among church congregations and prophecy writers changed with the times and the quest to uncover the false and the demonic assumed new forms. As the pursuit of Bill Clinton shows us, some of these discoveries had the effect of reconfirming the influence of the Antichrist at the highest levels of government in America.

Not all writers however, turned their back on the Gulf and not all church members became disillusioned with the teachings of the Bible. Just as Cotton Mather urged his congregation, at moments of disappointment, to redouble their efforts in pursuit of the Antichrist, so, in the aftermath of the Gulf War, prophecy interpreters like Pat Robertson refused to abandon their old faiths but reasserted them with renewed vigour.[1] For Robertson, the postponement of Armageddon had less to do with the mistaken prophecies of the Bible in

Kuwait and more to do with an absence of political will in Washington. Robertson's study of the period leading up to and including the Gulf war, *The New World Order*, sold more than half a million copies on its release and was on the New York Times best-seller list for many months. It focuses on the power of an ecumenical élite whose objectives are set by the secret societies that have infiltrated America's coalition partners in the United Nations.

In *The New World Order* Pat Robertson argues that the defection of the United States from its sacred task as a redeemer nation was 'consummated' when General Brent Scowcroft, 'longtime Council on Foreign Relations member', 'announced ... the beginning of a New World Order' (Robertson 1991, p. 252). This was an 'order without God and based on human potential', contracted by a 'one-world crowd of monied aristocrats' and their heathen agents in the Bush and Clinton administrations. The New World Order, 'based on aetheism or syncretism' and invented by nascent internationalists – Communists, Freemasons, international finance – also spawned a broad-based alliance between leftist and post-nationalist élites – homosexuals, lesbians, feminists, academics, liberal and multiculturalists – all of whom had ghettoised the academies and polluted the minds of the nation's youth. Dedicated to what Arthur Schlesinger has called the 'disuniting' of America (Schlesinger 1993), this liberal élite was descended from the Babylonians who rebelled against God 'and turned their worship to animals, heavenly bodies, demons, and other human beings' (Robertson 1991, p. 251). Obsessed with the doomed alliances of history which spring 'forth from the murky past of mankind's evil beginings' (253) they sought the end of American exceptionalism and demanded that 'the Babylonian humanistic and occultist traditions ... unify against the people of the Abrahamic, monotheistic tradition' (258). Their leaders in the United Nations, where a one-world language is spoken (in translation), worshipped a 'god of light, whom Bible scholars recognize as Lucifer', a deity whose faith is moral relativism and 'anything-goes syncretism' (238).

Syncretism came of age, says Robertson, in the Persian Gulf, when an unholy consensus of the duped and faithless conspired together in a Babylonian cabal. The Gulf task force compromised America's role as world policeman and undermined its status among the nations of the world. The construction of an international army was a godless errand on behalf of globalism, a prelude to the construction of an international judiciary by the constituent communities of the Illuminatus: the Council of Foreign Relations, the Trilateral Commission, the Bilderbergs and the United Nations. In the Gulf, these and other élite oligarchies sought to undermine America's constitutional sovereignty in the search for worldwide economic and political control.

Their aim was to administer a global, international bureaucracy which would regulate health, education, taxation, religion and the military. Responsibility for this would be entrusted to a multinational police force and a banking system like the Federal Reserve Board, staffed by officials from politically correct races across the Third World. The brainchild of secular Jews (displaced from Zion), Freemasons and international bankers who had infiltrated the Republican party, the Gulf War conspirators 'pushed Saddam into an unnecessary war in order to promote globalism' (Lind 1995, p. 23).

The money barons and monopoly bankers of Europe, such as the Rothschilds and their agents, Warburg and Schiff, had used this ploy on numerous occasions in the past. Just as the Cold War was 'a hoax designed to funnel money from taxpayers to High Finance' through deficit spending, so the First World War and the Gulf War were deliberately planned 'in order to boost military spending by various governments and increase the need for compound-interest loans' from the International Monetary Fund and World Bank (25). Politicians like Woodrow Wilson and George Bush may have 'sincerely' wanted 'a larger community of nations living at peace in our world' but 'in reality' they were 'unwittingly and unknowingly carrying out the mission and mouthing the phrases' of a secret society, 'whose goal [was] nothing less than a new order for the human race under the domination of Lucifer and his followers' (22).

The stand-off in the Gulf was a 'false peace', a *ruse de guerre* initiated by the Antichrist who had used Saddam as a pretext for multinational one-world government: the real design of new world history. The Gulf was a staging post. Planned as a deception it allowed a confederate superstate of nations the opportunity to practise a one-world-order conspiracy 'based on atheism and syncretism'. In examining 'the invisible hand shaping US government policies' Robertson sees the influence of a 'one-world crowd of monied aristocrats' (Robertson 1991, p. 253) and their heathen agents at the executive level. The New World Order has brought together Communists, Freemasons and international financiers, all of whom have been instrumental in the rehabilitation of Russia and its allies.

The ending of both the Cold War and the Gulf War proved conclusively, to Robertson, that agents of the Antichrist had deployed a delaying tactic and were managing to accumulate, on the basis of the war effort, vast sums of international capital in pursuance of a counterfeit economic utopia. America's political and economic influence in the world was no longer the result of what Charles Krauthammer describes as 'benign hegemony' (Krauthammer 1991, p. 25). It had been replaced by the collusion of a secret international order: the World Bank, the International Monetary Fund, the monopoly backers of the Illuminatus and occult organisations such as the Trilateral Commission and the Bilderberg Group.

In *The New World Order* Robertson manages to rehabilitate prophetic scripture and snatch a dramatic victory for Christ from the jaws of one-world-order defeat. The peace accord that concluded military action in the Gulf is doomed to failure. Isaiah 2: 2.4 is prophetic proof that a temporary peace will prevail prior to the rise of the Antichrist. During this period, says Robertson, the monetarist forces which financed the Gulf War effort will be supplemented by free-trade agreements and shifts in capital. This secular agenda will allow the Antichrist to create a one-world government through the efforts of secret societies and occult organisations like the United Nations and the Federal Reserve Board. In this, God is not found wanting, even though His fallible believers – with their mistranslations of signs and portents – certainly are. The refusal of Christ to intervene in our affairs is the result of human error, a failure on the part of His congregation to read correctly God's predicted time of arrival and to abandon assumptions that, if not premature, are incorrect.

If Europe's right wing see the devil in the Jewish diaspora, Christian conservatives in the United States are more preoccupied with Arab élites and a secret monetary order. Fundamentalists in the United States locate the devil in demon technology, in schemes of electronic and computer surveillance, in the worldwide growth of corporate bureaucracy and multinational confederacies. They emphasise the menace of personality and the political influence of the 'counterfeit' minister who feigns responsibility for his congregations. We will know the Antichrist, says Hal Lindsey, as he who attempts to 'deify himself' through 'a Satanic counterfeit of the resurrection' (Lindsey 1970, p. 97). Because of his 'magnetic personality' he will appear 'personally attractive and a powerful speaker' and 'mesmerize an audience with his oratory' (97). In fundamentalist prophecy the Antichrist is confirmed by Daniel (11: 37 and 9: 27) as a person of Middle Eastern, possibly Syrian, origin. In his novel *The Illuminati* (1991), Larry Burkett traces his support to a druidic society whose ultimate goal is a one-world economic system controlled and directed by an Arabic fraternity. For Hal Lindsey, the Antichrist is a 'Future Führer,' 'an implacable enemy of the new State of Israel' (55). He has links with an ecumenical order, like the Freemasons, who dedicate themselves to the implementation of his wishes as a one-world 'dictator' (97).

In religious fundamentalism the threat that exists to the righteous nations of the world is based on biblical prophecy. All pre-millennialists accept the endtimes as inevitable and work in accordance with an arranged system of signs and portents. In millennial thought the endtimes are always apocalyptic, part of a supernatural plan for humanity that will bring about a just and peaceful future. The apocalypse is 'the mother of all Christian theology', says Ernst Kasemann, and its maternal influence on writers and artists is overwhelming. Pre-millennialists appear 'overtly fatalistic', says Daniel Wojcik, because they are 'powerless to avert the destruction to come'. As creative writers they readily accept that freedom of expression is severely curtailed by 'the esoteric language and ambiguous allusions' of the Bible (Wojcik 1997, p. 31). Theirs is an obligation to anticipate the symbolism and ceremony of the Rapture when God lifts up His believers to heaven; to acknowledge the havoc wreaked in the Tribulation period by the emerging Antichrist; and to acknowledge the persecution of the Jews that prefaces Christ's final triumph at Armageddon.

The scripted events that frame the last days are curiously reminiscent of the dramatic conventions that inform the formula fictions of Hollywood. In 'the peculiar vacant fervor of Hollywood', says Joan Didion in her essay 'Good Citizens', and in the morality and motion of its films, 'political ideas are reduced to choices between the good (equality is good) and the bad (genocide is bad)'. A 'curious vanity and irrelevance' characterise so many of Hollywood's 'best intentions', she writes. These 'intentions' of good citizenship are apparent in the way 'social problems present themselves ... in terms of a scenario, in which, once certain key scenes are licked ... the plot will proceed inexorably to an upbeat fade'. In the predetermined language of 'a well-plotted motion picture', the prevailing ideology

is faith in dramatic convention. Things 'happen' in motion pictures. There is always a resolution, always a strong cause-effect dramatic line, and to perceive the world in those terms is to assume an ending for every social scenario ... There are no bit players in Hollywood politics: everyone makes things 'happen'. (Didion 1981, pp. 86–9)

In pre-millennialist literature the power of 'convention' also results in an equally 'curious' level of 'vanity'. The patterns of history cannot be altered; things work out for the best in the endtimes. God's 'upbeat fade' will bring about the conversion of the Jews, the salvation of Israel and His millennial rule. These events are part of a design that orders the universe and are evidence of what Hal Lindsey calls 'Christ's credentials' (Lindsey 1970, p. 22). Christian literature must operate on the basis of these 'credentials', none of which can be changed, disputed or improved. Literary Christians must recognise, says Lindsey, that 'He [Jesus] told us that seven signals – war, revolution, plague, famine, earthquake, religious deception, and strange occurrences in space – would alert us that the end of the old world and the birth of the new was near' (Lindsey 1981, p. 19). Although 'attempts to prevent worldly disaster through social action are considered to be hopeless and human responsibility concerning the improvement of this world is discouraged' (Wojcik 1997, pp. 57–8), the duty of every Christian writer is to dramatise the wonders of the natural world and clarify the evidence that God has given us in the prophetic endtimes. If history is a narrative 'designed' (53) by God and foretold by the prophets, the foremost duty of the writer is to reveal the meaning of His unique 'signs', the arrival of which will lead to the triumph of good over evil.

The problem with following a received narrative which puts each of us at the mercy of 'God's great time-clock of eternity' (Lindsey 1984, p. 280) is that His chronological order cannot be adjusted to suit the interpreter's imaginative needs. Since literature is a weapon in the war against the Antichrist, the Christian writer is constrained by prophecies which censor his inventiveness, forcing him to act in accordance with an unalterable plan. The constant recycling of 'ancient apocalyptic ideas' (Wojcik 1997, p. 58) has a curious effect on the writer's work. Contemporary Christian prophecy tends to be a mixture of conceit and powerlessness and while its writers claim to know the fate that awaits us all, they also know that nothing they say can alter the coming catastrophe. The existence of a 'rigorous' timetable for history means that 'current crises' can only be explained 'as part of a design that orders the universe' (143). Dispensational writing offers us a 'fatalistic interpretation' of the world and a joyous record of the 'signs that foretell the imminence of Christ's return'. While 'many of these signs are appalling in themselves', says Hal Lindsey, 'their tremendous significance should gladden the heart of every true believer in Christ'. Disasters are 'preordained portents' (Lindsey 1984, p. 65). The Antichrist's decision to move against Israel in the endtimes and his eventual defeat brings with it the promise of salvation and an end to suffering.

By aligning biblical prophecy with current examples of moral and physical decline – AIDS, abortion, ecological devastation – prophetic writers are able to provide a coherent explanation for the random and the meaningless. In books such as Hal Lindsey's The Late Great Planet Earth, Larry Burkett's The Illuminati, Salem Kirban's 666 and Pat Robertson's The New World Order, the signs and portents that accompany life in the endtimes are revealed by prophets who have been specially chosen by God to provide a special insight into His prophetic word. It is their gift which allows us to witness the onset of His plan and their intuition which accompanies the ubiquitous signs of doomsday.

In The Turning Tide Pat Robertson tells us how the rebellion of the unbelievers, lead by a resurgent Antichrist, is about to wash over

Israel. Civilisation is already under threat, writes Robertson, and the 'tide' of history is 'turning' against us. Without His help the 'tide' will become an apocalyptic flood. The 'curses' that are being sent upon us daily in the form of natural disasters and satanic confederations like the Gulf War alliance, are testimony to our moral decline.

The superlatives of disaster amount one upon another. Hurricane Andrew hit the Homestead area of Florida with killer winds that included the phenomenon of 210 mile-an-hour tornadoes within a massive hurricane. The devastation from that storm cost $25 billion, the most costly in America's history. Hurricane Andrew, coupled with Hurricane Hugo, which devastated Charleston, South Carolina, at a cost of $3 billion, and the San Francisco earthquake, which did $10 billion in damage, make up the three most costly disasters in US history. They were the worst until the rains came in July and August 1993 and produced the worst flood in the history of America, with initial estimates of financial losses at £12 billion, and the possibility that losses might be much higher. (Robertson 1993, pp. 298–9)

These disasters, says Robertson, are a punishment for 'what is taking place' in the United States, a nation 'wasted by drugs, rebellion, illicit sex' (297). The precedent was set by the Israelites, once 'considered a peculiar treasure of God', a 'chosen race' and 'heirs of the patriarch Abraham, who had received a special covenant promise from the Lord' (299). But the Israelites 'turned away from God' and there came 'a time when the sins of the chosen people were too great to ignore anymore'. Assyria's invasion of Israel was permitted by God in 721 BC and a similar fate awaits the United States. In spite of 'a genuine spiritual revival' among fundamentalist denominations like the Southern Baptists and the Assemblies of God, the nation risks an eventual slide into 'moral oblivion'. Under President Clinton the United States is 'operating on borrowed time', its spiritual decline overseen by a 'ruling liberal élite' whose political leaders 'are clearly committed to a radical, unbiblical agenda' (300).

In *The New World Order* and *The Turning Tide* Pat Robertson projects himself as an Old Testament seer, able to address the needs of 'millions of Americans' who 'are embarking on a search for the sacred in their lives' (Begley 1994, p. 39). He provides us with a text on election and salvation, together with a dynamic interpretation of signs and clues for the coming apocalypse and an instructive reading of His role in our future lives. Robertson's popularity confirms the importance of dispensational pre-millennialism 'as an interpretive scheme through which scripture is understood' (Ammerman 1987, p. 45). Prophetic literature is consulted because those who read it believe it can be trusted. In Nancy Ammerman's *Bible Believers*, the parishioners of Southside 'enjoy reading about prophecy even more than they enjoy reading their Bibles'. Bible prophecy is unswervingly predictable. It is said to report 'accurately the events of the past' and present 'detailed predictions of things that are yet to come' (44).

As an aid to understanding the Bible, Southside fundamentalists rely heavily on the interpretetive schemes of their teachers. In *The Late Great Planet Earth* – the largest-selling American nonfiction book since the 1970s – Hal Lindsey provides his readers with a route map for discovering the works of the Old Testament. Lindsey tells his readers 'that for the prophetically knowedgeable ... the words of scripture do not always mean what they seem to mean' (45). Only those who are blessed with the gift of divination and insight can locate the figure of the risen Christ in the scriptural weave of the biblical carpet. As a visionary who claims to know more than his readers, Lindsey bears witness to a rabbinical love affair with scholarship. He adopts for himself 'the role of prophet, calling the nation back to morality' (200), while warning it of the dangers of backsliding 'into terrible sin' (Lindsey 1990, p. 17). In each of his books, Lindsey's predictions are formulated, like those of Robertson's, in order to make sense of current political and economic trends. Through quirky deduction and prophetic inference, Lindsey interprets Biblical symbolism to explain the signs of the coming Tribulation. Flashes of lightning are interpreted as missiles, hailstones refer to ICBMs, and beasts and 'locusts with scorpion tails' are armoured tanks and Cobra helicopters 'spraying nerve gas from their tails' (Wojcik 1997, p. 39). Prophecy affects the lives of fundamentalist communities at 'ground level', says Charles B. Strozier (Strozier 1994, p. 34), and tends to focus attention not on a God of a love or compassion but a divine being who is preoccupied with 'a mankind ... bent on its own destruction' and in desperate need of 'dire remedies' (quoted in Cox 1987, p. 295).

Lindsey's 'belief in apocalyptic prophecy', writes Daniel Wojcik, has its origin in an 'ancient Jewish prophetic tradition' which 'has an extensive legacy in American culture' (Wojcik 1997, p. 6). As a scholar, Lindsey relies on 'the failure of previous prophets and Bible students' correctly to 'interpret the signs of the end' (38). Although his 'scholarship may be questionable and somewhat indiscriminate, his books give the impression that he has a vast knowledge of contemporary events' (46). For this reason 'his interpretations of current events in terms of biblical prophecy convey a sense of privileged information and an understanding of the present and the future'. In the hands of a diviner, scriptural history is never capricious. Lindsey's 'assurances that biblical predictions are being continually fulfilled in God's countdown to Armageddon', are offered as a rational judgement on the future (46). Since God has blessed Lindsey with superior powers of

intuition and scholarship his ability to 'decipher symbolic information about the future as revealed in the Bible', is strictly scientific.
Lindsey claims to possess 'unique insights and special abilities in
interpreting the Bible' and 'special skills in interpreting the prophetic
meaning' of key passages. As a charismatic reader he has '"exceptional
powers or qualities" ... that enable (him) to unravel and decode God's
blueprint for the end of history' (50).

Over the last thirty years the literary prophecy movement has become
a major growth industry in the United States. Its stock-in-trade are
publications which expose their readers to the horror of the gothic in
The Rise of the Antichrist and *Secrets of the Gathering Darkness*. The
emphasis, overwhelmingly, is on the attraction of evil. Writers devote
themselves to an investigation of *Satan's Mark Exposed*, *Satan's Music
Exposed*, *Satan's Angels Exposed*, *The Mark of the Beast*, *The Occult*,
The Devils Playground and *The Seduction of Our Children*. Evangelical
prophecy finds it more profitable to ask its readers 'Why do bad things
seem so fun?' (Russo 1994) than provide them with an outline of
the spiritual benefits they can expect to receive during the Rapture.
'The constant recourse', 'to the Old Testament', says A. G. Mojitabai,
'and to [its] most bellicose sections ... strangely negates the "good
news" of the Gospels and the First Coming'. Harvey Cox agrees. By
ceasing 'to proclaim the central kernel of the biblical message – that
God calls human beings to repent and to change their evil ways' and
that His 'grace makes such repentance possible' – fundamentalism
forgoes any claim to being a merciful theology. Instead, it chooses an
ominous fatalism and 'a cynical sense of powerlessness' that provides
the basis for 'a religious pathology' (Cox 1987, p. 295).

Prophetic Christianity offers its readers a blueprint for survival in
a dangerous age, allowing them 'to recognize Satan's influence' and
'to develop a personal "battle plan"' to counteract 'his attacks' (Russo
1994). Prophecy abhors complacency. 'If you're not paranoid', write
Peter and Paul Lalonde in *The Mark of the Beast* (1994), 'it's because
you're not paying close enough attention to the imminence of evil in
the last days: the Soviet Union's continuing threat to the State of
Israel, the threat from so-called world peace organizations such as
the United Nations and the World Council of Churches, and the
ten-nation confederacy [the European Union] mentioned in the Book
of Revelation' (Lalonde and Lalonde 1994, p. 105). In *The Mark of
the Beast*, the Lalondes examine the role of advanced computer
technology, laser scanning and electronic surveillance in the Antichrist's system of social control. The introduction of a universal mark
('The Mark of the Beast') in the form of a silicon chip implant is
seen as the first step in the creation of a totalitarian state and a
numbering system, 666, as a framework for devil worship. The rise

of the computer mogul is also a standard concern, and with Bill Gates as president of Microsoft a new False Prophet is already using computer technology to facilitate, worldwide, the worship of 'the Beast'.

In *Satan Is Alive and Well on Planet Earth* (1972) Hal Lindsey identifies the satanic influences and expressions of evil that have overtaken modern civilisation and infiltrate all aspects of western life. Lindsey shows himself to be fascinated with satanic phenomenon: parapsychology, drug addiction, blood sacrifice, the sexual excess of America's youth and an American culture that is deeply corrupt. As a dispensationalist he is able to enter the mind of Satan in order to warn us of the coming Tribulation, but in the act of narrating the apocalypse (and recording its signs and portents) he is also compelled by the cerebral intrigue that Satan relies on and the artifice of his schemes.

Lindsey prides himself on his scriptural intellect and powers of divination, even though the practice of divination is condemned by the Bible (Deuteronomy 18: 9–14; Isaiah 44: 25; Jeremiah 29: 9) as false prophecy. In Ezekiel 13: 8 the Lord calls the word of the diviners a lie and cuts them off from cohabitation with Israel. In Jeremiah 14: 4 God makes fools of the diviners by showing their divination to be a deception. Although it is not always clear what the Bible permits as a legitimate reading of His signs, Lindsey's predictions often 'resemble', says Daniel Wojcik, 'the speculation of futurologists'. There is often no truth to them and no contrition is forthcoming in the event of failure. Unfulfilled predictions are 'disregarded or modified in subsequent books' (Wojcik 1997, p. 53) rather than explained. The failure of prophecy also results in the structured amnesia of those who author it, as happened after the Gulf War when prophecy writers failed to predict accurately the outcome of Saddam Hussein's attack on Kuwait but refused to admit it.

The desire to predict future events in the working of Satanic rituals differs little from the occult practices of futurism and precognition, which fundamentalists find disturbing. Religious analysis of contemporary history, moreover, is no less speculative than telekinesis or parapsychology as a way of verifying Bible prophecy. Damning the clairvoyant in no way inhibits the fundamentalist from trying to imitate his confidence trickery, as if the righteous would like to disempower the occult by utilising a secret ventriloquism.

The ploy of attaching the number 666 to the name of the beast is a common example of the way fundamentalism reduces scripture to a mechanistic numerology, but does nothing to clarify the meaning of Revelation 13. 'The Bible does not have an intricate numerical pattern which only a mathematical expert can discover', writes

Oswald T. Allis. 'The strict and obvious meaning of words ... and numbers should be adhered to unless it is quite plain that some further meaning is involved.' A mathematical theology which attempts to make 'a biblical case' for numerology 'by pointing to the number of the beast (666) in Revelation 13: 18 (59) and then relates that number to incidents that confirm its power in the present day, is an "idle" attempt "to find a mysterious or mystical meaning in [a] simple historical fact"' (quoted in McDowell and Stewart 1992, p. 60).

Anthony Hilder sees numerology as an answer to the 'Faustian' conspiracy behind the styling of the dollar bill.

In 1934, an Egyptian pyramid – with all its masonic implications – was worked into the dollar's design, atop which is the all-seeing eye of Lucifer. Underneath is the inscription: Noval ordum seclorum – 'the New World Order' ... Beneath that are Roman numerals for the date 1776, the date of the founding of the order of the Illuminati. There are 13 layers in the dollar's pyramid, 13 stars above the head of its eagle, 13 berries, 13 leaves, 13 arrows, 13 stripes – everything is in 13s, the mystical number of Satan, except for the eagles' wings, which are 32 and 33, for the highest degrees of masonry. (Vulliamy 1995, p. 23)

In the act of exposing Satan as an occult intellectual, folklorists like Hilder are fascinated by the constructions of his mind. As a fallen angel, Satan's beautiful and intricate prodigality demands attention. While God's salvation in the Old Testament tends towards the archival and the formulaic Satan's errant divinity offers the prophecy writer an opportunity to investigate a mercurial intellect. Those who do so have a tendency to commemorate Satan's 'magnetic personality', to emulate the scholarship on which his occult theology depends and to replicate his idolatrous following with their own.

Satan is alluring to the prophecy writer because, says Norman Mailer, his intellect contains something of the mind of God as well as the disfigured intellect of a 'beautiful' degenerate (O'Hagan 1997, p. 21). In this sense he is not simply a brutal or brutalising presence but a figure in whom the paranoid style is invested with the power of the divine and charismatic. Prophecy literature becomes embroiled in the mesmerism of someone whose beauty has gone astray, a 'virtual' Christ (Russo 1994, p. 101), a parasitic minister whose love affair with numerology, the science of mathematics, messianic practice and resurrection motifs is evidence of an original divinity he shared with God. It is this remnant of divinity which allows the devil to retain possession of the kind of personality that Jesus can never have. As a 'supernatural' emissary (97), Satan is both fallen angel and fallen Jew, a 'Criolian degenerate' who can never be reformed, a 'miracle worker', a promiser of peace with the 'deifying' power of a 'new Caesar' (95).

As the False Prophet, says Hal Lindsey, he is believed to be descended from the tribe of Dan (Lindsey 1970, p. 101). In Larry Burkett's novel *The Illuminati* we know him as Amir Hussein, a 'dark' (Burkett 1991, p. 128) charismatic who is born of a Jewish mother in Israel, his features resonant with the beauty of the ancient world.

In the 1980s the most popular course taught at the Fuller Theological Seminary (the leading evangelical teaching college in the United States) was C. Peter Wagner's 'Signs, Wonders, and Church Growth'. The unique feature of the course was that it analysed 'signs and wonders' in the Christian church today and included 'practical sessions' (Anon. 1983, pp. 31–4, 63) in which these signs were interpreted in class. The course also emphasised the supernatural element in fundamentalism: biblical inerrancy, the virgin birth, the miracles of Christ, bodily resurrection, the Second Coming and the incidence of divine intervention in history. Wagner suggested that Christians would be wise to exorcise demons from their homes, especially if they had travelled to pagan temples in foreign lands where demons might have attached themselves to their persons or luggage. In the act of damning the occult Wagner came close to exceeding his purpose as a chosen servant of the Christian church. The advice he gave broke down the barriers between legitimate prophecy and parapsychology. In claiming to know the existence of the occult, Wagner was prepared to practise it himself, extending his own supernatural belief in 'psychical gifts' with a clairvoyance that lacked 'a biblical base' (McDowell and Stewart 1992, pp. 94–5).

At the root of all fundamentalist theses, says Umberto Eco, lies an obsession with plot, one in which the followers of a movement feel 'besieged' (Eco 1995, p. 27) and intrigued by the presence of an alien force. In Richard Hofstadter's essay, 'The Paranoid Style in American Politics', plots take the form of apocalyptic warnings, irrefutable proof that history is a conspiracy, set in motion by demonic forces of almost transcendent power, the meaning of which can only be revealed by the ferocious 'scholarship' and genius of the scholar (Hofstadter 1966, p. 32). Plots are the product of a paranoid style in which those who believe in the power of conspiracy exploit the occult in order to act as the controllers of narrative. Threats are contrived, but eventually overcome through intuition. The conspiracy theorist is extravagantly gothic, fearing the occult and the Dionysian, but relishing the power that comes to those who claim to understand it.

Those who 'solve the plot' acquire the status of a semi-divine, but in order to know what the plot contains they must first imitate 'the enemy'. This enemy, says Hofstadter, is 'the perfect model of malice, a kind of amoral superman, ubiquitous, powerful, and sensual, luxury-loving'. He is finally (and only) outdone by an opponent who pays the enemy the 'implicit compliment' of taking on his 'vast and terrifying quality' (32). The paranoid mind exploits ignorance on the basis of secrecy: secret knowledge, secret intuition, secret speculation. Detection through secrecy confers a mystical, charismatic power on those who display it. The fundamentalist leader is powerful, says Umberto Eco, because he appears an 'exceptional being', a luminary who detects the message in the runes, a saviour who derives his legitimacy from God – a 'fantastic power' – on the basis of a revealed text or inscription (Eco 1995, p. 27).

Fundamentalist fascination with the beauty of deviance is overwhelming in Salem Kirban's *666* (1970), one of the first fictional attempts to assess 'the depraved conditions of today's world' (Kirban 1970, p. 7) in the Tribulation period. Kirban is intrigued not only with deviance but with an 'ominous fatalism' which delights, as Harvey Cox puts it, in the 'spreading' of 'bad news' (Cox 1987, p. 295). *666* is thus a fictional casualty of Kirban's reluctance to write outside a prescribed dispensational formula and an extravagant desire to plot the course of a charismatic satanism. Kirban unravels history through a 'specific pattern of world events' which 'are precisely predicted' by the Old Testament (Lindsey 1970, p. 31). On the evils of a 'United World Church' Kirban quotes from a passage in Timothy: 'But evil men and seducers shall wax worse and worse, deceiving, and being deceived' (2 Timothy 3: 13). He describes the inventions of the future – the picturephone, the ruby laser and the flying belt – to show how the Antichrist uses technology to incapacitate his opponents. Since all present and future events are based in biblical 'fact', writes Kirban (Kirban 1970, p. 11), the responsibility of the writer is to accept the guidance of a preordained form and faithfully to interpret the narrative of the ancients. 'God's complete panorama of prophecy' relieves Kirban of the need to conduct his own imaginative enquiries and leaves him free to criticise those who ignore the moral and spiritual challenge of Christianity.

Throughout *666* the story line 'corresponds with prophetic scripture' and Bible verses accompany the text with supporting 'facts'. The writer's view of the 1960s – the satanism of nuclear disarmament, campus riots, illicit sexuality, 'the Goliath of Churchdom' (8) and the 'watered down religion' (249) of ecumenism – are an illustration of the endtime trajectories forecast in the Bible. *666* shows how the 'Antichrist and his associates' 'apply' scientific 'discoveries' in order 'to achieve their own sinister goals' (11). Science and technology are a threat to salvation because they deify human ingenuity and abandon the need for spiritual guidance.

From a command post on the Mount of Olives, the Antichrist, Brother Bartholomew, decides to attack Jerusalem by deploying an army of 'flying men' who wear jet belts and a special virus spray stored in a 'tabular section on their back'. A lever on the belt releases 'a fine spray over a 150 square yard area'. Bartholomew calls his force '"ABADDON"', which is '"Hebrew for The Destroyer"'. His attackers emerge from an underground complex in a cloud of smoke and are referred to by George Omega as '"almost like a plague ... a plague of LOCUSTS!"' (232). The account of the attack is supported by extracts from the Book of Revelation in which locusts with tails like scorpions and the power to poison are released from a smoke-filled pit by their king, Abaddon. The sequence of events which Kirban chooses owes its origin to the dreams and visions of the biblical prophets. It is they who lay down the foundations of the narrative and it is their account of 'God's prophetic timetable' which Kirban uses to stimulate his chronology.

A similar pattern is revealed during a cavalry attack on Israel, organised by the anti-Semitic Russian Premier, Alexi Bazenoff. Bazenoff leads the campaign on horseback on a 'blood red horse' (Revelation 6: 4). The dust from the horses casts 'an ominous cloud' over Israel, causing great fear among the people (Ezekiel 38: 9). The attack is repulsed when God intervenes by causing Mount Tabor to erupt. In an act of divine providence Bazenoff is killed by lightning, his cavalry retreat in panic allowing 'The Lord' to give 'His remnant people, the Jews ... victory' (Ezekiel 38: 18–22) (134). The intervention accelerates the conversion of the Jews to Christianity and frustrates the plans of Brother Bartholomew to wreak further havoc on Israel.

The idea of a cavalry invasion of the Middle East has long been a staple of fundamentalist literature. It is also an article of faith that the state of Israel will be 'plagued' by the threat of invasion from the northern nation of Gog and that this invasion 'has been clearly forecasted' in the Bible (Lindsey 1973, p. 48). As an endtimes device the judgement of Ezekiel that Israel will be attacked by a godless confederacy was intensely popular throughout the Cold War. Thirty years after he first made this claim in *The Late Great Planet Earth*, Hal Lindsey is still repeating it. In *The Final Battle* (1995) Lindsey suggests that the real Gog announced in prophecy is not the old Soviet Union but a confederacy of 'ethnic Russians' (Lindsey 1995, p. 4).

Following the collapse of the Soviet Union, the menace of Russia as an agent of the endtimes could not be denied. In the late 1980s and early 1990s Pat Robertson and Robert W. Faid depicted Mikhael Gorbachev as a satanic threat whose reforms were a hoax. In 1994 Grant Jeffrey reminded his readers that Gorbachev and Boris Yeltsin were in league with the Prince of Darkness and had stage-managed the death of Communism to distance us from the old objective of Communist enslavement. In other dispensationalist texts, the focus is to warn us against a new, pan-Islamic brotherhood of Gog, an assembly of countries that were once part of the Soviet Union – Turkmenistan, Kyrgyzstan, Kazakhstan, Tajikistan and Uzbekistan – and who now plan an attack on Israel.

Many of these prophecies struggle under the weight of a morbid fascination with endism. Cataclysm, they say, is unavoidable. The road on which the writer must travel does not require that he blaze new trails but recognise the signs that others have given him. The task requires, as Kirban puts it, that he demonstrate prophetic knowledge of 'THE SEQUENCE OF EVENTS' that frame 'the entire Millennial Age' (Kirban 1970, p. 10). His gift, if he has one, lies in the ability to match these events with a corresponding narrative outside the Bible. In order to synchronise biblical events with events current in *666*, Kirban supports his novel with a pictorial and photographic record of the endtimes. This artwork graphically reveals the journey we are about to undertake towards Armageddon. So desperate is Kirban to bring to our attention the fact that we live in desperate times, he is prepared to go to extraordinary lengths to convince us of the problem. His pictures are the product of trick photography, photocopied treatments of original work that lack an acknowledgement of source or context. The illustrations accompanying the text in the Tribulation depict scenes of violent death, torture and execution. In many of them, consumer entertainment gets the better of art and sensationalist photography mirrors the worst excesses of the tabloids. So intrigued is Kirban by the 'hoax' (8) methods of the Antichrist that he feels compelled to perpetrate them himself. In reproducing and plagiarising the work of others, we are reminded of Kirban's own warning about the danger of 'strong delusion' (Thessalonians 2: 11) and the trickery of those whose 'miracles and wonders' seem 'convincing' (26).

While Kirban claims to have written a 'novel' which is 'true' to life in its use of 'facts', his fictional account of the Tribulation period 'and its judgements' (279) lack any grounding in realism and give limited attention to the creation of character through dialogue or plot. So enthralled is Kirban by the horror-pornography of science fiction and the epic dimensions of the Antichrist's wizardry that alternative social activities are abandoned. Characters are dwarfed by supernatural force. They become the product of a fatalism which denies them the chance to be emotionally confronted, spiritually challenged or intellectually enriched by the questions they ask or the decisions they make. Where His divine plan is unalterable, life lacks an independent status and the novel loses energy and integrity.

666 begins on the day of the Rapture when George Omega and a friend are flying back from the United Church Fellowship in Rome. In the 'twinkling of an eye' George loses consciousness, only to regain it with the immortal line: '"I don't remember exactly what happened. There had been two stewardesses standing next to me; but when I woke only one was there!"' (34). The disappearance of the stewardess is quickly followed by that of George's friend, Bill, together with the pilot and half the passengers. The remaining stewardess tries her best to explain:

Ladies and gentlemen ... something rather unusual has happened. We are not sure what ... but please be calm ... everything is under control. Our pilot has vanished ... perhaps some mysterious celestial illness. This caused the abrupt dive ... (35)

For readers who are inclined to see the loss of a pilot as more than 'rather unusual', Kirban offers no further explanation. Understatement is a key weapon in Kirban's Christian armoury, a writer with the ability to move, at the speed of light, from total ignorance to blinding revelation. In the above scene, George Omega begins to realise that since he is conscious, what he is experiencing on the plane must be real. 'And suddenly it came to me. I WAS HERE!', he announces. The shock of the moment, with its laboured reflex, is wholly disconnected from the language that evokes it. The meaning of suddenness sinks without trace. So do many of the characters in the novel. They, like George on the day of the Rapture, are unable to generate an emotional identity in a form which matches the drama they are encountering.

The problem of language divorced from experience recurs when the False Prophet, Bishop Arthur, tells George and his daughter, Faye, that the guillotine he is about to use on them has an electronic release mechanism that will allow both heads to '"roll at the same time ... in unison!"' (253). Kirban's response ruins any hope that Arthur has achieved the effect he is looking for. 'Faye's heart sank, her eyelids dropped. George was furious and was ready to unleash a tongue lashing at both Prophet Arthur and Brother Bartholomew' (253). Condemned to serve out his life as a cartoon George has lost the power of speech. Instead of cliché he falls back on 'Scripture' and lambasts the 'confirmed monsters of iniquity' (254) with a passage from Isaiah. In an aside to Faye, George also quotes from Romans 11: 33 to explain their predicament: 'O the depth of the riches both of the wisdom and knowledge of God! How unsearchable are His judgements, and His ways past finding out!' The dynamic of the moment is completely lost. George is refused permission to speak. Instead, biblical epigrams speak on his behalf. The reader is forced to conclude that, in times of crisis, Kirban believes it is less problematical to have a character register an emotion through the 'word of God' than independent thought.

Kirban's fascination with the endtimes embodies many of the flaws that are common to dispensationalist fiction. Not only does Kirban not understand the characters he has created, he is not concerned with the flaws and fault lines in their social psyche. The problem is that Kirban believes his characters cannot think for themselves because freedom of expression is a sin against God. This becomes clear when Faye's husband, Bill Saunders, refuses to accept Brother Bartholomew's branding mark, 666, and is executed by guillotine. Faye screams but is less aroused by the sight of her husband's severed head floating in a glass bath than by God's decision to save the soul of Tom Malone, an old ally of Brother Bartholomew. Faye's joy, at the divine rescue of Tom, is far more important than the death for which Malone has been responsible. Faye translates her emotion, from anguish into ecstasy, at the moment of Malone's repentance. The ease with which she does this is unhealthy and Kirban's response to it is dubiously prurient. Faye appears bored with her mortality and the time she has spent – during a misspent youth – away from God. She has even confessed as much to her husband, Bill, before his death:

Oh Bill, Bill, Bill, why does life have to be this way? ... Why did I turn my back on God for so many years? Helen, little Sue and Tommy. They're in Heaven now enjoying the blessings of God. But we're here on this miserable, sophisticated, progressive, godless, everything-goes earth. (171)

Faye says she '"can't go on"' without God. This is the reason she appears overjoyed when, after her husband's death, God is the only man left in her life. Faye now awaits the sexual 'terrorism' of the 'demon' (Morgan 1989) lover, a God whose rapturous promise allows her an emotional release from a life in which she was trapped by marriage. If Faye is lucky, the Rapture will allow her further escape from a prose whose spirit is cryogenically preserved in the embalming fluid of Bible-speak and the abstract emptiness of a righteous religion.

Although Faye must achieve the release she dreams of in the arms of the Lord, her orgiastic plea for help falls on deaf ears. On a 'pretend ... honeymoon' (170), Bill cries in sympathy with her, but does not have the faintest idea of the wet dream of heaven his wife is possessed by. Nor, one suspects, does Kirban. Faye, who hates her marriage and the 'miserable' world in which she is forced to live, keeps herself sexually alive by imagining that God will come and Rapture her away. If God is powerless to resist the fetishes of the righteous, and the idolatry that inspires them, Kirban is unwilling to dismiss them from the text. The idea of death masquerading as Rapture belies a false understanding of divine intervention, which Kirban tolerates. Rather than clarify the meaning of an emotion, he allows it simply to run away with the character. In so doing, he permits what could have been an intriguing relationship to collapse into a kind of pathetic martyrdom.

Faye's love affair with God does nothing to improve her standing with the reader. In a sense, her relationship is with the wrong person. Faye is inexplicably attracted to a God who is the social inferior of Satan and unable to achieve his intellectual and imaginative dominance in the text. Kirban's strategy lends weight to this argument. He tells us that because 'the days are critical' Christians should 'become concerned and active in what they believe'. Satan's influence over world events is undeniable, he concedes, and is 'already paving the way for a world dictator!' (11). Kirban feels compelled to devote his artistic attention to the morbid ministry of the Antichrist and the counterfeit productions which steal Christ's thunder. He is so intrigued by the aesthetic possibilities of Satan that he tends to become his greatest advocate. As a result he displays all the deviant urges of the errant Christian in pursuit of the Indian in the forests of New England. In a three-hundred-page novel we have to go two-thirds the way through before God is allowed to make his presence felt. God may unsettle the Antichrist with his earthquakes and eclipses and fabled white horses, but He hardly does the same to us.

As an illuminating presence in *666*, God is about as dim as a 40-watt bulb. He shines His light on the world's faithful from a vast and inscrutable distance, finally intervening to obstruct the Antichrist through natural catastrophe and cosmic occurrence. But God is a remote and absent avenger, whereas the Antichrist is a gregarious adventurer who reveals himself by 'going to and fro in the earth, and . . . walking up and down in it' (Bernières 1998, p. 21). Set against the occasional tidal wave or eclipse of the sun, Satan's theatricality is lively and compelling and the infrastructure of his organisation provides the writer with much of the fabric and framework for the plot.

Kirban relishes the moment when Brother Bartholomew tells his assistant, Bishop Arthur, about his plan to control 'the populace' with public executions in the Colosseum in Rome. The prospect of a 'spectacle' of terror as the 'trip levers go off in sequence' allows Kirban to project the Antichrist like Cecil B. De Mille and to have him 'stage the whole thing like a big Hollywood production' (Kirban 1970, p. 221). Satan is the grand, experimental idealist with a flair for the dramatic. He is unafraid of new technologies: laser rings, heliojets, a lavishly equipped TV studio in which he performs as president of the United States in front of sixty hundred and sixty-six people, seated in six 'cushioned' tiers. There is a stylishness in his parody of the Resurrection when he arrives in Israel in a robe and cape, fanfared by the Israeli Army Band, 'as though Christ himself were returning to the Mount of Olives ... not on a donkey' but in a 'space craft' (117). His formality and idolatrous reception on the Day of Atonement is invested with a natural gravitas. As an elected leader of a united world church and a man of peace and reconciliation, Satan brings to an end America's war with China. His knowledge of the Scriptures is impressive, so is his ability to enter the minds of the people he is cajoling, as if he has 'taken a course in psychology' and knows 'how to quell factions and make them the best of friends' (55). While God is supercilious, Satan retains his fatherly appeal. As George Omega puts it (Kirban 1970):

I had confidence in him. Many had asked me what he looked like. To me he looks like a prophet. In him there is no hypocrisy, and his followers love him. Tall, well shaped, his hair is not too long, just long enough to portray that fatherly appeal ... that appeal of confidence. (43)

Satan's apparent humanism gives him a compelling advantage over God. In *666* he is a saviour in possession of a personality, a patriarch redolent with light and shade that a country can warm to as it faces the prospect of being 'swallowed up in [its] own wickedness': rampant crime, urban pollution, a workforce on welfare, sexual promiscuity (60). An America that has never recovered from the cancer of the 1960s and feels overwhelmed by the legacy of 'sex filth', is obliged to cry out for a 'strong man', someone like Brother Bartholomew who can 'speak one word and the bullets would cease ... [who] can take one step and walk on water'. There is 'something special' about the Antichrist, we are told; 'something that demanded respect and inspired confidence' (45).

The problem, says Peter Handley, is that since we do not know who he or she is, God remains indescribable. The difficulty for any novelist who uses a 'sublime language ... to describe God' is that His personality will 'be wrong', as well as aesthetically unappealing. In *666*, Kirban's mistake is trying to make God into 'a perfectionist', which he clearly is not. God 'is a chancer', argues Handley, who has chosen 'a world in which chance has a role to play'. This means there are 'problems' with 'God's character' which require explanation: the first one being that 'God somehow botched the job of making this world' a better place and of peopling it with 'risk-takers' who, like Him, make calamitous decisions. As 'a projection stemming from human fears, neuroses and abject needs', God's decision to make a humanity in His image requires us to see in Him a character who is not inscrutably good, but 'vulnerable', 'self-sacrificing', 'permissive', 'forgiving'. God's various 'attributes' 'ought to be more widely appreciated', argues Handley. If they were, and if the God we worshipped was not truly pure, but 'jealous, wrathful, indifferent, loving', novelists like Kirban could offer us a more intriguing personality (Handley 1998, pp. 6–7).

In the dispensationalist struggle between the forces of good and evil, says Daniel Wojcik, evil continues to be 'regarded as an overwhelming, uncontrollable power that is foredained to dominate in the endtimes' (Wojcik 1997, p. 165). Since the endtimes are always imminent, Satan remains the compelling alternative to a Christ who does not come (and a God who does not make him come). The Christian message needs Satan for its dramas and a Christian congregation to recognise his appeal. As long as vigilance remains the key to survival for a faith like fundamentalism, and as long as that faith embraces the watchfulness of a Jeremiah or an Ezekiel, then Satan will remain the dominant partner in any artistic production: the 'primary' protagonist 'in the apocalyptic drama' (162).

Notes

1. The psychologist Leon Festinger and his associates, in their study of prophetic movements, conclude that while there are limits beyond which belief will not withstand disconfirmation, the introduction of contrary evidence often serves not to destroy the belief but rather to strengthen the conviction and enthusiasm of the believers (Festinger *et al.* 1956). The dissonance resulting from the clash of a belief-system and facts which tend to discredit it produces anxiety which can be reduced in one of three ways: by discarding the disconfirmed belief; by blinding oneself to the fact that the prophecy has not been fulfilled; by reconfirming the belief in the hope that if more and more people can be persuaded that the system of belief is correct, then clearly it must be correct. Although millennialist believers have exhibited all three tendencies after the Gulf, the latter two, and especially the third, constituted by far the most prevalent response.

   A similar reaction can be seen in the response to the failure of the messianic prophets, Sabbatai Sevi and William Miller. In 1666 gullible millennialists were 'taken in', says Richard H. Popkin, by the arrival of Sabbatai Sevi, an Ottoman Jew who claimed messianic powers. Sevi proclaimed 1666 as the start of a new messianic age but was exposed as 'an impostor'. 1666 – 'a year many Christian millenarians had forecast as the beginning of the millennium' (Popkin 1980, p. 79) – was not a year of 'wonders', 'revolutions' and 'blessings to the Jews' (80), and the effect 'on the Jewish side' was to dampen 'messianic expectations' (85). This was not the case, says Popkin, on the Christian side, where millennialism 'went on undaunted' and 'Believers' chose 'to recalculate the date of the wondrous year when the millennium would begin' (83). 'As millennial expectations in England receded', says Popkin, 'American Puritans devoted themselves to reconfirming an apocalyptic tradition within the Protestant church and increasingly found prophetic meaning in their own history' (68).

The incentive to reconfirm the importance of prophecy is often born of adversity. In the nineteenth century the Baptist preacher William Miller spent much of his life calculating the date of the endtimes. Miller decided on 22 October 1844 as the exact date for the end of the world, and he and his followers stood on a hill waiting for Christ, in an 'any-moment Rapture', to carry them away. Although Christ's non-appearance created much disappointment ('Our fondest hopes and expectations were', said one distraught Millerite, 'blasted, and such a spirit of weeping came over us as I never experienced before' (Boyer 1992, p. 81)), the disenchanted Millerites refused to abandon their apocalyptic beliefs. Rather than denounce God for having abandoned them, they turned to other millennialist churches, like the Seventh-Day Adventists, and, in the middle to later years of the nineteenth century, the preachings of John Nelson Darby.

4

Bill Clinton:
the South's Lost Cause

If the 'phenomenon of fundamentalism' has become a 'universal' condition (Ruthven 1993a, p. 31) in the United States, its political and economic power base continues to lie in the 'moralistic South', a place whose 'militant evangalism' finds a home in the 'Puritan values' of the Bible Belt (Wilson 1980, pp. 52, 80–1). Southern fundamentalism came of age in the years following the Civil War. In the 1870s the principle of an ideal Christian civilisation, morally and spiritually superior to that of the North, was transformed, into what Charles Reagan Wilson calls, a 'Southern civil religion'. Conservative religion became the core of a southern culture that was preoccupied with understanding defeat and honouring the memory of 'the Lost Cause'.[1] Under the social and economic stresses of post-war dislocation and the grinding poverty of the postbellum era southerners turned to the reassertion of nostalgic values to make themselves right with God and to express disdain for the liberal Christianity of their former enemies in the North.

Failure in the Civil War gave the South, writes Wilson, a feeling that theirs was a history which had been more righteous and more sacrificial than that of the North. As a result, the South's pursuit of redemption became the basis for its spiritual and civil faith. 'The Enlightenment tradition played virtually no role in the religion of the Lost Cause', says Wilson. But 'the emotionally intense, dynamic Revivalist tradition' and the 'secularised legacy of idealistic, moralistic Puritanism ... helped form its character' (13). Confederate defeat offered confused southerners 'a sense of meaning, an identity in a precarious but distinct culture', a 'mythology' which 'taught that Americans are a chosen people, destined to play a special role in the world as representatives of freedom and equality'. For the South, suggests Wilson, the religion of 'the Lost Cause' was 'a creation myth', the story of the attempt to create a southern nation as a testament to chosenness. 'The myth enacted the Christian story of Christ's suffering and death with the Confederacy at the sacred center.' This Christian drama of suffering and salvation would remain 'incomplete' until the Confederacy, which had 'lost a holy war', achieved 'resurrection' in the endtimes (Wilson 1992, pp. 47–8).

If the idea of the South as biblically 'chosen' reminded southerners of their link with Israel it did so by combining a literal reading of the Scriptures with the emotional intensity of a memorial faith in history. 'The Religion of the Lost Cause' combined the devotionalism of the 'nomadic Confederate army' with that of the wandering Israelites who were 'wont to set up the tabernacle and offer sacrifices to the God of battles', says Wilson (Wilson 1980, p. 43). This particular faith was resurrected a hundred years later in the immediate aftermath of the Vietnam War as a result of the nation's political failure to articulate a clear and coherent vision of errand in Southeast Asia. Defeat in Vietnam was keenly felt in the South, which had retained a strong tradition of military service and sent a disproportionately high number of recruits to Vietnam. Southern troops, it was thought, had not lost the war in Vietnam; they had been stabbed in the back at the eleventh hour by liberal politicians in Washington.

In the aftermath of war – and the scandal of Watergate – national politics appeared to be in a state of moral collapse. In the later years of the 1970s the quest to explain the reason for collapse, by southern politicians such as Jimmy Carter, did much to enhance the moral authority of those who bore witness to the truth in public. In the crusade to redeem the United States, southern ministers like Jerry Falwell, Oral Roberts, James Bakker, Jimmy Swaggart and Pat Robertson also celebrated the moral supremacy of the South as a 'chosen' race and a 'Redeemer' nation. They also 'resuscitated a theme from earlier eras by looking upon America as God's New Israel providentially designated for moral leadership in the world'. From its campaign headquarters in the South, the New Right sought to preserve the traditional moral ideals of the 'lost cause' by providing an 'unequivocal alignment of Christian zeal and political conservatism' and by signalling 'a return into public life of traditional moral forces that had gone underground after the public defeat of the fundamentalists in the 1920s' (Bakke 1983, p. 454). For the conservative church in the 1970s, the cult of 'piety' based on the notion of 'insight' enshrined the principle 'that faith must be personal', proclamatory and authoritarian (Enroth 1983, p. 473).

In the aftermath of Vietnam evangelical leaders were willing to identify with any politician who (in finding a pretext for restoring the credibility of the Protestant faith) committed himself to the principle of a redemptive errand. Fundamentalists were much less threatened by Ronald Reagan and George Bush, politicians with no social or cultural affiliation with the South – but who accepted the need to undertake a compelling commission against the Antichrist – than they were by Bill Clinton, a small-town southerner from Hope, Arkansas, who had served as his State's governor but had gone to Washington without the righteous egotism of the Puritan or the moralistic piety of the southern traditionalist.

After his election Clinton's opponents in the South quickly convinced themselves that their President lacked a chivalric faith, a redeeming belief in a biblical cause that would inspire a call to arms and infuse his presidency with a sense of southernness. For southern fundamentalists the nation under Clinton became a lost cause, made worse by the man's spiritual and emotional disloyalty to the South and his refusal to engage with its military traditions. This disloyalty had already been highlighted during the Vietnam War when Clinton preferred the company of anti-war protestors to that of Vietnam veterans and opted for the decadent lifestyle of a Rhodes scholar in Oxford to that of a soldier in South Vietnam. As a student at Georgetown University and Yale and a protegé of another southern apostate, William Fulbright, Clinton created an impression, says John Lichfield, that here was an individual with 'the confidence swings of a teenager', but 'no rooted sense' of himself. In the 1992 presidential election, argues Lichfield, the feeling that Clinton could never 'behave as a father to his children' (the American public) was expressed as a worry about his 'incapacity for the paternal, story-telling part of the job' and his lack of an 'all-encompassing myth' for the nation (Lichfield 1992, p. 19).

In later years, the stories the White House told about Whitewater, Vince Foster, Paula Jones and Monica Lewinsky were condemned by the Christian Right as fabrications, stories without a moral centre or, as Jimmy Carter would have put it, 'a solid base' to support them. (Reston, Jun., 1984, p. 187). Clinton's occasional confessions of adultery – with Gennifer Flowers, for example – merely exposed the moral hypocrisy of presidential power rather than a need to bear witness to the truth through personal testimony. As a southern politician Clinton lacked what the evangelical Carter had in abundance, a clear belief in the importance of personal morality as a guiding principle and a genuine understanding of the importance of testimony – the making of a private stand on a public mission – as a crucial determinant of the individual's right to membership in the church. Clinton's experience of testimony – to investigative counsels, Special Prosecutors, prayer meetings, Grand Juries, TV interviewers – was seen as little more than a mockery of the principle of unabashed Christian witness.

For David Thomson, Clinton is 'a natural, even a chronic denier' with 'a sad history of legalism, evasive phrasing and bare-faced deception in his "confessional" mode'. Congenitally unable to speak the truth (except only as a last resort) during the whole six months of the Lewinsky crisis, Clinton pulled 'every trick of spin, delay and legal manoeuvre to force the issue into obscurity' (Thomson 1998, pp. 1–2). Elsewhere, he relied on the guidance of Hollywood producers like Harry Thomason, who flew into Washington in January 1998 and, for nine days, coached the president to produce 'a televised cameo performance' during which he bluntly and categorically denied sexual relations with Monica Lewinsky. Clinton, says John Carlin, 'did not fail his instructor. When the lights came on, he trained his laser eyes on the cameras and, like John Wayne facing down the bad guys, delivered his script' (Carlin 1998, p. 20).

Christopher Hitchens is certain that Clinton 'is never happier' than at a National Prayer Breakfast in the White House where he is able to intone 'scriptural platitudes' for the assembled religious leaders (Hitchens 1998, p. 28). At the White House prayer meeting on Friday, 11 September, the day the report of the special prosecutor, Kenneth Starr, into the President's eighteen-month relationship with the former White House intern, Monica Lewinsky, was made public, Clinton resorted to the Puritan practice of plain speaking and public testimony as he faced the prospect of political annihilation in the coming days. The 'maneouvre' was a way of 'outcharming' his guests and disarming his opponents (Marshall 1998b, p. 3). Clinton, in effect, used the strategy of the disgraced fundamentalist Jim Bakker by tearfully repenting while positioning himself to counter the legal charges brought by the Starr inquiry. In acknowledging that he had not been 'contrite enough' and that 'I don't think there is a fancy way to say that I have sinned', Clinton publically and unashamedly plagiarised the Puritan conversion narrative. This form of address, says Elizabeth Caldwell, professes feelings of inadequacy, frustration and spiritual incapacity and does not seek to hide them away. In his confession, Clinton distanced himself from the sin of 'soul speech', the manipulation of an audience by verbal means, 'swelling words of humane wisdom' and 'blubber-lipt Ministry' (Boorstin 1965, p. 24). His testimony was enacted as a matter of sincerity, of plain style rather than rhetorical performance, of contrition rather than eloquence designed to elicit 'external applause' (Caldwell 1983, p. 96).

Clinton has proved himself a shallow recipient of the Puritan tradition of bearing witness, and a degenerate exponent of its legacy. In Puritan New England signs of a true, confessional nature were proved by expressions of speech, attempted speech rather than colourful effusions or extraordinary statements of faith. The demonstrated willingness to speak for oneself and to do this before friend and foe, even allowing for feelings of inadequacy and the mystery and imprecision of verbal expression, was a central requirement of church membership. To express publicly one's own experiences – feelings of guilt and joy and sinfulness – was seen as the beginning point of confession and a necessary preliminary to spiritual conversion. As a southerner Clinton understands the residual value of Puritanism and the extent to which personal narratives can satisfy the standards of witness and adjudication that are expected in matters of faith and testimony. Clinton's performances are not spiritual but emotional. As a politician, says David Thomson, he 'knows' he is acting and he is consumed by 'the dynamic of acting'. This allows him to exploit the 'intimacy' of the actor's charms and to revel in a 'consummate smartness (a kind of piercing instinct)' that makes him 'aroused and excited by the great game he is playing' (Thomson 1998, p. 2).

As someone who absorbs 'the inner rhythms' (2) of an audience, Clinton's presidency is frequently described as a projection of its needs, a postmodern conspectus of macro- and micro-policies: feminism, multiculturalism, teenage curfews, school uniforms, forty-eight-hour hospital stays for new mothers, a $500-a-child tax credit. Clinton fails to offer, says Jonathan Freedland, 'an all-encompassing doctrine or core ideology' on the grand issues of education, healthcare and the environment (Freedland 1996b, p. 2). His policies, agrees Norman Mailer, are like 'a cosmetician's catalogue ... developed by a consummate pitchman' (Mailer 1998, p. 1). And because they are shapeless, they serve to remind the conservative faithful of what can happen to a southerner when he abandons his past or when a Methodist enters the White House but lacks the sustenance of a sacrificial religion.

The real irony of President Clinton is that he does not so much defect from the South as play out a version of the structured amnesia with which he grew up. The Arkansas South of Clinton's youth was not a dynamic, revivalist South but one which appeared, momentarily at least, to have lost its faith in the all-encompassing myth of religion. In Pete Dexter's *Paris Trout* (1988) the South, in the early 1950s, is indifferent to the Lost Cause and has yet to witness the nascent ministry of revivalist preachers like Billy Graham and Oral Roberts. In Cotton Point, Georgia, the church is conspicuous by its absence and provides no leadership or spiritual guidance in the town. In *Paris Trout*, children like Bill Clinton are the product of a society that is morally rudderless and more than willing to substitute an arid contractualism for the zealous exceptionalism of the Lost Cause. The 'Southern Way of Life' (Wilson 1980, p. 12) that worked as a 'pact' (Dexter 1989, p. 162) between friends – business associates, marriage partners, legal acquaintances – and formed the cement of a southern 'cohesiveness' (Wilson 1980, p. 15), has also come undone. In the enclosed society of small-town Georgia, the homogeneity of traditional alliances has broken apart; racial and gender affiliations cannot be taken for granted, nor can marital relationships or the outcome of jury verdicts or the social conventions that once moderated the cultural behaviour of race and class.

Traditionalists, like Paris Trout, no longer attend the church and resist the erosion of 'normalcy' (Dexter 1989, p. 152) through punishment beatings. Retaliation against those who have abandoned the status quo takes place within the family and among those who are politically disobedient outside of it. When Paris Trout murders a black girl he does so in order to protect his reputation as a moneylender in the community. Trout kills Rosie Sayers because she interrupts his plans to collect on a debt. He then brutalises his wife, Hannah Nile, because she offers her sympathies to the dead child's family. As a principled southerner, Trout is 'afraid' (142) of his wife's unwillingness to 'associate' herself with his actions and her refusal to keep up the 'appearance of normalcy' (152) in a world which has lost its Confederate shape.

In Cotton Point, patriarchal ordinances are not what they were. Hannah Nile Trout swims in places where she does not belong and is sodomised with a bottle for her liberal enquiries. '"You're sorry for every child ever come out of its mother's pussy barefoot"', says Trout, '"and people that's old, and all the sumbitches play with their own toes up to the asylum, but you ain't sorry for me"' (106). Appalled, when the first stirring of civil rights begins to make its presence felt in his marriage, Trout is scared that '"rules ... that was here before any of us"' (94) can no longer be relied on to protect the southern male. The church is no help to him either and has allowed its belief in an all-encompassing myth of the Confederacy to atrophy into a secular network of élite supremacist structures: segregated housing, banking practices, education and gender conventions.

Trout discovers that marriage no longer offers the same opportunity to own a woman 'the way he owned his own hands' (142). Like Carl Bonnor, whose cage birds are killed 'unexplainably' (233) by a storm 'from the South', Trout is the victim of a volatile, internal energy. He finds people 'out of control' and actively 'working against his interests' (142). His position as moneylender and murderer comes under attack from a loose alliance of assertive women, feisty blacks with literacy skills and rogue lawyers who have fought overseas in integrated units. Confronted by those whose behaviour '"you can't predict"' (65), Trout feels betrayed and besieged by the changes that are taking place in the South. In his post-Confederate consciousness 'a negro debt' cannot be discharged until the South has recovered its independence and the status of its citizens returned to what it was. Trout ignores the way age has taken its toll on Cotton Point. Once 'a rich place' and 'the centre of the States agriculture and law' (206), it is now a home for 'asylum' patients. Trout, who tries to reconstruct his family tree during a court hearing, finds his mother in a deteriorating state in the Ether Retirement Home. She sits naked in a wheelchair, her legs 'thin and bruised, and unshaved', her body splashed with dirty water by 'a fat negro woman in a green uniform'. Like his mother, Trout struggles unsuccessfully to regain his composure but only succeeds in getting '"excited"' with those who try to attend to his needs (175).

Trout is prepared to die for his convictions – '"I make my deals and live by them, and Jesus save those that don't do the same"' (105) – in order to atone for what has happened to the South. But his death is a travesty of southern sacrifice and few of the convictions he claims to uphold involve him in a ritual celebration of the dead. Instead, he satisfies himself in the abuse of women and the murder of a girl (already) rabid from a fox bite. In reality, Trout is a martyr to the heroism of commerce and to 'a contract he'd made with himself a long time ago' (59) about the sanctity of an agreement made between gentlemen. What Trout ignores is that his contracts were only guaranteed because they were underwritten by the landed gentry. A store-owner all his life, Trout has been granted economic protection by the 'rich families' of Cotton Point. Following the killing of Rosie Sayers the families cast him adrift and he finds himself no longer 'part of their safety' (58).

Angered by the comment of his lawyer, Harry Seagraves, that '"There's some people you can't predict"' (65), Trout sets out to prove the value of unswerving principle by targetting the symbolic enemies of the South: its new women. When Henry Ray, the black gigolo, defaults on a debt in a public street, it is Ray's mother, Mary McNutt, who is shot by Trout as punishment for her son's humiliating banter. Trout's wife, Hannah, is similarly punished 'for her (personal) ambitions' (100), her refusal to 'lie' (101) about the state of her marriage and her desire to come 'clean' (101) in her diary. When violence fails, Trout fortifies his bedroom with locks, lead mattresses, glass floors and fittings. Trout's agoraphobic celebration of sovereignty, sexual and cultural, exposes the inarticulacy of the South in the 1950s. It also exposes a patriarchal agenda that feigns an avoidance of sexual contamination with a woman who has started to reject him.

In *Paris Trout*, Hannah Nile surfaces from the depths of a suffocating marriage and a feral sex to which she has been subjected by her husband. Although Trout gives 'no sign' that he understands the new sexuality of the world he is living in (a world, in which, as

Harry Seagraves says, '"isn't anybody safe"' (202), his survival is ensured, momentarily, by the principled legalism to which he clings. When he is finally shot Trout is born again in the contractual evangelism of Pat Robertson, a minister who bases his Christian Coalition on the mannered medievalism of the South's 'Lost Cause'. Robertson's complaint against the Clinton presidency incorporates a claim that Trout is fond of making: '"They ain't nobody gets in trouble if they live up to their obligations"' (115).

A common complaint against Clinton is that he has never been 'principled in the truest way' (59) and has ridiculed the South that Robertson speaks for. When Hillary Clinton complained of a 'vast right-wing conspiracy' against her husband – as she did during the Monica Lewinsky affair – she was acknowledging the impact of her husband's decision to live outside his southern 'obligations'. The result of that refusal to act like a southerner in the Oval Office was, in the case of Monica Lewinsky, '"the cause" of this "whole mess"' (115).

At their annual convention in Salt Lake City in 1998 the Southern Baptists specified the meaning of 'obligations' for their 16 million followers, declaring that a wife must 'submit herself graciously' to her husband's leadership, 'as the Church willingly submits to the headship of Christ' (Coles 1998, p. 3). Clinton's inability to exercise a restraining influence, either on his wife or his mistress, infuriated the Southern Baptists who, in the summer of 1998, called for the president's resignation.

They could hardly do otherwise. As Nancy Ammerman shows us in *Bible Believers*, family authority in the fundamentalist community is derived from church authority and in any congregation the most powerful 'man of God' is the pastor.[1] In fundamentalism, 'women are ... thoroughly outside the official power structure', says Ammerman. The church recognises 'the biblical injunctions against women "speaking" in the church (1 Corinthians 14:35)' and 'takes those injunctions to mean that women should never have a major role in decision making' (Ammerman 1987, p. 125). When Paris Trout, the embryonic fundamentalist, goes to collect a debt from Henry Ray, he does not shoot Ray's mother, Mary McNutt, because she attacks him. He shoots her because she is 'not afraid' (Dexter 1989, p. 181) of him and speaks out of turn: '"There's no call to hurt nobody here"' (51), she says. The point is not that Trout disagrees with what Miss Mary says, but that she has not been invited by him to say it. As a daughter of Ham, Miss Mary has assumed a right of consultation. She has awarded herself an unnatural status, one she has come by in dealings with her son.

The most vigorous opposition to the Clinton administration has always come from southern fundamentalists, much of it focusing on the president's relationship with his wife, Hillary. Hillary Clinton is repeatedly portrayed by her opponents as a 'New Age sorceress' who talks with the dead (Carlin 1996a, p. 12); a False Prophet who leads the way for a revived Roman Empire headed by the Antichrist (Wojcik 1997, p. 164). She is said to be an embodiment of the great southern nightmare, the 'mystery Harlot' that Hal Lindsey speaks of in *The Late Great Planet Earth*. As an 'overbearing first lady' (Edsall 1994, p. 6) her liberal sympathies for '"the sumbitches [who] play with their own toes"', have aroused great hostility among fundamentalists.

Hillary Clinton has become the symbol of a special treachery for the Right, for it is she who defected from the southern Methodism of her youth and renounced the lifestyle of the 'ultra-wasp' or 'Puritan' she was 'raised' to be. She is seen as a woman who 'overvalues the verbal realm' and encapsulates 'the arrogance and self-delusion' of the baby-boom generation 'with its evangelical sense of social (not religious) mission'. With 'her chameleon-like blonde hairdos and charismatic smile', says Camille Paglia, Hillary is 'actually a drag queen, the magnificent final product of a long process of self-transformation from butch to femme'. Worst of all she is 'addicted to sermonising' and has become preoccupied with 'her own moral superiority and infallible IQ' (Paglia 1996, p. 2).

If the 1960s helped to bring about 'an end to patriarchy', says Daniel Bell, then recent fundamentalists have reaffirmed its value. The emergence of male conservative movements, like The Promise Keepers, testifies to the political muscle of those who have become embittered with feminism. Part of this reaffirmation of male cultural and sexual identity is aimed at politicians like Bill Clinton, a president seen to be lacking in moral fibre, unable to resist the advances of the harridan Hillary and her equally domineering sisters on the left.

Male discontent features strongly in Pat Robertson's critique of the Clinton Presidency. In *The Turning Tide* Robertson documents the ease with which Clinton has been distracted by the false prophets of political correctness and leftist feminism. In his first administration, says Robertson, Clinton attempted to undermine the patriarchal traditions of his office and the pietistic traditions of the South by lifting the ban on homosexuals in the military and AIDS-infected Haitian immigrants. Robertson is particularly angered that Clinton tried to make abortion on demand, and federal funding for abortion, among his first priorities as president. In his first hundred days in office, says Robertson, Clinton fell under the influence of gays, feminists and multiculturalists, and was promoting policies that were alien to the church. This was evident, says Robertson, in Clinton's attempt to bring the French abortion pill, RU-486 – 'known to cause bleeding, sever systemic reactions, and even death in some patients' (Robertson

1993, p. 56) – into the country. It was also evident in his appointment of a 'known liberal activist from the Children's Defence Fund, his own wife, to head the national task force on healthcare reform', which she did 'behind closed doors with no qualified medical personnel as members' (56–7), and in the former Democratic National Committee Chairman Ron Brown – who had lobbied for 'Baby' Doc Duvalier and Japanese industrialists – to head the Commerce Department. One of his appointees, Zoe Baird, employed an illegal alien as her child's nanny and then failed to pay Social Security taxes, while Donna Shalala and Roberta Achtenberg were given positions in his administration, 'despite the fact that Shalala is widely known as the "Queen of Political Correctness" and Achtenberg is a radical lesbian' who attempted to 'smear' the Boy Scouts of America because they 'refused to have homosexual scoutmasters' (57). Lani Guinier, his 'ill-fated nominee for the Justice Department', is an 'author of flagrant and questionable scholarship', while the 'confirmation of Ruth Bader Ginsburg to the Supreme Court' indicates Clinton's preference for liberal Jewish feminists, p. c. bureaucrats, radical abortionists and academic 'thought police' (57). Such nominations, argues Robertson – including that of Jocelyn Elders for Surgeon General – prove that Clinton had 'reached out' to radical, alien, unchristian 'elements in society', all of whom were 'associated with the lunatic fringe' (158–9) of lesbianism and socialism.

For the Conservative Right, Clinton's first administration was the prey of all patriotisms, the purveyor of fickle initiatives and whimsical agendas and the victim of circumstance rather than its master. Politics in the White House was regarded as a form of 'flexible pragmatism' (Jenkins 1991, p. 63), as a revolutionary engagement with the styles and strategies of postmodernity. Clinton was seen to have disengaged himself from a 'traditionalism' which had 'its roots in the small-town life of America and its fundamentalist Protestantism', and had surrendered himself to 'modernity' and 'the expression of liberal and cosmopolitan attitudes in the city' (Bell 1988, p. 4). In his first administration he quickly alienated small-town opinion, especially in the South, and compromised his proud association with his birthplace – an association he had heavily relied on during his first presidential campaign – in favour of the opinions of an east-coast, liberal intelligentsia. As a counterfeit southerner, Clinton seemed to have become part of the wider movement and sweep of history, an opportunist who was willing to incorporate into his presidency those styles and strategies which challenged the traditions of mainstream thought.

Clinton's decision, in the early days of his presidency to establish new trading links with Latin America, Asia and the Pacific appeared as yet another indication of a willingness to challenge the 'old organising frameworks' of 'Euro-centric' and 'western thought' (Jenkins 1991, p. 60). To his critics his economic policy suggested that he 'no longer regarded' these frameworks 'as legitimate and natural ... but as temporary fictions which were useful for the articulation ... of ... very particular interests' (60). His decision to unsettle the security of these 'certainist' traditions threatened the very survival of those meta-narratives which had underpinned the Cold War agenda. For a time, this included the special relationship with Britain, which, during the Major years, 'no longer resonate[d] with actuality and promise' (63) and was ready to be ditched in favour of new and zany complicities.

To be freed from what Keith Jenkins describes as 'the desire for certainty' may, in some contexts, be wonderfully liberating, but in the South it looked like an excuse for woolly thinking. For the southern conservatives, in particular, Clinton's postmodern agenda was woefully lacking in political and moral 'certainty'. Not only had Clinton been unfaithful to his wife, he had demonstrated the same infidelity toward the South, in particular, and the nation in general. Because he lacked a moral ideology he had to be resisted and because he supported a plurality of narratives – to which no one course of action could ever be assigned – he could never be trusted. For most conservatives Clinton's policies were impossible to fathom. He was unreliable because he lacked a singular vision of history and a recognisable political discourse.

Clinton's early presidency, like the composition of his cabinet, was considered little more than a heteroglossia of competing voices: women's voices, ecological voices, ethnic voices, babylonians who spoke for those who played 'with their toes up in the asylum'. If a vote for Clinton was a vote for diversity, it was soon depicted as a vote for weak-kneed liberalism, especially in the South, where the stigma of Clinton as a draft-dodging, dope-smoking, delinquent, overly fond of gays and blacks and loose women, had a powerful resonance. As Carl Douglas, a retired miner from Tracey City, Tennessee, put it: 'We elected him and in the first 30 days he is harping on about gays and lesbians and homosexuals' (Usborne 1994, p. 15). In his first term Clinton was forced to back down on a number of policy issues, including rights for homosexuals in the military, which merely confirmed conservative suspicions about his devious nature.

Other opponents pointed to his foreign policy in which he removed the embargo on the supply of arms to Bosnia's Muslim population, yet intervened in Haiti in order to appease the Black caucus in Congress. In the week that he supported the granting of a visa to the Sinn Fein leader and convicted IRA terrorist, Gerry Adams, he also announced strict controls on the sale of domestic firearms. Mindful of entangling the United States in a land war in Bosnia and wary of committing troops to Rwanda, Clinton's stewardship of foreign policy in his first term of office served to underline his domestic reputation as a 'fumbling', ineffectual president. In 1994, prior to the mid-term elections, polls on Clinton's ratings for foreign affairs were the lowest ever and showed an administration whose foreign policy was 'rudderless' and in 'chaos' (Freedland 1994, p. 9).

To many of his critics the absence of leadership in international relations resulted in 'wild oscillations' 'between cultural introversion' (in the Balkans) 'and messianic intervention' (in Haiti and Somalia) (Gray 1994, p. 18). During his first term of office, says Jonathan Freedland, the absence of a 'unifying force' in American politics and the collapse of the nation 'into hostile camps' (Freedland 1994, p. 14) was underpinned by 'righteous nihilism', a conservative mood which expressed itself not in a demand for more government – the activism of the Clinton administration – but in a crusade against the excesses of government: 'the belief that government is always the problem, and can never be the solution' (Young 1994, p. 24).

In the figure of Newt Gingrich, speaker of the House of Representatives, the American Right appeared to celebrate its contempt for Clinton. The idea that politics had got in the way of order and that the duty of politics was 'the abolition of all government services save policing and the military' (24) was designed to appeal to those very qualities which the Clinton administration had abandoned. Although Hugo Young may be right to argue that in the 1990s conservatives did 'nothing more ... than let the people swing slowly in the bitter wind of market forces and Darwinian individualism' (24), it was an individualism, none the less, that was strictly defined by righteous principles: opposition to abortion, feminism, gay rights, environmentalism, gun control, creationist teaching, excessive taxation, government surveillance and positive discrimination in favour of welfare-dependent minorities.

In the first Clinton administration fundamentalism emerged as a powerful coalition of right-wing Republicans, Christian evangelists and southern conservatives, all of whom were determined 'to undo the cultural impact of the 1960s', a period of perceived waywardness, profligacy and moral laxness. In seeking what William Kristol calls, 'a historic shift back to individual freedom and limited government' (Walker 1994, p. 14), Christian fundamentalists sought to retrieve the nation from the slough of despond to which the Clinton presidency had succumbed and the financial scandals and sexual peccadilloes that dogged his administration. For the New Right, Clinton was a weak and vacillating playboy whose problems could be traced to what Newt Gingrich called, 'the nihilistic hedonism of the counter-culture' (14). Those on the Right wanted Clinton 'driven out as an act of cultural vengeance', writes Martin Kettle, not just for the elections, 'but for feminism, for abortion, for affirmative action, for rock 'n roll, for the triumph of the anti-war movement over Vietnam, for irreligion, and for everything bound up in the cultural revolution of the conservative right's ultimate hate word – the Sixties' (Kettle 1998a, p. 2). Bill Clinton was, as Toni Morrison puts it, 'the first black US president': the product of a broken home, an alcoholic mother and 'the under the bridge shadows of our ranking systems' (Freedland 1998, p. 3).

For long periods Clinton found the image of the prodigal son, the gifted but wayward child, difficult to shake off. Republicans projected him as the reckless adolescent who searched in vain for an absent father and the kind of guidance he had lacked as a child. By 1994 the conservatives seemed to have won the day. The Midterm Congressional elections appeared to indicate that large numbers of voters had given their support to 'the Protestant Ayatollahs of the Christian Coalition', men of the church who could 'barely contain their hunger to impose the rule of the godly' (Walker 1994, p. 24). The Republican victory further illustrated that the Clinton administration had aroused 'the resentments and suspicions of millions of Americans' and was now regarded, in the words of Rush Limbaugh, 'as a hostile force' propelled by a mixture of élitism and fake egalitarianism. The 'dictatorial programs' of the Democratic party had been forced 'on an unwilling electorate' by an 'administration dominated by liberals greedy for personal gain' (Edsall 1994, p. 7) and presided over by a man who, from one day to the next, did not seem to know what he was committed to.

The conservative South led the attack on Clinton after 1994, depicting him as a spendthrift president, chastened by his parents – the Republican Congress – for having been feckless with the nation's money. By campaigning aggressively on moral issues like family breakdown, single mothers, abortion, pornography, homosexuality, creationism and the death penalty, the New Right eschewed compromise, believing it could do for the 1990s what the Moral Majority had begun to do in the late 1970s: slow down the pace of change, reverse the secularisation of political life and bring to an end the erosion of authority at the presidential level. It also believed it could close the gap between a duplicitous 'cultural élite' (Freedland 1994, p. 14) and a public for whom Clinton had been a major disappointment, a president who had shown that he was 'prepared to compromise on government's role in programme after programme and to trim traditional principles from the death penalty to universal health care' (Walker 1994, p. 24).

The inability of the conservative coalition to overturn the Clinton administration in 1996 was the result of a remarkable turnaround in Clinton's political fortunes, much of it due to the political complacency and moral arrogance of his enemies. In the years that followed Clinton's Congressional reversal in 1994 the Christian Right overreached itself, overhyped itself and was finally undone by its own ambition, especially that of its leader in Congress, the Speaker of the House, Newt Gingrich, who fell foul of the House Ethics Sub-Committee and was charged with financial misconduct. Clinton, who was more than a match for Gingrich between 1994 and 1996, proved himself able to master, as Jonathan Freedland puts it, the art of politics 'in the age of scepticism'. His skilful handling of domestic crises – for example, the bombing of the Alfred Murrah Federal building in Oklahoma in April 1995 – and his refusal to buckle to Republican threats to shut down Congress during the budget crisis, carried more weight with the American public than his 'continuing failure to offer an all-encompassing doctrine or core ideology'. In an improving economy voters proved less susceptible to 'the grand visionaries of the Republican Revolution' (Freedland 1996b, p. 2) and their daily diet of Protestant fatwahs, and more responsive to Clinton's political pragmatism and fiscal conservatism.

Between 1994 and 1996 Clinton cherry-picked many of the more voter-attractive Republican ideas – such as balancing the budget and welfare reform – and claimed them as his own. He also jettisoned the grander strategies of universal health care, *habeas corpus*, liberal immigration laws and federal benefits for children, all of which had proven an electoral liability with the nation's floating voters. Under the influence of his new adviser, ex-Republican consultant Dick Morris, Clinton's lack of 'core conviction' appeared to matter less than the personal embarrassments suffered by Gingrich and the Right's inability to find a strong presidential candidate in 1996.

In that year Americans opted for low-ambition projects and the 'small, achievable and verifiable plans that might actually work'. The prospect of an ideologue laying down the law with unwavering conviction, like Bob Dole, with his 'big idea' of a 15 per cent across-the-board tax cut, proved unconvincing. America had 'moved on' (2). High-flying talk about the morality of the presidential character or overhauling education or reforming healthcare or banning guns was not what counted, nor did the old conservative tactic of blaming Clinton for every conceivable misdemeanour in office.

Conservatives – and fundamentalists in particular – appeared not to grasp the significance of Clinton's victory in 1996, believing they could raise the political temperature by making his character a centrepiece for public opposition. As they had done prior to 1996, the religious right did not so much generate debate on issues of great ideological importance, as fix in the public eye an image of Clinton as serial adulterer and hen-pecked husband, who could only maintain his self-esteem by throwing himself at defenceless women. The significance of the Paula Jones case to Christian fundamentalists was not that the president had exposed himself in a hotel room to white 'trailer trash' (Vulliamy 1997a), but that a girl from a poor, religious family in the Bible-Belt town of Lonoke, Arkansas, who 'observed the Holy Scriptures' had been propositioned by a fellow southerner with a long history of philandering. Jones's case was announced at the Conservative Political Action Conference of 1994 (funded by southern religious groups, including the Christian Defence Coalition and the Legal Affairs Council). It was soon embraced by evangelicals, like Pat Robertson and Jerry Falwell, and became a perfect catalyst for born-again Christians who harboured deep suspicions about a draft-dodging, sax-playing President with a history of sexual misconduct over many years.

Fundamentalist preoccupation with Clinton's morality and fitness for office remained a priority throughout the 1990s. During the Whitewater scandal, Jerry Falwell used the full range of technological aids – e-mail, internet, talk radio, video, television as well as religious broadcasting – to promote the idea of a seedy alliance between the Clintons and the underworld. The conservative church, says Martin Walker, relied on what they saw as 'an American pathology', 'a distrust of government and a readiness to believe absolutely anything' of politicians. Their imaginations invented the bizarre scenario of 'Godfather Clinton growling out orders for contract hits, or Gangster Moll Hillary fleeing the bed of a doomed lover' (Vince Foster) whom she subsequently murdered (Walker 1995, p. 2). Here and elsewhere, says Walker, the fundamentalist crusade consistently miscalculated the extent to which the American public was prepared to embrace conspiracy theories, especially those which proliferated, as Whitewater did, at an exponential rate and seemed to assume a life of their own.

Conspiracy theories flattered to deceive throughout the Clinton presidency. Their appearance resembled what Douglas Rushkoff calls, a 'media virus' (Rushkoff 1996) feeding the public with expectations that are impossible to fulfil. Rushkoff argues that in the era of AIDS, those who rely excessively on the media to communicate opinion are liable to witness a breakdown in their own immunity from it. According to Rushkoff, 'media viruses spread through the datasphere the same way that biological viruses spread through the body' (9). But instead of travelling through blood circulation, a media virus spreads through the organs of the media: newspaper, radio, cable networks, satellite systems and the internet. Media viruses are likely to occur in a complex communications system, where the various branches of the media tangle and overlap, where distinction between fact and fiction is blurred, and where a major public anxiety is in play, such as Whitewater or the JFK conspiracy. A media virus flows through a circulatory system of inference, information and pure paranoia. It attains the status of a cult narrative or fabulation; it is so plausible and extreme that immediate denial in the short term has little effect. Stories that become viruses, such as the one picked up by Gore Vidal that Lyndon Johnson had sex with the wound in JFK's head while the dead president's body was being flown from Dallas to Washington, spread a contagion that feeds on crisis. The more virulent the virus the greater the demand for a fresh injection of narrative theory. The more heightened the exhilaration which the accusation or charge elicits, the more voracious the need for a drama of presumption. As Mark Fabiani, White House associate counsel said of the Whitewater affair:

There is an incredible cross-pollination of ridiculous and bizarre conspiracy theories. They start upon the Internet, get pushed by privately-financed publications like the Strategic Investment Newsletter, broadcast on talk-radio, fed across to rightwing newspapers in Britain, and then seep back over here into the conservative press like the Washington Times and American Spectator. And they pick up steam with each stage. There's an awful lot of smoke, but still no fire. (Walker 1995, p. 3)

Media viruses must find somewhere to settle and if no available host is found the virus regresses. A virus that does not create its own attachments or lasting, parasitical relationships is dangerous to those who transmit it. If the theory which feeds the virus is not supported by conclusive evidence the virus, says Rushkoff, can change direction and behave as if it were an anti-virus; feeding on those who were originally responsible for its incubation and transmission. Conspiracy theories implode when the narratives that feed them can no longer be nourished and the accusations and innuendos on which they rely are not upgraded or dramatically improved. 'Thus the virus continues, spreading a contagion of fact and fiction, going deeper into the depths of postmodernity, where the truth finally evaporates in a mist of invention' (Cosgrove 1995, p. 9).

By the mid-1990s practically anything that could be said about Clinton – accusations of murder, drug-running, larceny and fornication – was being said. The temptation to indulge in spoof was turning corrosive. Such a fate befell Pat Robertson in *The Turning Tide* when he argued that the Clinton government had 'politicised' AIDS 'and made it into a killer epidemic' by deliberately allowing into the country AIDS-infected immigrants.[2] By supporting homosexual and lesbian victims, said Robertson, the government had allowed AIDS to become 'the first disease in history to be endowed with civil rights'. It was 'absolutely contrary to common sense', he continued, 'to say that a virus has civil rights, but that's what the government has done' (Robertson 1993, p. 205).

Throughout the Clinton presidency such accusations, alongside those that depicted the Clintons as 'wickedness personified ... the head capos of an Arkansas mafia prepared to commit serial murder[3] to preserve their power', were the ingredients for 'a brew of irrelevant facts and half-truths' (Walker 1995, p. 2) that were put together to unseat the president. Narrative became a collaborative venture to which anyone could contribute; a plot without terminus, an argument based on inflationary rhetoric that few fundamentalists were able to control. The lack of any 'hard evidence of crime', the inability of 'the big guns of the American media' (3) to uncover any links between the death of Vince Foster and the Whitewater scandal, created a mood of such disappointment and anti-climax that, during the Monica Lewinsky affair, Clinton's popularity increased. The idea that Clinton could be driven out of office, as Pat Robertson believed, on the basis of his video testimony before the Grand Jury, 'backfired' badly, says Andrew Marshall. Although the Republican Right in Congress had long pursued a 'holy war' against the president, the release of the video was 'a grudge too far'. Clinton was perceived by the American people as 'a man ... more sinned against than sinning' (Marshall 1998a, p. 27).

The consistent clumsiness of the right-wing attack on the Clintons neutralised the effectiveness of the accusations made against them. The constant swirl of accusations regarding their sexual and criminal tendencies proved more diverting than politically acute. The scandals, says John Carlin, made the Clintons look like 'figures in a soap opera', not demonic conspirators who would 'do anything, but anything, to stay in power' (Carlin 1996a, p. 12; Carlin 1997a, p. 12). To claim, as Pat Robertson frequently did, that the president was a sexual celebrity who gave his allegiance, not to the American people who elected him but to the world of the super rich, the beautiful and 'bountiful' (Carlin 1997a, p. 12) donors of Hollywood with whom he loved to rub shoulders, was not to damage his reputation in any significant way. During the impeachment debate in the House of Representatives, Clinton's approval ratings with the American public improved. This, despite the adverse publicity surrounding Robert De Niro's attempt, at the end of 1998, to persuade Republican congressman to vote against the president's impeachment by the House of Representatives (Kettle 1998b, p. 3).

If there was foul dust floating in the wake of Clinton's dream then for the American dream it was the dust of Jay Gatsby – mythic, not political dust – the dust of an 'idealist'. Like Gatsby, Clinton studied at Oxford but was rumoured to have retained his links with the underworld. He was a socialite who threw fabulous parties for the rich and famous in the nation's White House but who lived a life of 'romantic' desire in search of the ineffable: the beautiful woman who always lay beyond his reach. For a vicarious nation who wanted politics to look more like tabloid journalism Clinton's charm was that of 'a playboy'. As a youth he was the renegade who had lost his chivalry the day he avoided the draft, in Washington he was an 'outlaw' with a 'streak of self destruction in him' (Thomson 1998, p. 2). In spite of – or perhaps because of – his 'secret trysts', Clinton came across as a child of the imagination whose 'heightened sensitivities to the promises of life' (Fitzgerald 1953, p. 2) were those of a naif, a bewildered innocent compelled by the colour of the green light that burned at the end of Daisy's dock. In the supersensual world of the White House Gatsby lived on as a figure of hope for a nation of dreamers, an entertainer in pursuit of an audience – gangster, bootlegger, holy man, fool – a child born of humble origins, born again in the redemptive fire of east-coast society.

For those who supported him, says Martin Jacques, Clinton transformed the political process into a celebration of 'the consumer market' (Jacques 1998, p. 23). Lacking 'a political language', he eradicated 'all the old ways and institutions in which people learnt about politics' and made sex a key issue of public life (23). In supporting Clinton for as long as they did Americans voted to escape themselves, to transfer their affiliations to 'a roguish charmer and his interesting wife' who continued 'to provide a diverting TV spectacle' (Carlin 1996a, p. 12).

Clinton's willingness to market himself as a west-coast celebrity carried with it much of the promiscuous promise that the American nation yearned for in the 1990s. Clinton – intelligent but shortsighted, caring but manipulative, slave to the masses yet a charlatan in personal relationships – was an ideal figure for Joe Klein to develop in his novel *Primary Colours* (1996). Whatever his failings, Clinton spoke for a nation desperate for sensation and a life of apparent moral deniability. Complicit in its fantasies, he was willing to pursue what the nation yearned to be: rich, famous and roguish with it. Like Fitzgerald's Gatsby and Klein's Jack Stanton, Clinton reinvented himself in the East. He wandered between material and mythical explanations of history, often deliberately confusing the two in order to allow those who followed him to construct their own vicarious fantasy about his life. In his fabulously opulent home Clinton threw lavish parties for the benefit of Hollywood stars and starlets. On behalf of the public he opened up the Lincoln bedroom and Queens bedroom to Steven Spielberg, Richard Dreyfuss, Jack Nicholson and Barbra Streisand. John Carlin writes:

It was such fun for the rascalous groupie-in-chief; celebrities who your average American would kill to shake hands with actually stayed under your roof and then – wondrously, unbelievably – bought into the whole scam ... by handing over loads of money and then going out and giving campaign speeches effusively praising the Saint. (Carlin 1996a, p. 12)

If Gatsby is 'a story of the West, after all', so is the South's perception of Clinton, hence the reason southern fundamentalists were affronted by the man's relationship with Hollywood. His was a breach of style and etiquette, an insult to the 'Lost Cause', a morality whose faith was expended on the amour and glamour of west-coast society and the sexual thrill of its *femmes fatales* like Monica Lewinsky. In Clinton's inaugural period an evangelical conservative ministry jealously sought to undermine his dependency on popular culture in order to expose his moral failings.

For Pat Robertson, the Clinton White House was 'Sunset Strip', an adjunct of Hollywood that reduced politics to 'all-star entertainment and glitzy packaging' (Robertson 1993, p. 52). Under Clinton, the executive function of government had been penetrated by an 'entire constellation of stage and screen idols'. The symbols of screen immorality and marital infidelity, an 'élite' (53) of movie-stars, rock stars, singers, dancers, celebrity junkies were given access to the inner chambers of the White House. They attended its banquets and state dinners, used its stationery, slept in its bedrooms, sat in on 'confidential' meetings with the president and participated 'in cabinet meetings, strategy sessions on marketing the president's new investment programs, and high-level policy briefings previously reserved for heads of state' (53). The 'new face' of government, claimed Robertson, was that of an office whose leader was 'star-struck' (54) by the media, who basked in the limelight of its visual splendour and who gleaned the secrets of the charismatic. Politics became a product of the charm school, which is hardly surprising for a man caught up 'in a 1960s time warp' (56). Clinton's associates were people whose private lives contained little or no public morality. Under his régime the country was losing sight of the need to rearm itself morally in an age of trash culture, cheap pornography and media salaciousness. The United States had entrusted itself to a man who had 'the bodily repertoire of a charmer, the eyes of a charmer and the smooth-as-honey speech of a charmer' (quoted in Robertson 1993, p. 54). Norman Mailer tends to agree. Buying Clinton, he argues, was 'reminiscent of the products you buy when it's late at night, the critical powers are weak and the TV infomercial becomes convincing' (Mailer 1998, p. 1).

If Clinton's role models were the heroes of popular culture, his sponsors, argue his opponents, were international bankers and financiers such as Citicorp, Goldman Sachs and other Wall Street lords. Clinton was the spokesman for 'a godless law of the jungle' which exposed children to 'clever manipulators' who 'weaken character' with atheistic agendas and 'a hatred of God' (Robertson 1993, p. 151). His liberalism was an excuse for 'secular humanism', infused with a strain of anti-Christianity. It led directly to 'the tragedy of broken homes', 'out-of-wedlock babies' and the 'ethical jungle' of modern America. It was hardly surprising that among the 'media élite' – the 'sex and violence' clique (151) to whom Clinton was personally and politically attracted – there were no 'practitioners professing to be fundamentalist, born again or evangelical' (148).

Clinton's greatest offence to the South is that whilst he portrayed himself as a devout Methodist, he willingly renounced the ideals of the evangelical and sought liaisons with unregenerate Jews like Monica Lewinsky. Clinton's promiscuity obstructed the prophetic events of the last days and interfered with His divine plan for the return of the Jews to Israel. Clinton's sexual dependency on the brattish and the wealthy and his political dependency on campaign contributions from 'Hollywood's liberal luminaries' (Robertson 1993, p. 54), confirmed his status as a lost southerner, a prodigal son morally tainted by the Jews of Hollywood and the slick troubadours of the mass media.

In Bill Clinton's collision with the Special Prosecutor, Ken Starr, we can see the contrasting fortunes of Jews in America, as well as the contrasting fortunes of professing Christians. While Clinton, the Methodist, was infatuated with a star-struck Jewish intern (and did nothing spiritually to retrieve the situation), Ken Starr, the son of a Texas fundamentalist minister, had married a Jewish girl, Alice Mendell, from Mamaroneck, New York, in the Church of Christ, thereby fulfilling his Christian obligation towards his religion (Winerip 1998, p. 2). As if fearing he had been trumped by Starr, Clinton reaffirmed his belief in Israel by quoting a passage from a Jewish liturgy book, *Gates of Repentance*, on the day that Starr released his report. In that reading, Clinton admitted the need for repentance and revival in Christ; an admission that was neither believed nor accepted by the Southern Baptist leadership.

For Christian fundamentalists, the Jews of southern California – as represented by Monica Lewinsky and her family – were the holders of a particularly poisoned chalice. They had forsaken the righteous opportunity which God awarded them (as exiles) in His promised land. The origin of this bias against California can be traced to the early Cold War and the threat posed by 1940s Bolshevism. In President

Truman's administration, writes Stephen J. Whitfield, Los Angeles was regarded by fundamentalists as a city of sin, crime and immorality which, because of its suppressed reliance on Communism 'merited destruction as much as Sodom and Gomorrah' (Whitfield 1991, p. 77).

For the radical, Bible-reading millennialist Herman Husband, writing in 1792, California was a place set aside for the Lost Tribes of Israel, the Indian Jews, who would settle in California and be redeemed as Christians. The visions of the prophet Ezekiel had convinced Husband that a 'New Jerusalem' would arise in the western regions of North America and would extend far beyond the 1792 boundaries of the United States. But later 'emigrants' to California – immigrant Jews especially – turned aside from this prophecy and abandoned themselves to secular humanism, forgetting their obligation, as 'governors in Judah' (Lazenby 1940, pp. 147–50) to honour Ezekiel.

In the promised land of California the Jews proved resistant to Christian ministry, preferring to create, what Neal Gabler calls, 'an empire of their own' in Hollywood (Gabler 1989). In its films, says Pat Robertson, mainstream Hollywood turned its back on the promise of salvation, extolling, instead, the virtues of the wilderness and moral primitivism. Robertson is extravagant in his condemnation. 'The essential core' of Hollywood's 'liberal philosophy', he argues, 'is a hatred of God and religion. Its adherents also hate our Western civilization, which is based on Christianity, and they want to tear it down.' The Jews of Hollywood believe in the idea of 'the noble savage'. In their films they portray the Indian not as an enlightened man but as a pioneer (an unreformed Jew) who, like them, has escaped the obligations of biblical Christianity. Robertson asks whether or not we should idealise this 'environmental' world which is such a feature of godless Hollywood, 'the purpose of which' is 'to exalt a tribe of primitive Indians as if they were the ultimate example of virtue and wisdom'. Such 'humanistic thinking is preposterous', for it idealises the pre-Christian tribalism of 'jungle-dwellers' and the uncivilised ceremonies of 'naked, unlettered primitives' (Robertson 1993, p. 151). Hence the reason for Husband's vision of a redeemed savagery which later generations of Jews in Hollywood turned aside from. Christian America, on the other hand, teaches us the 'freedom' to exist 'in an enlightened Christian civilization', not in the suffering of 'subsistence living' (152).

In order to ensure that Hollywood cinema is spiritually appropriate for a Christian audience Robertson created 'The 700 Club', a television channel that doubles as a redemptive ministry for those in the media who are looking to convert to Christianity. Such a person 'featured' on the 'Club' is the actor Chuck Norris, who, says Robertson, 'decided' he wanted 'to make a difference in the lives of children' and committed himself to Christ in his work. As well as making films which are 'wholesome' and full of 'warm, good humor', he continues, Norris has gone into 'the toughest, inner-city schools' to teach young 'hoodlums self-respect, respect for others, and important principles of discipline and responsibility'. Connors 'was thrilled to see that the programme was working' and 'touching the lives of kids who desperately need something to believe in'. He is 'a man who made a fortune in violent movies' but wanted 'to give something back to the people who supported him' (150–1).

Fundamentalists are attracted to Hollywood for political as well as pastoral reasons and the lure of the media has long proved a powerful drug for the tele-evangelist ministries of America. Pat Robertson's emphasis on the evangelical crusade in 'The 700 Club', and his purchase of a Hollywood studio to produce 'wholesome' entertainment, confirms his belief in technology as a profitable way to market religion. It may also explain his jaundiced critique of Bill Clinton, a rival southerner who ignores his evangelical commitment to the Jews and is seduced by the splendours of Hollywood society. Southern evangelists, like Robertson, find Clinton's behaviour treacherous and offensive. At the same time, they remain envious of his celebrity status and his ability to dominate the nation's media and its mass audiences. Clinton is despised not because he is involved with something that is fundamentally corrupt but because he threatens the special relationship with Hollywood which the church has nurtured and on which it has based its populist mission. In his public embrace of Hollywood Clinton violates this relationship, by making the myth of celebrity an end in itself. Clinton is dangerous because he unbalances the righteous integrity of techno-evangelism and its cultural dependence on secular technologies outside the South.

Harvey Cox senses a contradiction in this. 'Fundamentalism', he argues, 'is a highly traditional religious expression. Television is a tradition-smashing phenomenon. Yet rarely has any religious movement embraced an artifact of modernity as enthusiastically and uncritically' (Cox 1987, p. 296). Cox wonders about the process of resolution 'when a profoundly antimodernist attempt to reassert the primacy of traditional values utilizes a cultural form that is itself thoroughly modern and antitraditional'. He sees a 'tension between content and form' (297) when those who have been opposed 'to the powerful, modern, liberal and capitalist world that [is] disrupting their traditional way of life' (289) are forced to reconcile themselves with an enemy. An irreconcilable conflict between pragmatism and piety profoundly alters the meaning of fundamentalism, as religion begins to detach itself 'from the domain of tradition'. The act of shifting 'from the revivalist's tent to the vacuum tube' has given the 'defenders of tradition' a national identity but 'made them more dependent on the styles and assumptions inherent in the medium itself'.

Foremost among these is the decision to embrace religion as 'entertainment', an idea popularised by Pat Robertson, who copied the format of late-night talk shows on his '700 Club' where a 'succession of splendidly dressed guests tell the audience how the Lord has brought them success, health, money and power'. The 'contradiction' between 'the system' and 'traditional morality' results in a conundrum in which 'the technical and organizational means' chosen by fundamentalists 'to fight the battle' against modernity 'may be destroying precisely the religious resources most needed to save traditional morality' (298). In relying on the camera and the worldwide web, 'fundamentalism may have unintentionally sold out to one of the most characteristic features of the very modern world that it wants to challenge. If the devil is a modernist, the television evangelists may have struck a deal with Lucifer himself' (299). [4]

For Harvey Cox, fundamentalism is inherently flawed by capitalist imperatives: the desire to expand its market, appeal outside the local community, and generate a response from a mass audience through the non-traditional discourse of film and internet. As Cox sees it, the 'contradiction' of a religion that finds itself enamoured of technology represents an unacceptable deviation for those small-town congregations whose way of life J. Gresham Machen enshrined in *Christianity and Liberalism* (1923).

This contradiction is writ large in the release of Bill Clinton's testimony before the Grand Jury, 'an epic moment in the long siege of public life by the media-dominated popular culture of the age'. What is ironic is that the conservative Right should have lead the charge through the media to make Clinton 'the supreme victim of the unrelenting smut-driven popular culture of the age'. It is also ironic that the video of his Grand Jury testimony should align the Right with a filmic society whose work it finds so offensive elsewhere. In releasing the videotape of his evidence Republican conservatives, many of them affiliated with the religious Right, utilised the format of a 'gruesome televised confessional' (Kettle 1998a, p. 2). Politics became a version of the Jerry Springer show. Republican conservatives surrendered themselves to the quasi-pornographic horror of the video, as well as 'the jury of the television audience and the unelected pundits and personalities of the media world'. Media religion became an end in itself, not an agency through which the right in Congress were willing to translate the presence of the Antichrist. Here was a process, says Martin Kettle, 'in which the demotic' triumphed 'over the democratic' (2). In the person of the Witchfinder-General, Kenneth Starr, the American public could observe that 'psychological connection between persecuting orthodoxy and sexual prurience'. The lesson of colonial New England, that 'the springs of sanctimony and sadism are not far apart', was again reaffirmed (Harris 1998, p. 15).

Fascination with the media represents, in one sense, a fascination with an industry and an art form whose history is tied to that of the Jews. It is also the fascination of a religion that has long regarded the Jews in exile as an object of love and loathing in America. Hollywood's studios were founded by Jews – Adolph Zukor, Louis B. Mayer and Harry Warner – and, as such, they are the legitimate domain of the evangelist.[5] Wherever the Jews have decided to congregate, so must the fundamentalist. Israel in Hollywood is the South's Lost Cause, a secular place whose Jewish enclaves require redemption as a millennialist task. As an evangelical, Pat Robertson can look towards a righteous conversion of the studios and the appearance of films, such as *Schindler's List* which celebrate the return of the Jews to Israel. Hollywood provides glimpses of the 'dark beauty' of Israel and, so far as the Indian is concerned, the promise of a 'wild, passionate and alluring people' (Axtell 1981, p. 154). But Hollywood, as moral wilderness, is no different from New England, whose settlers were 'charmed' by the 'power of beauty in a savage' (Kornfield 1995, p. 309). In both locations the ministers of the church proclaim their opposition to the 'shadowed corners of the land' (Axtell 1981, p. 159), but harbour a desire to enter into it and replicate its features. Attracted by the 'living light' of 'Hebrew fountains' and 'the gleam of Palestine' in the American West, Robertson sees the legacy of Israel imprinted on the screen in a glorious celebration of colour and adventure. Whatever his complaint, Hollywood is home to a religious impulse which, although buried deep within an errant secularism, can always be redeemed through the Christian witness of 'The 700 Club' and the Family Channel. Hollywood is where the culture of the homeless – the Jew in exile – is displayed as art. For Robertson, it is a place of millennialist pilgrimage. As testimony to the experiential past and the utopian promise of a chosen race, it is also an industry which can utilise the power of technology to reconstruct a religious illusion.

What Pat Robertson declines to mention is the extent to which the evangelical love affair with Hollywood, and the backlot productions of the Jews, carries with it a long history of tawdry and profligate activity. Jim and Tammy Bakker's *Heritage USA*, a Christian theme park in Fort Mills, South Carolina, is a good example of Hollywood pentecostalism at its most overstated. The charges of sexual and financial profligacy which were levelled at the Bakkers' *Praise the Lord* network in 1987 were borne out by the chaotic commercialism of *Heritage USA*. With its bricolage view of world religion and its indiscriminate use of celebrity, *Heritage USA*, writes Susan Harding, was 'a kind of postmodern pentecostal mecca' (Harding 1993, p. 65), which abandoned the history and traditions of the Bible Belt and the rural ecology of the Lost Cause. In *Heritage USA*, Christendom's Disneyland, 'performed a ceaseless, if implicit critique of fundamentalism's restraint, its sacrificial logic, its obsession with authority, hierarchy, rules' (66). As a theme park, *Heritage USA* created an imaginary world in a 'placeless location', from

an ensemble of replicas, relics, facades, imitations, simulations, props and sets drawn from Biblical Jerusalem, the Old West, small town America, Hollywood, model suburbs and tourist resorts. Nothing simply was itself, everything was palpably a production, a reproduction, or a performance. (67)

In the desire to appeal to an audience, contrivance became more important than conviction and spectacle more valuable than story. Metaphors of displacement and appropriation made *Heritage USA* into a 'narrative-free zone in which history, fiction and the Bible were equivalent figures and frames, and the boundaries between the religions and the secular were called into question' (58).

The earliest example of the studio backlot reconstructed as a religious temple is Aimee Semple McPherson's Foursquare Gospel Church. In the mid-1920s, McPherson taught an evangelical creed of Biblical infallibility to a mass audience of southern Californians. From 1921 to 1926 'Sister' McPherson's Angelus Temple was a gaudy expression of religious burlesque. As a Jazz Age 'messiah' in southern California McPherson transformed the fundamentalist church as a place of worship into a Hollywood studio. 'Sister' sought her salvation in crowds and power, says Carey McWilliams, but was enslaved by the 'music-hall pornography of the time' and the 'cheap sensationalism' of the screen and its heroes (McWilliams 1964, p. 77). Throughout the twenties her private life reflected the tawdriness of popular culture and the trashy sensationalism of Hollywood society. With no evangelical strategy to redeem her and no reformed community of Jews to protect her, McPherson eventually fell foul of a 'glacial fundamentalism' and an anti-Semitic resentment against the 'un-Christian Jews' of Hollywood whose work she appeared to impersonate (79).

In Gore Vidal's fiction, the origins of 'Sister' McPherson's sexual ministry and the secular excess of the PTL network in South Carolina can be traced back to the pentecostal church in Asia Minor. In *Live from Golgotha* the promotion of religion is contingent upon the conversion of the Jew, yet the motive for conversion remains questionable. In the early Christian church, disciples like Saint Paul who are attracted to the 'living light' of 'Hebrew fountains' and 'the gleam of Palestine' are inspired by a sexual dream. Physical conquest is the basis of their evangelism and sex is a mechanism in the promulgation of faith. It is also enjoyable in its own right and is a way of distinguishing the work of the disciples from the ascetic legacy of the Old Testament. As a novel excuse for sex, Christianity corrupts the Old Testament legacy of a celibate, solitary and disciplined priesthood. Saint Paul's religion inspires a revolution in sexual values. As the word becomes flesh – and is experienced in it – Saint and the disciples pay homage to the past through the beautiful legacy of the Hebrew people.

As a method of ministry, sex allows Saint to pursue his love affair with the young Jewish boys of Ephesus and Macedonia. Saint grasps them by the hand and 'the balls' (Vidal 1992, p. 108), explaining his friendship as a Christian gesture. The opportunity for chance encounter lies at the centre of his apostolic mission and promiscuity is a consequence of the inflationary principle underlying his beliefs. The profit of godliness can only accrue to those who search for new acquaintances in one-night stands and multiple relationships. Saint's sexual gregariousness – his love affair with bodies as well as hearts and minds – is the reason behind his expanding congregations in Rome and Lystra. His crusade among the Jews forces him to 'call on every synagogue in every town', which is where he meets boys like Timothy, with their 'flashing cornflower-blue eyes and hyacinthe golden curls' (24). Since sex sells religion more beautifully than anything, there is no such thing as surplus friendship. Those, like Saint, who are suffused with love for their fellow man, accumulate within themselves the sexual energies of the celibate Christ. The passion for godliness which they are obliged to expend is explained by Saint as an evangelical requirement: '"You never know when or where you'll make a convert"' (25).

Saint's Christianity is an exercise in marketing; his is a people's religion underpinned by business principles, promotional stunts and a deviant leadership that promises things it cannot deliver ('the Great Embarrassment' of the Second Coming) (31). As the post-hoc recipient of 'the notion of the Trinity', formulated 'two or three hundred years' after Christ's death, Christians worship the fabulations of Saint and the inventions of others whom Saint has inspired. 'The Message' of 'Good News' is an invention kept alive by the early disciples (reform Jews), who display an irresistible tendency to interfere with God's divine plan on the sacrificial cross. Disciples, like Saint, abrogate the power of the ancient prophets, making themselves personally responsible for the old meta-narrative. Saint's faith is not the expression of an angry God, but of individuals to whom he has granted unparalleled powers of invention. In the divine supermarket of Asia Minor, Saint's Christ is the marketing tool for a new, product-centred community of historians who narrate the past from a corporate perspective. Under their regime the past is merely a notional concept which exists only on the basis of the present-minded discourse of those who articulate it.

Since the advent of a remythologised Christ reform Judaism, says Vidal, has anointed itself on the altar of adventurism and abandoned its integrity to the reckless pursuit of entrepreneurs. Whether it is Saint Paul at Ephesus or Philippi with his 'beautiful speaking voice' (30), or the time-travelling computer genius, Dr Francis Cutler, who returns to ancient Rome in order to transform the Gospel of Timothy 'into one of [his] own devising' (63), lying about history is a precondition of Christian testimony. Informed by a history of revision, Christianity lends itself to a joint invention of the virtual world and the evangelicals who have tampered with it. Under these influences it has come to resemble the diary entries of the Ephesian socialite, Priscilla, who 'constantly rewrote ... as her views of those recorded changed' (89). As the masquerading Christ, Marvin Wasserstein, realises, Christianity is '"what you say it is"' (101).

The problem of how to deal with excessive or inappropriate revision comes to light when a cyber-punk, known as the Hacker, uses a computer virus to erase the tapes that describe the mission of Jesus Christ and His Gospel ('Good News'). The Hacker is unhappy with Saint's version of Christ's life and decides to give Jesus an improved profile: a gambling problem, a youthful marriage and twins at twenty. In an attempt to contain the damage, yet sensing commercial opportunities in a crucifixion documentary, NBC–General Electric and Gulf and Eastern 'channel back' in time to reinstate an approximate version of the lost story. Through the miracle of time travel they plan to transport an entire television crew to Jerusalem to pre-record the Crucifixion from Golgotha in order to boost their ratings. Like the Hacker they see the advantage in creative testimony and approach Timothy, now a senior citizen in Rome, to write his version of the Gospel in a form acceptable to TV audiences and New Age religion.

The channellers believe in a flexible ministry and encourage Timothy to introduce 'more local colour' into the 'original gospel' (64) so that it will go down better with satellite viewers. Chester Claypole (Chet), Vice-President of Creative Programming at NBC–General Electric, chooses Timothy, as 'a bona fide witness to the Crucifixion' (67), not only to resurrect the Gospel but also to act as the anchorman on the telecast from Golgotha. Timothy is appropriate because he has led a promiscuous life and will, it is thought, strike the right tone in the new millennium. The television controllers want a gospel of true confession – religion as titillation and tabloid trash – as well as a kiss-and-tell account of Timothy's relationship with his girlfriend, Priscilla, and his mentor, Saint.

In another retrospective, Saint is also visited by Chet and agrees to work with him 'to restore the Christian message' (18) through Timothy. Saint, who is 'in on it' (116) from the start, encourages Timothy to collaborate with the television companies in the revival of Christianity. Since 'show business' (76) is Saint's life he, more than anyone, is responsible for the embellishment of Christ and the idea of promoting the crucifixion as box office. As a habitual liar and a 'charismatic' (30) Saint places a high priority on the kind of opportunism which the television companies are looking for. As the dominant influence on evangelical Christianity, Saint is the principal source of its need to fabricate a historical identity for Christ. Although he does not meet Christ ('except as a sort of ghost on the road to Damascus') (30), he testifies that he has. His instruction to Timothy and the disciples, 'not to teach the real cause for the Crucifixion but only the cover story' (119), means that for years he has been 'changing the whole show' (123) in order to disguise Christ's physical appearance on the cross. 'In the end', like Jim and Tammy Bakker, 'his cheapness', we are told, 'did him in' (129) and he is martyred for blasphemy and causing a riot.

Saint shares with other corrupt pentecostalists a love of spectacle, exuberant testimony and financial extravagance. He is also a pederast with a 'fantastic double standard' who advocates celibacy in his public ministry yet 'never stopped fooling around' (45) in private. 'There was no way you could say no to Saint if you were a Christian lad and wanted to be saved' (108), says Timothy. The link between sex and faith is indissoluble and the word of God no more sacred than the willing flesh of an adolescent. Saint's sexual and evangelical impulses are twinned in a kind of reformist zeal, the purpose of which is to venerate the Jews at all times.

Saint is indiscriminate in his pursuit of flesh. In his worship of bodies – the corpse of Christ on the cross at Golgotha and the living body of the young stud Timothy – he is both necrophiliac and paedophile: a man who, like Gore Vidal's LBJ (Rushkoff 1996, p. 261) would have sex with the dead as well as the under age. Whether it is circumcision or sexual ransack, Saint's needs become 'more and more insatiable' (45). At the circumcision, he is the one who holds the knife, exploiting 'a Jewish notion' of assistance as he leaves his mark on the bodies of boys with their 'huge uncut cocks' (4).

Saint's religious philosophy is highly suggestive and subject to prurient interference. He reconstructs the body of Christ to make it look more beautiful than it is and he does the same with the youthful

Timothy as he awaits 'the nightmare' (3) of circumcision in the family home at Lystra. Timothy's acknowledgement that 'the knife was with Saint Paul' (3) is an example of Saint's surgical prescriptions. His need to make Timothy as beautiful a Christian on the kitchen table as Christ is on the cross testifies to his love affair with the recon-struction of physical bodies. His devotion to 'the foreskin set' (25) and his life of wandering, requires a sexual and evangelical attachment to the Jew which sends him 'sashaying around Asia Minor' (4) with the zeal of a crusader.

Timothy, who is 'truly sick' (45) of Saint's obsessions, nevertheless, feels empowered by what Saint has done for him. 'Like every red-blooded Asia Minor boy', Timothy has 'been brought up to lust in dreams after the priestesses of Diana' (75). Saint's knife work carries benefits for the patient, Timothy, who has 'the largest dick in our part of Asia Minor' (34) and can now satisfy his sexual needs 'under the right "religious" circumstances' (75). As Timothy acknowledges to Priscilla, sex and Christianity are always 'fun' (3) and can hardly be compared to an act against nature fit only for 'a nance'. Even though Saint has had him 'by the balls' on a number of occasions he has never required him to act like 'a guy who takes it in the rear' (147).

Timothy is not without loyalty to Saint who discovers that the Christ (he thought) he saw on the road to Damascus was really a hoax. Christ avoided the tomb at Gesthemane, while the man crucified at Golgotha was Judas, the victim of a set-up and Christ's stand-in. Dr Cutler, a 'dedicated Zionist' at General Electric, rescues Christ to 'continue his messia-ship' in Cutler's 'time frame' (215–16). Christ is channelled into the future and turns out to be a computer genius who assumes the identity of Marvin Wasserstein. Wasserstein, how-ever, is 'horrified' (216) by the legacy of Saint's Christianity and knows that a corpulent Judas on the cross on prime-time TV will destroy the image of Christianity that Saint has cultivated. For this reason Wasserstein decides to erase the primary tapes, in collaboration with Cutler, the purpose being to discredit the Christianity that Saint has promoted. On discovering this, Saint realises that Christianity is 'out of business if the Crucifixion goes through with that lard-ass, Judas' (203). His solution is to 'get' Wasserstein 'crucified' (205), instead of Judas, on the prime-time rerun.

On the day of the crucifixion Wasserstein returns to Golgotha, accompanied by Oral Roberts, in order to start a rebellion against Rome and bring about the end of the world. It is Timothy who comes to the rescue of Christianity (and Saint's fabrication) by exposing Wasserstein as a traitor. The apocalypse is thwarted. Wasserstein is denounced and hung on the cross instead of Judas, thereby reaffirming the Christian story as told by Saint. In the 'dark beauty' of the body of Jesus – 'slender, bearded, ladylike' (204) – the Christian fascination with Jewish sexuality and the naked form it assumes on the cross, is allowed to live on.

Notes

1. Promiscuity is a concern of all fundamentalist religions, especially when caused by disobedient women. In the United States, unrelenting sexism remains a prominent feature of the Christian Right, says Sara Diamond and 'evangelicals frequently cite Ephesians 5: 22 – "Wives, submit to your husbands as to the Lord"' – in order to justify 'female subordination' (Diamond 1989, p. 104). Christian Right women, says Diamond, frequently recite the Old Testament account of Queen Esther (Esther 4: 14), who marries the non-Jewish King Ahasuerus in order to beg him to break a murderous agreement with his aide Haman and rescue her people (the Jews) from destruction. Esther is celebrated by the Christian Right for her heroism as well as her subservience, says Diamond. 'Nothing can be accomplished without co-operation with males in authority', which is why Esther is obliged to obey her stepfather, Mordecai, who counsels her that she has been granted the divine opportunity to save her people (108). Christian women are expected to submit to 'male domination' in a fundamentalist marriage (Ammerman 1987, p. 139), a position that has been dramatically re-enforced in the late 1990s by the arrival of the Promise Keepers, a conservative, Christian evangelical movement who seek the empowerment of American males.

2. In the 1990s what Susan Sontag calls the 'imagination of disaster' resonates with ideas of interception and exclusion. In *The Turning Tide* Robertson associates plague and virus with the movement of human and animal population in border states like New Mexico. The virus-carrying rodents that cross the Mexican border, he says, remind us of the Black Rats that travelled from Asia into Europe during the fourteenth century carrying infected fleas as a result of poverty, overcrowding and poor sanitation. Sensing the hostility to Mexican immigration in the 1996 presidential campaign, Pat Buchanan argued that a perimeter fence should be built across the desert to halt the transmission of virus by physically excluding illegal immigrants. In claiming this, Buchanan may have been acknowledging the recrudescence of HIV infection in sub-Saharan Africa. In *The Hot Zone* (1994), Richard Preston claims that the paving of the Kinshasa Highway was one of the most significant events in the medical history of the twentieth century. This transportation artery allowed HIV to be swept out of Central Africa and distributed worldwide. The accompanying movement of the world's poor from regions affected by atmospheric warming, widespread chemical pollution, environmental destruction, war and famine created a refugee movement well in excess of 18 million by 1992. As a result of these demographic

trends a broth of infection swirled around the planet requiring a co-or-
dinated effort to control the spread of infectious organisms.

3. The Reverend Jerry Falwell issued a number of videotapes in which he
accused the President of murder. See Wills 1996, and Lieberman 1996.

4. Throughout *The New World Order* Robertson warns of the dangers of
modern technology. He shows how a 'one-world credit system, a one-
world currency and a one-world central bank has been the centre-piece
of all significant planning for The New World Order' (Robertson 1991,
p. 30) and how modern technology makes this feasible. Robertson claims
that the Book of Revelation notes how all credit could one day be
controlled by a central one-world financial authority. (He notes how the
supercomputer in Brussels handling worldwide bank clearings at the
Society Worldwide Interbank Financial Telecomm (SWIFT) is nicknamed
the 'Beast') and is fearful that every citizen will be marked by the sign
of the Beast, using social security numbers and barcodes in supermarkets
as evidence of such marking. He marvels at how technology will be
used to destroy Christianity and discrete notions of liberty and nationalism (216). Robertson cites every form of modern technology as evidence
that the world is heading toward a 'New World Order' which, one day,
will control all communications: 'Modern technology has performed
wonders in this Century. In just the last ten years we have seen an
exponential increase in the sophistication of global communication.
Think of how satellites, computers, faxes, etc., have changed the way
we communicate. Think of how this same technology has given a powerful central government the ability to inform, indoctrinate, monitor, and
control the will of the people' (211). Having set out such a consistent
argument against technology as a product of evil and a sign of evil to
come, Robertson then advocates the need for it. He suggests the need
for a 'telefax network to activists all over the nation who can relay the
truth' (263). He even argues that America's free press might be used in
the ultimate battle against Satan: 'With America still free and at large,
Satan's schemes will at best be only partially successful. From these
shores could come the television, radio, and printed matter to counter
an otherwise all-out world news blackout' (256). To this end, Robertson
details how Romanian television has asked CBN for religious and fam-
ily-orientated programmes to be broadcast at peak-viewing times daily
in a bid 'to instruct their children in the ways of God' (290).

5. Of the eight major studios, writes Roland Flamini, six were started by
pioneers of orthodox Jewish parentage such as Adolph Zukor, Louis
B. Mayer and Harry Warner. 'Few more tycoons continued to follow the
orthodox practices, but Mayer's father was a Hebraic scholar and his
wife the daughter of a rabbi. Zukor's mother was also a rabbi's daughter,
and his brother became a distinguished rabbi in Germany' (Flamini 1994,
p. 14).

5

Israel in Idaho: Political Extremism and Right-Wing Religion

Critics who amalgamate conservative, political and religious activists into a single right-wing, racist fraternity practise a sleight of hand on their readers. Similarities between the orthodox, high church movements of the Bible Belt and the Christian Identity and patriot militias of northern Idaho, Michigan and Montana clearly exist: the shared acceptance of dispensational theology, the importance of biblical inerrancy in scriptural interpretation, fear of the United Nations and the New World Order as agents of conspiracy and infiltration, the idea of America as a New Jerusalem or Temple Nation whose people have been given a manifest destiny and covenant with the Lord. Yet, as James Aho has correctly argued, while there is 'an element' of religious 'fundamentalism' (Aho 1990, p. 53) in many of the patriot or paramilitary communities of the United States, those who profess millennialist convictions may differ theologically in their attitude to race.

Many of those political fundamentalists whom Aho calls 'Identity Christians' – Aryan Nations Church, Mountain Church, National Alliance, White American Resistance – subscribe to an anti-Semitic theory of origin, proof of which they claim to find in the King James Bible. The Christian Identity Movement practises 'cosmic dualism' and sees a crucial 'distinction between the House of Judah and the Kingdom of Israel, between Adamic man and pre-Adamic man, between the sons of light and the sons of darkness, the attribution of diabolism to "Jews", and the genealogies supporting the Anglo-Saxon's Israelitish identity' (105). As Wesley Swift, an early leader of the Christian Identity Movement argued: the Bible preaches 'the idea that there are two species of human being, Adamic man and Satanic man: true man – the Aryan European descendants of Israel – and homo bestialis – the sons of Lucifer, including among others, the Jews and Satan's footsoldiers, the black Africans' (55).

According to Michael Barkun, Christian Identity constructs 'a Manichean universe, divided into realms of light and darkness. The central figures of each, God and Satan, are in combat. Each is aided by coalitions made up not only of allies but of literal-descendants, white Aryans who are the children of God and Jews who are the children of Satan' (Barkun 1997, p. 249). In 'a universe structured along dichotomous lines', the idea that there are two species of human beings, Christians and non-Christians (who are led by a confederacy of satanic Jews) is the basis for 'a politics of ultimacy', one which 'rejects' all forms of 'compromise' and 'coalition building' (249). In the political programme of the Christian Identity movement the 'racial redemption' of the Jews – Satan's spawn who are delivered to earth, as Wesley Swift believed (248), in an armada of spaceships commanded by Lucifer at the time of the rebellion of the fallen angels – is 'non-negotiable' (258).

On the face of it this is a far cry from the fundamentalism of Hal Lindsey, who regards anti-Semitism as a thing of satanic derivation and 'the Core of Nazism' (Lindsey 1990, p. 5). The crucial difference between religious fundamentalism and political fascism is rarely noted, in literary, critical and academic debate. Critics of religious fundamentalism, like Michael Lind, find it preferable to complain about Pat Robertson's 'elaborate' conspiracy theories and the fundamentalist neuroses that originate in the fascism of the 1930s (Lind 1995, p. 23).

For Christopher Hitchens there is no difference whatsoever between the 'bucolic' fascism of America's 'wigged-out millennialists' in their Christian Patriot and paramilitary communities and the covert fascism of the religious right in the southern Bible Belt. Nor is there any significant difference between these groups and other 'neo-fascist movements in Italy, Germany, Japan, and France' (Hitchens 1995, p. 2). Michael Barkun concurs. In *Religion and the Racist Right*, Barkun discusses the link between European fascism and American anti-Semitism. He specifically notes the debt that Pat Robertson owes to Nesta Webster, an English anti-Semitic writer of the 1930s, and Eustace Mullins, a protegé of Ezra Pound and a prolific writer on the Jewish conspiracy.

Barkun subscribes to Jonathan Raban's thesis that the heart of the 'bucolic fascist movement' in America (Hitchens 1995, p. 12) lies in those rural, small-town communities of the West and Midwest who feel betrayed by the political élitism of Washington. In *Bad Land* (1996), Raban shows us how the agrarian militias in the 1980s, like the Posse Comitatus, exploited the decade's farm crisis to spread the belief that farm foreclosures were part of a conspiracy led by Jewish bankers in America's Christian heartland. Feelings of agrarian grievance, says Raban, reawakened memories of the Homestead Act of the 1860s and the failure of government promises on dry-land farming in the Great Plains. In the prairie regions of eastern Montana, he argues, 'the misleading language and pictures of the [railroad's promotional] pamphlets would eventually entitle the homesteaders to see themselves as innocent dupes of a government that was in the pocket of corporation fatcats – and their sense of betrayal would fester through the generations' (Limerick 1997, p. 6).

The contemporary concentration of political extremists in the rural West – the Unabomber (Theodore Kaczynski), Aryan Nations, the Freemen of Montana – leads Raban to conclude that we can find among these anti-governmental individuals and groups a 'perverse legacy of the homesteading experience and its failure on the plains'. The festering sense of neglect among those whom Raban calls, the 'bad-blood descendants of the homesteaders' (6) – Bo Gritz, Randy Weaver, the Trochman brothers, Louis Bean, Timothy McVeigh – is satisfied only by mixing together conspiracy theory with a righteous brew of patriotic paranoia. In the 1980s the discontents of agrarian Americans whose economic prospects had radically declined turned in the 1990s into a resentment against the American government and welfare-dependent minority groups.

For the rural paramilitary, 'America became the imaginary war zone', agrees J. William Gibson:

Images of the enemy proliferated. Poor Mexicans who had immigrated to the United States became 'illegal aliens' and were accused of being disease ridden, drug dealing, and communist infested. New racist and neo-Nazi groups surfaced, each filled with dreams of killing blacks and Jews and federal officials of the 'Zionist Occupation Government.' Fears of 'terrorist' attacks by foreign and domestic groups ... prompted massive escalations in police arsenals. Ordinary people across the country ... felt that 'terrorists', foreign invaders, black gangs, economic collapse, nuclear war, or some other chaos-causing foe would soon appear. (Gibson 1991, pp. 390–1)

While Gibson generalises the sense of chaos, fear of the 'imaginary enemy' (391) was felt most acutely among rural paramilitaries. It was they who fervently believed that Russian troops were hidden in salt mines under Detroit, or that the United Nations had a secret plan to disarm the American public with the help of black gangs in Los Angeles and to implant all newborn babies with microchips, or, that Attorney General Janet Reno was a paid agent of Jewish Columbian drug lords and that Queen Elizabeth II was working through British conglomerates to regain control of her colonies by purchasing Burger King and Holiday Inn.

In paramilitary communities the fear of invasion, and the beliefs that sustain it, originate in an arcane reading of the articles of the Constitution and a generic fear that government has become the enemy of freedom. In the fight against 'creeping Socialism and Godless Communism', says Gary Wills, the government is said to have colluded in the process of invasion. It is also seen as unresponsive to the needs of the people, especially to the claim that the Second Amendment guarantees every citizen the right to own and use firearms. If the Constitutional right to bear arms is not respected, then the government is unresponsive to the people whose interests it is obliged to represent. Such a government, says Wills, disqualifies itself in the minds of extremists; it 'does not even exist', and since it has 'divorced' itself from 'the American people', it 'is not even' considered as being 'American' (Wills 1995, p. 52). If Russian tanks fulfil militia fantasies, it is largely because the New World Order has been appropriated in the Clinton administration by United Nations personnel, international bankers and Russian imperialists. The American government has surrendered the country's sovereignty in much the same way that a corrupt ministry in eighteenth-century England was thought to have severed the popular link between King and Parliament, invalidating the entire constitutional monarchy. Corruption of such magnitude, says Wills, 'points not only to degenerate or imperfect government but to a non government' (52).

In the 1990s fears that a New World Order would be based on a sinister one-world government (the original mandate of the United Nations) led to widespread anti-Semitism, especially among these militia movements who believed that a 'Zionist Occupation Government' was ready to overthrow the country with the help of Jewish finance in New York and Washington. Strong links exist between American militias and the white supremacist John Birch Society. Many of today's paramilitary sects are aggressively anti-black and adopt explicitly fascist titles such as Aryan Nations or Ku Klux Klan. The theological inspiration for their activities comes from archaic populists such as Pastor Richard Butler, head of the Church of Christ Christian Aryan Nation in Idaho, and from Pastor Rob of the Arkansas Church of Christian Identity.

The militia movement also has its roots in the older and more notorious white supremacist organisations of the nineteenth century. Martin Walker draws parallels between the 'angry white males' of the mid-1990s, who are opposed to the creation of a black middle class, and those responsible in the 1860s, through organisations like the Ku Klux Klan, for defeating Reconstruction and the attempt to bring the emancipated slaves into educated citizenship and prosperity. 'The angry white males are bent on dismantling the new version of reconstruction', says Walker, and the attempt through 'affirmative action to give minorities some modest preferences in education and public contracts.' These 'sullen' males demand the right to buy any form of gun they want, when they want, and insist on the abolition of a planned national identity card, 'the apparatus of dictatorship' (Walker 1995, p. 24). Drawing on the ideal of rugged individualism in pioneer America, they see the government as an arrogant and remote superstate seeking to emasculate the nation of its once-proud individualists, through excessive taxation and preferential hand-outs to a coloured underclass.

The nationalist faith of America's militias is avowedly populist. It combines a need for direct action with an insurgent anti-federalism and it behaves in ways which reinstate the rugged individualism of the colonial past. For America's militias and private armies the government of the country is in regular collusion with the enemy. At the executive level it is said to be sympathetic to the claims of immigrants, the aspirations of foreigners and any non-Protestant multi-cultural agenda. Fears that the government no longer wishes to protect the majority of American citizens from the forces that are conspiring to undermine tradition – from guerrillas and terrorists to United Nations agencies – have encouraged many conservative groups to mount a fierce attack on affirmative action; on schools that adopt a 'multicultural' or secular agenda; on confiscatory taxation; on the keeping of elaborate files on citizens' activities; and on the agencies that use surveillance techniques and bribe informers.

It was President Ronald Reagan who created the necessary vacuum of suspicion for the executive and who prepared the groundwork for political alienation in the 1980s. It was Reagan who told his audiences that government must be taken 'off the backs' of the people and that government bureaucracy was a major problem. But if the government could do nothing except fight the Soviet Union, then the justification for government was taken away when the Soviet Union was finally defeated. 'If the government is only good for fighting Communists', says Garry Wills, 'and it no longer fights communists, then what good is it?' The answer is: 'It is good for nothing, and citizens must take their own lives in hand again, vindicating their own liberties' (Wills 1995, p. 52).

For the armed patriots of the 1990s the authority of government can no longer be assumed. It has to be justified from the ground up. Yet this cannot happen as long as the government is seen to be shooting innocent civilians such as David Koresh and the Branch Davidians of Waco, Texas. Here is the conspiracy the militias are faced with. People who protect their own families on their own property can be killed by governmental agencies for trying to defend their religious beliefs with constitutionally protected firearms, while, under the smokescreen of the New World Order, the country is subjected to covert invasion. John Trochmann, founder of the Militia of Montana, argues that the United States government is guilty of treason for ignoring the threat of infiltration from old-style Communists and anti-Aryans: Jews, Russians, Chinese and Hispanics, masquerading as lovers of freedom. The fear of too much war has given way to a fear of too little. The nation's self defence is at risk as the government surrenders its right of self-determination to a one-world government of the United Nations and uses its supervisory energies as the World's Policeman in restrictive practices against the individual.

The search for scapegoats among the lower middle class, many of whom provide a bedrock of support for the militias, has, as I have suggested, an economic foundation.[1] Those who fear the loss of an American culture and the onset of, what Jonathan Freedland calls, 'balkanisation' (Freedland 1994, p. 14), are deeply suspicious of the role vested interests play in the running of the government, and the chronic legalism that sells the ordinary working person short. For Freedland, writing in 1994, the 'United States may always have been a divided nation ... but few Americans can remember a time when their society was more sharply divided ... Nothing less that two rival cultures have emerged, competing for the American heart and mind, and barely speaking the same language.' This 'growing fragmentation', says Freedland, and the loss of a 'unifying force', creates a deep sense of unease. Those who claim to distrust big government are often the ones who are marginalised by it: they see themselves as having 'lost out' to a new 'cultural élite' (14) who are in possession of an increasing share of the nation's resources.

In the late 1980s the relative suddenness of economic decline created a sense of confusion which found its outlet, says Mike Bygrave, in a 'frustration with foreigners' and 'an intense national distrust of government' (Bygrave 1994, p. 22). This confusion was no less apparent in the Reagan administration when social divisions 'widened' to an unprecedented level. Under Reagan, the decline in median family income among working-class families and the transfer of wealth on a huge scale from ordinary Americans to the already wealthy, meant that the top fifth expanded their share of total household income to 50 per cent after tax, while 'the bottom three per cent lost ten per cent of an already tenuous share'. For middle-income earners 'real wages fell throughout the 1980s while Reagan 'devastated organised labour ... to the point where today a scant 16 per cent of the private workforce belong to a union'. Reagan was a manager of economic decline, rather than a harbinger of economic revival. His 'tax cuts, deregulations and arms build-up enabled him to reward his supporters and advance his philosophy'. His economic 'legacy' was to bankrupt the government and to leave the country with a 'crippling 220 billion dollar United States federal budget deficit'. Yet his magic as a politician was to cast 'a kind of hypnotic trance' (24) over the country. He usefully provided Americans with enemies: from Latin America to the Middle East, from Panama and Nicaragua to the old Soviet Union. He also identified throughout the world a number of satanic centres of energy whose threat America could only overcome, in the popular consciousness, through military adventurism and paramilitary action. By relying on an age-old demonology Reagan managed to divert attention from social and economic problems at home and the very divisions his overseas errands did much to create.

The New World Order and the collapse of Communism in the 1990s may have opened the doors for politically disadvantaged societies in Eastern Europe but it did little to inspire the immediate confidence of the lower middle class in the United States. Those who should have benefited most from the ending of the Cold War – one they never shied away from supporting – believed they had benefited the least. Blue-collar communities who saw their sons die in the fight to secure freedom and democracy in Korea and Vietnam now began to question that sacrifice. They saw themselves as the target of bureaucracy; a government in Washington that was soft on crime yet fearful of self-reliance and individualism, obsessed with citizen surveillance but overly restrictive on the right to self-defence, tolerant of corruption in the nation's capital yet willing to impose taxation burdens on those who could least afford to carry them. The threat to America in the New World Order was from too much government – the intrusiveness of the United Nations – and from too little leadership: in particular, the absence of a strong, unifying executive. For the Christian Identity and patriot communities in the United States the principal offenders were the Jews whose power and influence had increased immeasurably. In the immediate post-Cold War era, Identity Christians saw the Jews as imposter Israelites, selected by Satan to create a multiracial society and morally to undo Anglo-Saxonism.

Much has been made, by writers like William Gibson, of the relationship between Christian Identity and the teachings of the British writer Edward Hines, whose pro-Israel theories of history spread to the United States in the late nineteenth century. Hines argued that while Adam, the father of Abel, slept with Eve, Eve slept with Satan and fathered Cain, the first Jew, who killed Abel before fleeing the Garden of Eden. Adam's other son, Abraham, was chosen by God to receive the Covenant and found the non-Jewish nation of Israel. The leaders of the tribes of Israel were sons of Jacob and in 586 BC Nebuchadnezzar seized the southern tribes of Judah and took them to Babylon, the place where Cain had fled after killing Abel. It was there he mated with wild animals and created non-white races, whom Identity Christians refer to as 'mud people'. Nebuchadnezzar then converted the tribe of Judah to Satanism and formed Judaism or Jewry – a race 'who killed Christ', and dispersed throughout the world. The children of Satan, who called themselves Jews, were not Israelites and arrived in America as latter-day emigrants or 'imposter Jews'. Since their Jewish character is counterfeit, these Jews 'cannot become authentic Christians through conversion'. They are 'born evil' and are under an obligation to 'ruin the people among whom they sojourn'. This they did by giving birth to Karl Marx and Communism, and by taking over 'the Federal Reserve Bank in the United States' (Gibson 1994, pp. 216–17).

In Identity Theology, says William Gibson, the white, Anglo-Saxons of America believe they are descended from the tribe of Manasseh who migrated westward into Europe and hence to America. The sons of Manasseh are 'the true Jews', a sacred race of chosen people who will be redeemed if they follow 'God's will'. Since 'the true Jews' cannot convert the imposter Jews to Christ they must prepare for the coming apocalypse and confront 'Satan's secular representatives – the Zionist Occupational Government – that runs the United States'. The best way of achieving this, in the post-Vietnam, post-Cold War era, is by per-petrating a 'New War' of vigilante violence against government agencies who are in hock to 'ZOG' money (217).

This 'culture' of violence provides paramilitaries, writes Gibson, 'with a world view that frames virtually all social conflicts … as potential life-and-death confrontations' (Gibson 1991, p. 390). In the post-Cold War era, this culture embodies what Umberto Eco calls, an Ur-fascist ethos which transforms the warrior into a sacred symbol of redemption and catharsis, able to achieve 'supernatural happiness' and 'occult' status. Fascism, says Eco, 'derives from individual or social frustration' and, historically, has appealed 'to a frustrated middle class' that feels it is 'suffering from an economic crisis or political humiliation' from the presence and 'pressure of lower social groups'. All fascists feel 'besieged' (Eco 1995, p. 27) by internal and external threats, says Eco, and in the 1990s the biggest threat of all are the Jews. Anti-Semitism is the glue that binds together an international network of alliances in Europe and the United States as well as a more general fear of multiracialism.

Christian Identity theology is usually described as an apolcalyptic faith which has abandoned its links with dispensational funda-mentalism in favour of an international fascist syllabus and an obsessive anti-Semitism. As a mainstay of paramilitarism, Christian Identity is commonly represented as a two-dimensional, adversarial faith which derives its sense of purpose from its enemies. As a cultural revitalisation movement, Identity Theology partakes of a global anger, says Martin Wollacott, brought on by a failure of expectation and a profound scepticism at the economic performance of nation-states in the New World Order. The regression into violence allows those who see themselves as economically marginal and socially neglected to seek redress in paramilitary rituals (Wollacott 1995a, p. 22). The solution which violence offers people in different diasporas is an example of a form that is permeated by the ideas and idioms of cultural transnationalism, a 'pathology' which has lost its insularity and local definition. In civil society, writes Wollacott, violence is inclined to 'borrow' the clothes, imagery and sometimes weapons from the world of war and international terrorism. Recent acts of political violence must be seen, he argues, in the wider context of the fragmentation of 'traditional systems', a fear of penetration from new diasporas and the escape of religion and nationalism 'from traditional controls and from traditional thinking' (22) into the arms of post-literate fundamentalism.

The sensuality of controlling and deploying weapons systems in violent theatres is not lost on the conscripts to fundamentalist causes who are poor and unemployed or who lack an obvious stake in society. In the present social climate, writes Martin Van Creveld, war is an economic rather than an ideological activity. In places where government has collapsed or someone is 'living a life of idleness ... war is a step up. It offers a break from tedium, the pleasures of comradeship, opportunities for enrichment and, for powerless young men, the thrill of control' (quoted in Stone 1994, p. 9). With the help of middlemen and entrepreneurs, like the *muvator*, Slavko, in Misha Glenny's *The Fall of Yugoslavia* (1992), the arms trade nourishes new militias. In places like Sierra Leone, Rwanda and Liberia, agrees Wollacott, 'degenerate armies have sucked in the disorientated young men of vulnerable societies'. In their 'feckless pursuit of the arms trade', western industrialised countries are assisting 'the suppression of dissent by undemocratic regimes' and are propping up military societies which 'are in a process of degeneration'. There is now around the world a 'panorama of military pathology ... a world-wide Rambo culture' (Wollacott 1994, p. 20) that feeds off the exports sales of western industrialised societies and the availability of guns within those societies to people who feel they are not protected. The Italian journalist Tiziano Terzani has described this culture as a budding fraternity of 'lethal poseurs' whose needs the West exploits but does not satisfy. There is, says Terzani, a 'silly ostentation with which many of them carry their arms, the way they size up each other's rifles, test their weight, and admire them, the pistols carelessly stuck in belts, the useless knives so many of them wear flapping on their thighs' (Wollcott 1994, p. 20).

The image of sensuous violence is sustained in American paramilitary culture and is especially attractive to those who feel that mainstream political leaders have failed them. *Soldier of Fortune* magazine shows us that dress codes and theatrical costumes are an integral part of the social identity of current paramilitary thinking. The imagery of war as a form of theatre has always been dear to the hearts of soldiers but, says William Gibson, military clothing such as uniforms and camouflage outfits gives men a way to play with costumes, accessories and make-up without feeling effeminate. Military uniforms disguise feelings of economic inadequacy which are responsible for driving the most vulnerable members of society into military, millennial and cult militias. Writes Gibson:

At a fantasy level, changing clothes means the warrior is no longer bound by the moral code governing civilian actions. To change clothes and put on make-up allows men to fantasise that they have become truly different from the ordinary, law abiding men they normally are. In the minds of psychotics, this fantasy transition marks a real transition. One man in San Diego changed into camouflage clothes, took over a McDonalds restaurant and murdered twenty-six people with his Uzi 12-gauge riot shotgun and Browning 9mm Hi-Power pistol (favourite paramilitary weapons). A number of similarly dressed and equipped killers have recently been reported in newspapers. (Gibson 1998, p. 31)

The interaction between war and theatre has grown at an exponential rate since the 1920s. 'Because war is communicated to us with satellite immediacy', says Cal McCrystal, 'we may find passions released by distant conflicts, permeating our own social fabric.' In other words, someone else's war 'can easily become our argument too' (McCrystal 1993, p. 39). The discourse of violence works by osmosis on civilian minds. As soldiers become international celebrities, so styles of war translate rapidly into styles of life. 'The entertainment industry', says Martin Wollacott, 'seizes on violence as an addictive fix for uneasy audiences.' The process feeds back to those who perpetrate that violence and has an 'unhappy legitimising effect on it ... Anyone who has watched Lebanese militiamen spellbound by American war and crime films knows that this culture of confrontation and violence has a worldwide impact.' Although 'there is less real experience of western societies than there used to be', adds Wollacott, there is a greater 'interchange of ideas, of weapons, of images, and of people' (Wollacott 1995a, p. 22).

One of the quirkier ironies of the New World Order, writes Simon Sebag Montefiore, is 'that warlordism' has come 'to America, the land of the victors of the Cold War, as well as to the land of the vanquished'. The outbreak of international 'warlordism' in the first half of the 1990s involved, on a global scale, 'the rise of private armies, privately funded, united by a single political or religious creed'. These armies were independent and hostile to government' and 'commanded by charismatic leaders' whose power depended 'on their ability to wage war' (Montefiore 1995, p. 7).

Arguments which stress a primary moral or aesthetic division, he continues, between the 'medieval warlords' of Georgia or Chechnya and the Christian militias of the United States, are 'obsolete'. American militias, like the Michigan Militia, replicate the dress codes, the methods of training and the 'charismatic' culture of the 'medieval warlords of Eastern Europe'. They are a version of the 'wild men of the Caucasus' whose struggle against a central government in Moscow embodies the same sense of alienation in the rural hinterland towards the nation's capital. 'The wild men of the US militias', says Montefiore, take their cue from the rural warlords of Georgia and Chechnya. Their uniforms, guns and training camps look 'exactly like those of the Caucasian fighters'. Both groups are kitted out to look like freedom fighters, pioneer heroes whose job it is to identify an alien force which threatens the cultural purity of the nation. In their camouflage uniforms and wilderness strongholds they are possessed by fantasies of backwoods nationalism, 'the cult of the bandit', the fairytale myth of the freedom fighter as populist hero. Each shares a pathological hatred of strangers, a belief that the nation is in the grip of the 'anti-Christ' and that a government 'conspiracy' exists to undermine the rights of the individual. 'The glue of a rebel army', writes Montefiore, 'whether in the Rockies or in the Causasus, is usually a fanatical combination of personality cult religion and nationalism. God, gun and general come together' (7).

In Georgia, Jabas Iosliani's Knights of Horseback 'wear insignia that combines a Christian cross with the "J" of the warlord's name and would not look out of place in today's Midwest'. Warlords like these are capable of leading men to their death. They are also 'entrepreneurs of chaos and alienation' who 'claim a special, often artistic ability to dazzle their constituency of outcasts' (7). Like David Koresh, or the Russian warlord Baron Ungern-Sternberg who saw himself as the son of God, these leaders, he continues, are profoundly religious and committed to the notion of a divine destiny. As a hieroglyph, the J represents the snake-like S of the swastika, a divine or supernatural symbol of energy emblazoned on the chest of the warrior hero as he prepares himself for battle. (Hester Prynne, the Salem guerrilla, does something similar with the letter A in Nathaniel Hawthorne's *The Scarlet Letter* and uses her own pagan alchemy to transform her badge into an artform based on magic and naturism.) 'The cultures that produce the Caucasian warlords and the Michigan Militia', says Montefiore, rely on the same channels of energy. 'America today is a place where thousands of men in camouflage uniforms, emblazoned' with '"hissing cobra" regalia, train openly as private armies with a fearsome modern arsenal of weapons' (7).

The correspondences that exist between quasi-fascist movements in politically unrelated or opposed societies should not blind us to the inconsistencies that bedevil the fascist syllabus and the contradiction which fascist personalities tend to reveal, not least of which is the urge to change one's clothing at moments of crisis and dress up in the kind of costumes favoured by children. The paramilitary dream of fascist rescue is that of the juvenile escaping from adulthood in a costume which releases the superhuman energy of the frontier and the motor energies of the Aryan race. Fascists and vigilantes who are unhappy with their own identity and are willing to disguise it by dressing up convey something of the psychic dislocation of the hero and an attraction to that which is incompatible with their manhood.

If contradictions such as these lie at the heart of fascist culture, as Umberto Eco claims, it is reasonable to assume they can also be located in fascist religions like Christian Identity. This is particularly true in the United States where Identity Theology is faced with the problem of reconciling the dispensational teachings of the fundamentalist church – from which it evolved in the nineteenth century – with the paramilitary rituals of anti-Semitism in the twentieth.

James Aho has argued that Christian fundamentalism is 'an element in all Identity doctrines' and that all Protestant millenarian faiths are 'variations' (Aho 1990, pp. 53–4) on the nineteenth-century Anglicanism of John Nelson Darby's dispensational theology. What Identity Theologies attempted, says Aho, was to reinvent dispensationalism through British-Israelism and the teachings of the English biblicist Edward Hines, especially his *Identification of the British Nation with Lost Israel* (1871). British-Israelism was 'imported' via Canada during the late nineteenth century and grafted onto American millenarianism. Whilst it subscribed to the idea that biblical history is periodised by the actions God undertakes towards His children and that ours is the final age (Last Dispensation), Identity Theology, writes Michael Barkun, has moved away from the 'futurist orientation' (Barkun 1997, p. 104) of orthodox fundamentalism. Specifically, it dismisses the promise of the Rapture, which it regards as a spurious way of avoiding the violence that is inevitable in the Tribulation.

As descendants of Manasseh, whose people came to the United States as the thirteenth tribe of Israel, Christian Identity equates

Anglo-Saxon America with Israel and parts company with fundamentalism in its willingness to single out the Jews as the children of Cain. As a contaminated race the Jews have forfeited the right, through intermarriage and idolatrous behaviour, to be considered authentic sons of Israel and worthy members of His millennialist theocracy. They are a mixed breed whose sole purpose is to create an occupation government in the United States and to destroy its children through the sale of drugs and abortion. In the work of race theologians like Wesley Swift and William Potter Gale, non Anglo-Saxon Jews are depicted as occult messengers, the product of Satanic fornication among the fallen races, all of whom have been brought to earth by Lucifer in one of his armada of spaceships.

For Michael Barkun, it is both possible and plausible to see clear evolutionary divisions between a domestic American fundamentalism, which believes that the conversion of the Jews foretells the end of the world, and a theology shaped by British-Israelism which sees the Jews as 'the personification of cosmic evil' (104). Yet the idea of two, discrete traditions operating from the same millennialist root, neither of which influences the other in the contemporary age, is difficult to sustain. Especially so, in a world informed by popular culture where reading habits do not always correspond with theological beliefs.

An example of this is provided by the eleven-day, armed encounter on Ruby Rudge, Idaho, in August 1992 between federal law officers and Christian paramilitaries who resisted arrest for non-payment of taxes and illegal use of firearms. Among the leading protagonists in the conflict were Randall and Vicki Weaver, 'Yahweh believers', who 'included in their religion', says James Aho, 'the doctrines of white separatism' and a belief that the Jews were 'Christ killers'. The Weavers awaited the Last Days and vigorously proclaimed their religious beliefs with sawn-off shotguns, but they also remained 'profoundly influenced', writes Aho, by the teachings of Hal Lindsey (Aho 1994, p. 57). Demonized as neo-Nazis for their extreme, racist views, the Weavers accepted Lindsey's teachings about the plight of the Jews and the imminence of the Rapture in the coming endtimes. Previous to this the Weavers were members of the Baptist and Mormon churches, as well as avid followers of Jerry Falwell and Jim Bakker, and other pentecostal miracle healers. Whatever the rhetoric of its more 'vocal proponents', says James Aho, 'blatant racist anti-Semitism is not intrinsic to the Identity message'. Aho quotes from the 'comparatively tolerant' J. H. Allen, a British-Israelite who did much to infuse Semitic ideas into America's Christian Identity sects:

Understand us: we do not say that the Jews are not Israelites. They belong to the Posterity of Jacob, who was called Israel, hence they are all Israelites.

But the great bulk of Israelites are not the Jews, just as the great bulk of Americans are not Californians, and yet all Californians are Americans. (Aho 1990, p. 53)

Followers of Christian Identity find it difficult to maintain an anti-Semitic position with any kind of intellectual or practical consistency. As believers in a patriot faith, they face the problem of exposing the Jew as the enemy of the nation, even though the country they defend was built on the principle of Jewish conversion. Hebraic theories of origin played a key role in the evolution of colonial religion and were instrumental in shaping attitudes towards America's native races. Yet Christian Identity has kept remarkably quiet on the subject, which is odd considering its obsessive preoccupation with the genealogy of Israel's lost tribes and the amount of anthropological and cultural evidence which has been amassed on the subject. While Christian Identity traces its origins to the arrival of the Puritans on board the *Mayflower*, those same Puritans developed their own millennialist theories, focusing on the presence of the wandering Jews and the lost tribes of Shem, whose history played a prominent role in the millennialist movement for the next three hundred years. It is hard to conceive that Christian Identity was, and is, unaware of this history.

The Indian as (errant) Jew has long inspired a scholarly theory of tribal origin within the pre-millennial Protestant church. In this reading the tribes of the north Kingdom of Israel resettled in Iran, Armenia and the region near Baku in the eighth century BC and chose a route to the Americas which took them across a land bridge in Siberia. For the seventeenth century Spanish historian Andrés Rocha, the Jews came via the Straits of Anian and their travels took them from Assyria and the cities of the Medes through Persia, Scythia and Tartary to Anian and finally Mexico. Portuguese historians in the 1640s and 1650s, like Antenio Montensinos and Menasseh ben Israel, also claimed that the Israelites got to the New World first, where they were driven into the mountains and 'hidden' places by the late-coming gentiles. These theories had a dramatic impact on the colonial mind and influenced the works of Roger Williams and John Eliot, as well as later generations of American missionaries.

The problem that Christian Identity faces with these first-arriving Jews is that in order to discount an Indian theory of origin it must also discount millennialism itself, as well as a religion from which it has derived profound, intellectual inspiration. In millennialist theory the Jew came to America from the East, a descendent of Shem who was blessed by Noah. This race of 'true Jews', says James Holstun, was said to have moved through Asia and the Caucasus 'in a complex utopian dialectic of enclosure, population growth and plantation'.

The names of Shem's descendants, Eber, Peleg, Ren or Regnu, signified 'confederation among the divided', making 'these archetypal pilgrims' forerunners of both the Iroquois Confederacy and 'the Old Testament types of the emigrating and planting Congregationalists' (Holstun 1987, p. 113). For Christian Identity, either the theory of Indian descent was counterfeit and the Indians were depraved (as were all coloured races) or they were 'true Jews', actual descendants of the lost tribes, whose authenticity asks to be recognised.

The response from Christian Identity to the presence of the Indian and a racial heritage which claims affiliation with ancient Israel is far from explicit. The surface view is that the Indian is an aboriginal whose atheistic and hostile intentions are typical of mud people and non-white races that mate with animals. Yet Christian Identity is also a form of fascism whose 'syllabus' is both 'syncretistic' and derivative, willing to combine 'different forms of belief or practice' in a system of occult 'contradictions' (Eco 1995, p. 27). In Identity Theology, these 'contradictions' are rooted in a millennial 'cult of tradition' (27) and echo many of the feelings and intimacies that have long characterised the relationship between Christians and Jews in the Americas. These feelings cannot easily be eliminated by an Anglo-Saxon theology like British-Israelism which demands that its followers renounce their heritage in favour of an imported cultural metanarrative. For this reason the Scythian descendants of Eurasia and the Orient – the descendants of Shem and Eber – appear to haunt Christian Identity and constantly petition the conservative churches to acknowledge their presence as travellers from Assyria. Christian Identity provides that acknowledgement in gestures which are not only introverted and secretive but theatrical, allusive and mythopoetic.

As the sons of Shem who came to America and lived in its 'hidden' places, the Indians are denounced by Identity preachers, like Gordon "Jack" Mohr, as members of a mongrel race whom Lucifer has deposited among a chosen people (Aho 1990, p. 94). Yet the Indian's elicit pathological sympathies of a less vociferous and covert nature. These sympathies remind us of the behaviour of the Reverend Hooper in Nathaniel Hawthorne's *The Minister's Black Veil*, a man obsessed with the symbolism of secret sin and the interior world of his parishioners. Like Hooper in Salem, or Randall Weaver in northern Idaho, the Christian patriot sees the world as tainted and withdraws into the nation's hinterland in order to preserve family values and rural traditions. By retreating to the 'tops of the mountains' the patriot, like Weaver, returns to the settlement long favoured by the sons of Shem. The transcendental embrace of nature is experienced, says Aho, not in the religion of a racist church, but in a physical encounter with an ancient world, a landscape of 'Big sky and roaring river', a

'Gem of the Mountains, with wilderness acreage alone that dwarfs several New England states' (21).

For America's Christian militias and paramilitaries the idea of an adventure in the form of a retreat means entering a spiritual and sacred world, a land reminiscent of ancient Israel whose 'Old World customs' were brought to the Americas, in the minds of early Protestant historiographers, by Native Americans. Furthermore, at the same time that British-Israelism crossed over to the Americas in the mid-nineteenth century, the quest to uncover the Lost Tribes of Israel was already a subject of intense discussion. The idea that the tribe of Joseph had reappeared in the Americas as the Lamanites, precursors of the Native American Indians, was one of a number of suggestions commonly discussed by millennial communities and would have been well known to nineteenth-century Bible students. Though the idea was not formally accepted by British-Israelism, it found expression in the United States where it featured as one of the prophecies of Joseph Smith, founder of the Mormons.

In the late twentieth century, writes James Aho, those Christian paramilitaries who carry their 'baggage ... into western and northern Idaho', are themselves 'emigrants' in the wilderness, re-enacting a history of tribal exodus. Northern Idaho is a memorial terrain in the history of that exodus, a transnational landscape which fuses American Indian country with Caucasian settlement in Georgia and Chechnya, a land of 'big sky' (21) and Eurasian space, a geography that is both American and pre-American. It is the New World home of those Scythian descendants who migrated to the Americas through the rebel settlements of Georgia and Chechnya on an eastward journey.

The warlord in the wilderness professes his need for what Richard Slotkin calls, 'intimacy with the Indians' (Slotkin 1973, p. 126). He responds to a landscape which embodies elements of a promised land, a residual Jewishness which has been sought out and preserved by a primitive people with their 'forests, mountains' and horses. Here is a synergy between people of a common seed, wandering Jews from the same diaspora, Anglo Saxons and Asian Israelites, rural idealists who wear the costume of a defiant Jew. In the uniform of the warlords of Georgia and Michigan, Montana and Idaho, we see beyond the battledress of the fascist to a race whose jackets are inscribed with a supernatural icon, the initials S and J (the sacred brotherhood of Shem and Japheth.)

The tribalism that links the descendants of Shem and Japheth is further secured if we juxtapose the tribal name which Identity Christians have assigned themselves – Manasseh – with the name of the rabbinical theologian, Menasseh (ben Israel), whose theories of Jewish Indian origin (in *Hope of Israel*) are among the earliest examples of

Jewish 'explorer literature' (Popkin 1980, p. 73) in the Americas. Menasseh ben Israel's genealogical history of the exodus of the Indian tribes was of 'central' (75) importance in the millennial debates of the seventeenth century, says Richard H. Popkin. Menasseh argued that the Indian's were lineal descendants of Shem's son Eber (Genesis 10), and were worthy recipients of the Christian message. His theories also provided the basis for the scholarly enquiries into Jewish-Indian descent until the late nineteenth century and were still active when British-Israelism was first formulated. That formulation, instead of refuting the work of ben Israel, used his name, with a change of vowel, to identify the house of 'Manasseh' that had come to America on board the *Mayflower*.

In the work of the Identity historian and genealogist Wesley Swift, the tribal leader who carries the lineage of Abraham to America is Manasseh, twin brother of Ephraim and son of Joseph. Manasseh, writes Swift, is, a direct descendant of Japheth who accepted 'Jacob's blessings to his sons' and told his followers to come to America, 'the place prophesied for the regathering of the Last Days' (Aho 1990, p. 110). The problem is that while ben Israel identifies the Indians as descendants of Shem, and Christian Identity associates the Puritans with the sons of Japheth, the risk of confusing the name Menasseh with the house of Manasseh remains considerable. By using what amounts to the same name to illustrate a different history of settlement, the impression remains that Christian Identity is willing to allow a confusion to exist. Given the proximity of Manasseh and Menasseh – one the tribe, the other a rabbinical spokesman for the Indian – it seems remarkable that Identity theory can run the risk of embracing its opposite without any warning.

The suggestion of a spiritual tie between the rural inhabitants of the American West, both white and red, would be regarded an outrageous conceit by critics and historians of the paramilitary movement. The political hostility of the Christian militias towards most, if not all, non-Aryan races, seems, on the face of it, inconsistent with any kind of sympathy for ethnic or Third World communities. America's ideological and spiritual opponents, Russia and China, remain, says Michael Barkun, a great concern for the Identity movement. Even though the Cold War is over, the Antichrist still retains a pressure among us and this demands a 'cleansing process ... before the Kingdom of Our Lord Christ can be established' (Barkun 1997, p. 108). As John Harrell of the Christian Patriots Defense League has argued: if a 'spiritual, political and moral housecleaning' is delayed, evil will triumph in an outcome that will be 'terrible, irreversible, and eternal'. Harrell's survivalist pamphlet urges 'retreat to an area in the center of the continent as a redoubt where the faithful can wait out the "ruthless Communist dictatorship"' and 'the total anarchy that will threaten to overwhelm North America during the Tribulation' (107). Bertrand Comparet is more specific about the threat to America. In an article for *Christian Vanguard* he reconfirms the idea that the United States is a new Jerusalem and that the Russian Zog will form a vast coalition of its satellites in the Middle East. Here it will be assisted by 'the mixed breeds of Asia and Africa and India, who … will ally themselves with anything which promises them that they can pillage and rape in the lands of the White Man' (108–9). The alliance between '"the Russian Hordes"' and their satanic associates will result in a direct attack upon the United States by '"nomadic warrior"' and '"Asiatic hordes"' who will cross the Bering Strait, disperse throughout Canada and '"roll in like a flood in our north-western states"' (109). It is this which requires, says Dan Gayman of the Church of Israel, an 'exodus to the land' and the implementation of a 'survivalist imperative' (111).

The rural quest for 'maximum self-sufficiency' (111) attracted its most celebrated Christian paramilitary the day Lieutenant Colonel James Bo Gritz established a Christian commune, 'Almost Heaven', in Kamiah, Idaho, in 1994. Gritz, whom Mark Hamm refers to as, 'the moral authority of the American radical right' (Hamm 1997, p. 27), is a charismatic paramilitary leader, who is often described as an anti-Semitic, Christian survivalist. For Michael Barkun, Gritz is a populist with fascist sympathies, a classic conspiracy theorist with a political agenda to end income taxes and dismantle the Federal Reserve. As a dedicated opponent of secular Jewishness and the Zionist Occupation Government, Gritz is described as a vigorous enemy of multiculturalism which the white supremacist leader, Pastor Richard Butler of Aryan Nations, has accused him of. As a dedicated opponent of Communism and a Green Beret who served with the Special Forces in Vietnam, Gritz was hired in the late 1970s by the billionaire industrialist H. Ross Perot to lead a search-and-rescue mission into Laos and Thailand to look for POWs abandoned by the US government.

Gritz's exploits became the basis for the Rambo films in the mid-1980s. These films, says Willian Gibson, made Gritz – and his progeny, John Rambo – into archetypal 'New War' heroes for America's emerging paramilitary communities. Gritz epitomised the revisionist doctrine of rewriting the war that was such an essential part of Reagan's America. Under this ethos, writes Gibson, paramilitary culture dedicated itself to erasing the memory of failure in Vietnam and to creating 'new mythic victories' in an 'imaginary war zone' proliferated by poor Mexicans and 'disease-ridden' illegal aliens (Gibson 1991, p. 390). Popular culture glamorised paramilitarism, providing an opportunity for the avenging soldiers or vigilantes to be 'reborn' as 'powerful' warriors who were 'fighting either criminals inside the United States or guerrillas, terrorists, drug dealers, or KGB agents abroad, on a world-wide battleground' (389). In films like *The Hunt for Red October* (1984), *Red Storm Rising* (1985) and *Rambo: First Blood* (1985) New War warriors were seen as:

Special men, men whose whole being is dedicated to fighting the enemy. Although they once led normal lives and had careers and families, something has happened to change them, to transform them into warriors perpetually in search of adventure, danger, and death. More often than not, New War stories have their origin in the Vietnam War. Most of the heroes served in Vietnam. Others did not serve in Vietnam per se, but fought in limited, undeclared wars elsewhere and were similarly betrayed by leaders who sold them out. Yet others suffered some form of Vietnam-like 'self-imposed restraint' at home, when major social institutions – particularly the police and the court system – failed to combat the enemies of American society. (Gibson 1994, p. 33)

In Gibson's thesis the 'warrior films' that were released in the mid-to-late 1980s remasculinise American society by fantasising a revisionist victory in Vietnam. In the revised war against Communism the élite paramilitary wins 'decisively' (11). Since 'paramilitary culture can be understood only when it is placed in relation to the Vietnam War', writes Gibson, and since 'America's failure to win that war was a truly profound blow' (10), the paramilitary is engaged, first and foremost, in a war against race. When 'illegal aliens inside the United States and hordes of non-whites in the Third World are returned by force to their proper place' victory not only affirms 'the country's fundamental goodness and power' (10), it reinstates 'an archetypal pattern' of 'regeneration through violence' (10). The success of warrior strength and virtue reaffirms a racist, neo-Nazi creed in which the death of the Vietnamese, as well as the elimination of 'blacks and Jews and federal officials of the "Zionist Occupational Government"' (Gibson 1991, p. 390), is a legitimate activity in defence of American racial purity. This 'appetite for destruction' identifies pacifism as 'trafficking with the enemy'. This is 'bad' for the fascist since 'life' is a matter of 'permanent warfare' and is 'lived' in order to maximise 'struggle' (Eco 1995, p. 27).

Gibson sees a link between the post-Vietnam paramilitaries in the United States and the Freikorps, a far-right battalion in post-First World War Germany who were bitterly disappointed by the terms of the Armistice in 1918 and felt 'stabbed in the back' by the liberals of the Weimar Republic. Both communities, he argues, emerge from a culture of disappointment and both share 'a similar despair and search for rebirth' (Gibson 1994, p. 32). In the United States the 'New War' warrior never gives up his 'war of vengeance' (50). The ultimate good of 'post-Vietnam mythic heroes' is to rewrite history and completely eliminate the memory of failure. What this requires, in effect, is to display 'a vicious appetite for destruction' (30) and the elimination of any adversary who represents an actual or symbolic reminder of the war.

All forms of Christian Identity, including its paramilitary units, are members of the same 'racist right', says Gibson, targetting 'nonwhites' as well as 'Jews' and 'Communists' in 'a fight for white supremacy' (214). As an explanation of the paramilitary activity of those who bring the war 'home' to America, as Aho phrases it (Aho 1994, p. 5), Gibson's thesis finds general acceptance in the academic community. But in so far as it relates to the war in Vietnam, the argument, I believe, has a dubious validity. For one thing, America's 'defeat in Vietnam' was not typically regarded by those who fought there (or those who formed covenanted communities as a means of opposing a tyrannical government) as 'the defeat of all white men' (Gibson 1994, p. 214), which is what Gibson claims. Nor is it accurate to see a patriot land development scheme, like 'Almost Heaven', not to mention Gritz's political activities as a presidential candidate for the anti-Semitic Populist Party, as a crude vehicle with which to impose control over the coloured races that threaten the United States. To argue that the war in Vietnam is seen as a triumph for 'the "yellow" Asian' (214) races reduces its value as a cultural resource to those who participated in it. This is to say that Vietnam can only be understood (by a white supremacist movement) as an aberration, a shameful and humiliating experience, 'mysterious and threatening' (214), as Gibson puts it.

Christian Identity and its paramilitary factions, learned as much about their own government during the Vietnam war as they did about the Vietnamese, and what they learned inverted their beliefs about the real identity of the enemy they were fighting. The feeling of betrayal towards the American government never left the paramilitary: the profound anger at those who had been responsible for the war effort – the managers, bureaucrats, academics and politicians who, by withdrawing decisive support, allowed the military to swing in the wind. One of these soldiers, the ex-Green Beret and militia supporter Randy Weaver, was shot by federal agents after an eleven-day siege at his cabin in the forests of northern Idaho.

The death of Vicky Weaver, Randall Weaver's wife, and the siege at Ruby Ridge, proved a defining moment for Randall's friend Bo Gritz, confirming his opposition to a national government which had betrayed not only its most loyal citizens – the veterans of foreign wars – but had actively conspired to undermine the freedoms of the individual. Gritz's opposition to federal income tax, foreign aid, the New World Order and the Federal Reserve was the platform on which he conducted his political campaign as Populist presidential candidate in 1992. But while Gritz had long been associated throughout his civilian career with a number of racist, far-right organisations (like David Duke's National Association for the Advancement of White People) it is also true that he had abandoned his relationship with them when he 'realised' how extreme their 'racial views were' (Pitcavage 1996, p. 1).

'The ambiguity' that surrounds Gritz's 'political activity' (1), says Mark Pitcavage, is also a feature of his millennial faith. In spite of its fascist associations, Gritz's Christianity displays a need for personal intimacy and physical association with non-white peoples. Richard Butler's throwaway description of Gritz as a 'multiculturalist' (Theroux 1998) has validity in the context of 'Almost Heaven', where Gritz lives with two half-Chinese children and an African-American godchild. At 'Almost Heaven', Gritz frowns on 'race-mixing' as contrary to biblical injunction, but denies this means support for white domination. 'Skin color means nothing', he is reported to have said. 'A bullet in combat doesn't have any prejudice' (Aho 1994, p. 64).

As a freedom fighter Gritz is also attracted to the racial 'other' – the alien, Third World race that he and his associates have previously claimed they want to exclude from the United States. 'Almost Heaven' is not an exclusively 'whites only' area – like Richard Butler's Aryan Nations compound at Hayden Lake, Idaho – nor is it created as a way of implementing the Northwest Territorial Imperative, a neo-Nazi plan to make the Pacific Northwest exclusively white. As Louis Theroux's film shows us, 'Almost Heaven' has a multiracial social base, and a vigorous commitment to eco-systems such as solar power and organic building materials such as hay and wood. The name 'Almost Heaven' brings to mind a pastoral Vietnam and suggests a need to reach out to nature and establish a synergy with the people of Asia. In his memoir of the Vietnam war *Remembering Heaven's Face* (1991), the pacifist poet John Balaban describes the importance of the celestial spirit in the Tao-Buddhist world of Vietnam. In Hue, Balaban notes the importance to the Vietnamese of addressing 'the sun', the 'face of heaven' (11), the countenance of Ong Troi, in the homes and places of worship of his friends. This is done through the use of mirrors on buildings or family altars and by painting the names of ancestors on a mirror's face and then covering the mirror with a red cloth. Balaban describes a secret meeting of old men under the eaves of a home where they cover their faces with cloth and lean back to 'tilt' their 'face skyward' while they 'dance in slow whirls' (12). For Balaban, the Vietnamese soul is 'the human spirit reaching toward heaven', a spirit that is 'watched by heaven where our moral efforts are judged and weighed' (12).

At 'Almost Heaven', Bo Gritz insists on maintaining a similar level of ceremonial privacy. Amidst all the violence that has surrounded his life in Vietnam, the peasant proverb 'Go out one day, and come back with a basket full of wisdom' (12) is integral to the culture that Gritz is seeking to create in Idaho. In 'Almost Heaven', as in Vietnam, those who leave 'the safe, unsurprising village' and take 'to the road', discover 'something new', something which they 'bring' 'home' (12) with them. What Gritz brings 'home' to Idaho is a belief in the power of nature and the idea of 'home' as a Tao or Buddhist community, one that requires protection from the world.

The ideal of the settled community in Idaho connects the bucolic enclave in Asia with a biblical ingathering of exiles in a promised land. When he founded 'Almost Heaven', Gritz purchased 200 acres of land in Idaho and subdivided it into smaller parcels to interested patriots. He created a community, therefore, that was both separate from the world and settled by those who had found themselves in flight from it; a place of retreat for a wilderness people who, like the sons of Israel, were looking for a home in a New Canaan. 'Almost Heaven' restored the ancient Israelite as American Jew to the mountains and focused attention on the Native American who had made the trek into those mountains long before Gritz and his people arrived.

In Idaho, Gritz celebrated his vision of the Jew as an Oriental and an American wanderer. This was the vision of Herman Husband, the eighteenth-century pamphleteer who was convinced that a 'New Jerusalem' would arise in the western regions of North America and extend beyond the 1792 boundaries of the country, westward to the Rocky Mountains. In fulfilling the visions of the prophet Ezekiel, Husband believed that the Indians would become 'governors in Judah', occupants of an area of land that was sovereign, independent, self-governing and 'cultivated'. At 'Almost Heaven', political and cultural sympathies exist between the paramilitary as settler and those whose history has derived from a biblical experience of exodus and settlement. In seventeenth-century scholarship, says Lee Huddleston, the Native American was seen as a descendant of Israel who had come to the new world not 'from one nation but from many' (Huddleston 1967, p. 146). The Indian was a composite of many cultures, agrees James Holstun, and was commonly thought to have roamed his way through India and China before arriving in the Americas. In the New World he trailed behind him a multicultural tradition, a historiography that connected him with the Scythian and Oriental communities of Asia through which he had travelled (and in which he had sometimes settled).

At 'Almost Heaven' Gritz restated the importance of the wilderness trek and an agrarian society he had seen at first hand in Vietnam. In the aftermath of war, Gritz struggled to reinvent himself, adopting, on the one hand, the rural persona of the Vietnamese peasant, while publicly professing Third World exclusion as a way of disguising his psychic need to emulate the enemy.

The wilderness of Idaho also enabled Gritz to encounter the millennial legacy of the Jews as Indians in their original homeland. In his quest for hiddenness he sought a kind of metaphorical acquaintance with the Lost Tribes of Israel. According to Mark Pitcavage, his scheme was to create 'a hideaway "Christian Covenant Community"' in a 'remote' region of Idaho (Pitcavage 1996, p. 2). As an adherent of Christian identity Gritz re-enacted the mythological arrival of the sons of Eber to a 'hidden' and mountainous region. He thus brought to mind the Indian adventurism of Roger Williams and the beliefs of Antonio Montesinos and Menasseh ben Israel.

Gritz has described his latter-day trek into the mountains of Idaho as the precursor of Armageddon:

I observed a pouring out of virtuous people from the metropolitan centers into the hinterlands. I beheld covenant communities standing separate from a tyrannical government ... It was Armageddon. Millions of massed soldiers − both men and women − were slaughtered, but the homeland was spared. (Pitcavage 1996, p. 2)

Gritz had witnessed an early version of Armageddon in the hinterlands of Vietnam and the terrible vengeance which the American government had wreaked on the 'soldiers' and civilians who had opposed the 'tyrannical government' of Saigon. The circumstantial similarity of Gritz's position in Kamiah, Idaho, to that of the Communists in the Mekong Delta cannot disguise the very real resemblances that exist between America's paramilitaries and the rural peasantry of South Vietnam.

During the Vietnam war the Viet Cong and North Vietnamese Army received most of its support from a rural hinterland of jungle, swamp and hill-land. Like America's militias twenty years later, theirs was a mission to expose the corruption that was rife in the nation's capital: an immoral presidency, a government that was bureaucratic and unresponsive, a military that was weak and ineffectual, an economy that was dependent on overseas investment and the 'foreign ownership of domestic soil'. Like America's paramilitaries, the Viet Cong were committed to the defence of local and national sovereignties, opposed 'intervention outside America's borders' and rejected a foreign policy that went against the national interest and 'national defense' (Stern 1997, p. 34).

In the wilderness, America's militias saw an opportunity to emulate a legacy of Third World insurgency. The ideal of the rural resistance fighter was certainly instrumental in assisting disaffected veterans like Randy Weaver to regain control of their lives. For other rural insurgents, stealth and hiddenness were a vital part of a new political strategy of opposition. As one right-wing commentator has put it:

It's like guerrilla warfare. If you reveal your location, all it does is allow your opponent to improve his artillery bearings. It's better to move quietly, with stealth, under cover of night. You've got two choices: You can wear cammies and shimmy along on your belly, or you can put on a red coat and stand up for everyone to see. It comes down to whether you want to be the British army in the Revolutionary War or the Viet Cong. History tells us which tactic was more effective. (Reed in 'The Quotable Pat Robertson')

As a beneficiary of Israel's legacy of wandering and her search for a homeland in Asia, Communist Vietnam had distilled the essence of a rural aesthetic into a struggle for independence. The nationalist crusade and the importance of territorial sovereignty were an indication of the country's sacred attachment to land and the traditional importance of ancestral, tribal and family values in a rural society. The goal of independence, like Israel's quest for the paradisal garden, had commenced the moment the country was conquered by China. It concluded in Asia on the day the final occupying power (the United States) was evicted. Vietnam's defiance in the face of colonial occupation was that of an Israel who stood its ground, its values those of an agricultural race where a network of cells provided a basis for political and military resistance in Asia. In Vietnam, the support of the peasantry in defence of their land was crucial to the success of the revolution, a fact which American policymakers did not realise until much too late. As Jeffrey Race says in *War Comes to Long An*:

No other factor looms so large in the consciousness of the peasant. Aside from the economic precariousness of owning no land a peasant feels a rootlessness particularly strong in Vietnamese culture, because the land has a special ritual significance for the Vietnamese: it is the focus of life and family activity. Closeness to ancestral graves and the fields the family has worked for generations provides the emotional security and strength which westerners generally draw from prophetic religion. (Race 1972, p. 6)

The link between prophetic religion and rural culture reappears in the Christian Identity movement. Those who are willing to live in a hostile world until the Second Coming share many of the same stoical features as the Communist guerrillas in the jungles of Vietnam. The

anticipation of 'imminent catastrophe' among many of the Christian
Identity survivalists, says Michael Barkun, creates 'a siege mentality,
a sense that one is surrounded by enemies and that the battle is even
now beginning' (Barkun 1997, p. 213). Biblical prophecy, like Marxist
prophecy, is underpinned by a logic of violence which must be
accelerated rather than delayed. The politics of 'radical localism'
which characterise the 'preindustrial' ideal of 'free Aryan yeoman
farmers, governing themselves under a common law that allegedly
allowed no outside political intervention', is based on a 'fear of
political and economic centralization' which threatens 'the independence of local communities' (218). It is the same fear which the
Communist Dong Lao Dong Party exploited in South Vietnam when
it opposed President Diem's land redistribution policies. The fear of
corruption, which Vietnam's farmers associated with these policies,
was exacerbated by the American government, both in its political
support for Diem and in its programme of rural resettlement. In the
1960s the Strategic Hamlets policy forced people off their land into
artificial urban environments and created the basis for a revolutionary
struggle among the peasant classes, through which the Dong Lao Dong
created a strong party apparatus at the hamlet and village level.

During the 1980s in the farming communities of the American West
and Midwest, fear of outside intervention fuelled a deep suspicion of
the government's economic policy on farm management. The belief
that government policy was underwritten by a 'Zionist Occupation
Government' (composed of secular Jews) and that the Internal Revenue
Service was merely a tool of Zionist international bankers led to the
creation of the Posse Comitatus, a radically decentralised, vigilante
movement or citizens' army, dedicated to protecting the interests of
farmers threatened with foreclosure. The Posse Comitatus was an
insurgent guerrilla movement representing the interests of the
local community against a government that was said to be robbing
Americans of their hard-earned income through punitive taxation while
surrendering its political sovereignty to overseas agencies like the
United Nations. Controlled by bankers, freemasons and liberals,
the United Nations was seen as an umbrella organisation that gave
shelter and protection to agents of the New World Order like the World
Bank and the Federal Reserve System, both of which were planning
an attack on the nation's agrarian heartland. This fear of urban intervention, says Jeffrey Race, was also expressed by the farmers of Long
An province in the 1960s and 1970s. It was the inspiration behind the
conviction that 'the soil could provide a bounteous life' and generate
'spiritual values' (Race 1972, p. 106) for those who worked it.

Christian Identity splices together rural self-sufficiency and biblical
prophecy in a war against the American government which, says

Christopher Goodwin, owes much to Vietnamese methods of rural insurgency and survivalism (Goodwin 1995, p. 17). Affiliated organisations like the Montana Militia Movement, led by the bearded 'Old Testament' prophet John Trochmann, adopt a survivalist ethic 'in the remote Bitterroot mountains of northwest Montana', where large quantities of weapons and food are stored 'in readiness for a hit-and-run guerrilla war' (17). All militia movements, writes Wayne La Pierre, accept the idea that there is no twentieth-century example 'of a determined populace with access to small arms having been defeated by a modern army'. Where 'the Russians lost in Afghanistan, the United States lost in Vietnam, and the French lost in Indo-China ... it was the poorly armed populace that beat the "modern" army' (LaPierre 1994, pp. 19–20). The militias brought the war home from Vietnam in all sorts of ways. John Milius's *Red Dawn* (1984), a film popular on the militia circuit, shows how Americans avenged the defeat by guerrillas abroad by becoming guerrillas at home. In William Pierce's novel *The Turner Diaries* (1979), the guerrillas turn their Vietnam experience against their own government by adopting the same underground strategies as the Communist Viet Cong.

The racist who acts as rural revolutionary and political guerrilla takes centre stage in Costav Gavras's film *Betrayed* (1988). *Betrayed* is a political thriller that examines the aspirations of white supremacist farmers in the Midwest at a time of economic decline and fore-closure. As a socio-historical drama, it deals with the rise of agrarian resistance movements in general and the political emergence of the Posse Comitatus, in particular. Gavras emphasises neither the utopian character of the rural underground movement in America nor its prolonged love affair with violence. What interests him is its proletarian and religious character: the impact of economic instability on an evangelical community that feels politically unrepresented, and the pressures that result from attempting to produce grain and cereal crops at marketable prices in the face of subsidised foreign competition.

In *Betrayed*, America's family farms are in crisis and, on the eve of the New World Order, the government appears to have lost interest in their survival. The frustration felt by farmers when their self-sufficiency is undermined and their farm income drops below subsistence level places an intolerable strain on a community that, for generations, has equated hard work with social stability. Deprived of self-respect and legitimate economic aspiration, the farmer turns to a politics of vendetta that is replete with all the racist contradictions of small-town, American fascism. In the farmers' support for the Posse Comitatus, the film provides a cogent explanation as to why the banks are foreclosing on farms: 'Jews incapable of farming', it is argued, have managed 'to control the world's monetary system in order to control the global food supply' (Stern 1997, p. 120).

Betrayed is, however, more than a simple-minded exposé of small-town xenophobia and rural anti-Semitism. From the outset, the film presents us with a group of likeable, Illinois farmers who have fallen on hard times and are forced to create a self-help militia in an attempt to identify the reason for decline. The local militia operates as an individual cell in a much larger, underground network. In order to preserve its anonymity this resistance network meets once a year at a summer camp. Here it professes a racist creed, practises military drills, trades weapons and promotes ideas on revolution and violence.

This fascist philosophy is seemingly confirmed at the outset when Sam Kraus, a Jewish talk-show host in Chicago, is gunned down and murdered for attacking a right-wing fundamentalist on a phone-in. Other executions follow, such as that of a black youth who is kidnapped in Chicago and taken to the country where he is set loose and then hunted with dogs. The need for vigilantism is underwritten by an Old Testament God whose Word is interpreted by a righteous ministry in the cornbelt. In his sermons, the Reverend Russell Johnson tells his congregation they are descended from the Lost Tribes of Israel and must protect themselves from the 'mud people', the blacks and Jews who are descended from Cain. Pulpit paranoia is superficially popular, especially with men like Shorty who, through no fault of his own, has lost a farm to the bank and a son to Vietnam.

Underneath the racist rhetoric, however, the real enemy of the farmer is not Vietnam or the multiracial city. It is a government which has been corrupted by overseas influence and is unresponsive to the needs of an agrarian hinterland. The xenophobia of the community is little more than a façade and its racist persona is full of discrepancies. The legacy of Vietnam is also a contradiction. The militia leader, Gary Simmons, has a distinguished career in Vietnam, and illustrates the difficulty of being both a racist and a revolutionary. As a Christian patriot, Simmons vilifies Communists and Jews but, as a point man in the war, has considerable respect for the military discipline and moral character of the Vietnamese. At camp, Simmons finds the neo-Nazi paramilitaries in their fascist uniforms little better than make-up artists and he despises their posturing and childish theatricality. Like the Vietnamese, Simmons is fighting to defend his land against the forces of corporate capitalism. As a patriot, he is determined to preserve the jobs, the products, the industries and living standards of the American working man, many of which are being swallowed up, as he puts it, by Arab tycoons with easy money from places like 'Abu Dabi'. As a result, Simmons carries with him a considerable empathy for the NVA grunts and Vietcong guerrillas and he resists any attempt by adolescent fascists to hijack the disciplines and military proficiencies that are earned in battle.

Simmons's position in Illinois is little different from that of the peasant farmer in South Vietnam during the Presidency of Ngo Dinh Diem. Just as the American government appears to have turned a blind eye to the activities of banks and businesses, so the Diem government in Saigon, says Gabriel Kolko, ignored the opportunism of the urban landlords, and pursued instead, a corrupt programme of land reform which allowed the landlords to retain their power at the expense of the peasantry. Vietnamese resettlement would have provided Simmons with evidence that policymakers in Washington have little understanding of the traditions of an agricultural society and are prepared, if necessary, to forcibly remove and separate families in direct violation of their rural heritage. Simmons would probably have seen the destruction of native villages and the forced removal of villagers as 'the necessary first step' in the 'reconstruction' of Vietnam from 'a rural agricultural society' to 'a modern urban society' (Gibson 1986, p. 226). If farmers who are hostile to the American government can shape such a policy, similar experiments in social engineering and pacification might also occur in the United States, should the nation's farmers ever become a political threat.

Betrayed suggests other linkages with Vietnam's rural poor. During the war, for example, one of the main casualties of urban resettlement were young women, many of whom were forced into prostitution in the cities to support their families in the provinces. In Robert Stone's *Dog Soldiers* (1973), John Converse notices the girls in the bar of the Hotel Coligny who eye him 'with suspicion and loathing', the 'war widows or refugee country girls or serving officers of the Viet Cong' (Stone 1973, pp. 26–7). Converse senses the hatred of the women but is unable to enlarge the scope of his sympathy and is left with a feeling of 'vague dissatisfaction' (39) that, eventually, a price must be paid.

Gary Simmons's reaction to the menace of prostitution is more principled and political in assessing that price. Simmons hates any suggestion of sexual promiscuity by the FBI agent Katie Phillips, with whom he falls in love. When Phillips buys a skimpy nightdress and parades it in front of him, Simmons calls her a whore. For Simmons, the real freedom fighter overthrows gender stereotypes. He prefers his women to earn their respect as working members of the family farm, either in the wheatfields, where they drive combines, or as militia members, like Ellie, a farm girl who trains alongside her colleagues and is accorded equal rights. A woman like Ellie who works and fights like a man, who wears jeans and combat fatigues, has the appearance of a paramilitary and a Viet Cong guerrilla. This idea of female equality comes not from the whorehouses but the battlefields of South Vietnam. For America's rural militias the woman's role is instrumental, just as it was, says Arlene Eisen, for the people of Vietnam who overthrew patriarchal traditions in their fight against colonialism.

In the 1990s political extremists and underground guerrillas mirror Vietnamese insurgents and experiment with survivalist and revolutionary strategies in ways that are designed to accelerate millennial conflicts. When Theodore J. Kaczynski, the 'Harvard Hermit' or 'Unabomber', retreated into the Scapegoat Wilderness region of Montana and launched his bombing campaign against the military-industrial complex, he too copied the tactics of the Vietnamese guerrilla. Kaczynski's blend of homespun violence and environmentalism resulted in a type of eco-fundamentalism that combined the freedom fighter's revolutionary zeal with the divinity of the Indian in a 'refuge' or 'retreat' (Reed 1997, p. 2). Kaczynski's opposition to technology's destruction of Third World society and wilderness habitat – spectacularly apparent in Vietnam – was framed by a religious and intellectual 'manifesto' published in *The Washington Post* and *New York Times*. His thesis was that the 'industrial revolution', in so far as it had been interpreted by the United States, was a disaster for the human race. It had led to 'widespread psychological suffering in The Third World' and had 'inflicted severe damage on the natural world' – a claim that comes straight out of the 1960s and the anti-war protest movement (Didion 1998, p. 17).

Kaczynski's idealism is shared by other paramilitary opponents of the technocratic state in the 1990s. In the case of Timothy McVeigh, opposition to hierarchical and technological power was visceral rather than philosophical, but was certainly a factor behind his decision to bomb the Alfred P. Murrah government building in Oklahoma City in April 1995. McVeigh's revulsion against the indiscriminate use of technological violence in Third World theatres originated in the deserts of southern Iraq where, as a soldier in the US army, he witnessed one of the most appalling massacres of modern warfare, the slaughter of retreating Iraqi soldiers on the Basra road. Until that point in his career McVeigh had been 'in love' with the army and, as an *aficionado* of Vietnam, had ignored the devastation which the military had inflicted on civilian society in Southeast Asia. The Basra massacre appears to have changed all that, focusing his attention on the atrocities and the horror of modern warfare. 'Everybody who saw that terrible event was deeply affected by it', says McVeigh's commanding officer, Captain Terry Guild:

The next morning, after the helicopter gunships had finished their work, we all wandered for miles through hundreds of blackened bodies. None of us took any pleasure in the sight and McVeigh, like all of us, was pretty sickened. I remember him as a fine young soldier who served his country well. If he did indeed do this terrible thing he is accused of, then all I can tell you is that something very bad indeed happened to him between the time he left the army and today. (Carlin 1995, p. 11)

The Oklahoma bombing was McVeigh's quasi-revolutionary statement against a government that was willing not only to massacre the innocent but conspire with its multinational partners in the New World Order to deprive its citizens of their liberty and freedom. After the Gulf, 'the tyrants' were to be seen holed up in Washington, says John Carlin, 'partners in a conspiracy with the other western powers to hand over national sovereignty to the United Nations' (11). For McVeigh, and his equally 'tormented' accomplice Terry Nicholls, the very concept of patriotism was at risk from a tyrannical government bent on taking away the individual's constitutional right, and, with the passing of the Brady Bill in 1994, violating his right to purchase arms in self-defence at a time of alien infiltration.

The icon for disaffected veterans of both Vietnam and the Gulf – and the original complainant against the over-technologised state – was the result of a twinning arrangement between the popular culture in Hollywood and the revisionist culture of the 1980s. The novels and films which featured John Rambo did not so much glorify 'New War' paramilitarism or demand revenge against a Vietnamese state that held American POWs in collusion with its Soviet masters. The principal target of the Rambo films, says Russell Berman, was the 'governmental machine with its massive technology, unlimited regulation and venal political motivations'. Like Timothy McVeigh and Theodore Kaczynski, Rambo was a prototype for the 'anti-bureaucratic non-conformist [who is] opposed to the state' (Berman 1984, p. 145). When told, in *Rambo: First Blood II* (1985), of the support he will receive on his rescue mission from sophisticated electronic surveillance devices and other technological hardware, Rambo replies: 'I thought the best weapon was the mind.' Motivated by a desire for purification, Rambo seeks to free himself from the world of high-tech computers and a technologically dependent American mindset. Murdock, the CIA chief in Thailand, who finally betrays him, controls this computer bureaucracy that Rambo finds odious. Murdock, says Adi Wimmer, is 'a representative of a degenerate, over technocratic and over-bureaucratic segment of American society' (Wimmer 1989, p. 189) that can no longer be trusted. At the end of the film when Rambo destroys Murdock's computers, symbols of modern American alienation, he demonstrates the extent to which, says Leslie Gelb and Richard Betts, 'the old American virtues have

already been eaten away ... the old national security and independence have been destroyed by treasonous plots'. These have as their
'agents not merely outsiders and foreigners' but those 'seated at the
very center of American government' (Gelb and Betts 1979, p. 27).

The two-dimensional view of Rambo is that he goes to Vietnam
to win the war the politicians lost. When Rambo asks Trautman,
his former Special Forces Commander, 'Do we get to win this time?'
it is usually assumed that 'we' refers to the American military. But
Rambo's 'we' could equally refer to his ethnic background and the
Native Americans who fought in Vietnam in considerable numbers
who, like Rambo, were betrayed and marginalised on their return.
What Rambo can 'win' back is the dignity and spiritual identity of
his people, an identity which, in Hebraic historiography, took shape
in the flight out of Egypt and brought the Lost Tribes to America
via Asia and the Orient. In accepting the assignment, Rambo decides
to reinstate a history that, on several levels, says Adi Wimmer, has
been 'taken away': a history that exists outside Adamic America
and which belongs to 'the original Americans, the Red Indians'
(Wimmer 1989, p. 190). In the act of severing his link with postmodern America, Rambo connects with a tribal Asia and resurrects
himself as an ancient Israelite. As a redemptive figure he revives
himself as a Wandering Jew, a modern-day son of Shem and Eber,
functioning outside the dominant power structure and the bureaucracy
of conventional military and law-enforcement units. He is an élite
fighter who 'relies on the tactics and weaponry' of an indigenous
race, of which he is a member. In his use of the combat knife
and long bow he seeks out the origins of that race, rejecting the
superior fire power of the American military in favour of the Vietcong
who 'fought with more primitive weapons and had greater tactical
skills' (190).

Like James Bo Gritz, Rambo empathises with the cultural artifacts
of ancient civilisations, the ancient tools and weapons of the woods
that the American military, with its corporate technowar, sought to
destroy. His ability to survive without the 'dubious paraphernalia'
of warfare 'in an untamed Asian wilderness', also suggests an innate
ability to see in Vietnam an America 'that no longer exists' (191)
back home. Rambo draws 'his strength from a mythical immersion
in the jungle foliage, in the water, even the soil of Vietnam' (192),
which is why his tendencies resemble those of the rural Vietnamese
more than they do those of a military that need to conscript him.
By seeking out the 'hidden' places, he exhibits the instincts of the
American Indian as Israelite, the wilderness manner of the cross-
country traveller who tames his hair with a sweatband and decorates
his chest with an oriental charm. For a white audience that misses

the connection, the charm behind that appeal lies, as it did in the seventeenth century, in a Semitic aesthetic.

The film *Rambo* appeared in the same month, May 1984, that the Chicano novelist and native American, Rudolpho Anaya, 'embarked' on a more benign adventure in Asia, 'a pilgrimage', as he puts it, 'that turned out to be one of the most incredible journeys I have ever taken' (Anaya 1986, p. v). Asia was where Anaya would seek out 'those simple secrets that hint at the deeper spiritual and humanistic relationship' of pre-Columbian societies. 'For those of us who listen to the Earth and to the old legends and the myths of the people', he writes, 'the whispers of the blood draw us to our past' (viii). In his pursuit of 'an integrated world', Anaya looks to the 'basement' of Asia as it 'speaks' (x) to the Chicanos about an ancient culture and draws them to it in order to examine their lost history.

In *A Chicano in China* (1986) Anaya returns to the place in which, as Mennaseh ben Israel had claimed in 1650, native Americans can trace their roots to a 'secret origin' (5). It is 'secret', says Anaya, because the explanation for it lies 'in the old Asiatic world that sent its migrations of people across the Bering Strait thousands of years ago'. This is the 'real source of the Mesoamerican populations' and 'the Native American Indians, and all the mythology and thought which has intrigued and interested me for many years' (3). In his journey, Anaya picks up the snake skin of history which the Asian migrants brought with them and deposited on the 'earth of New Mexico' (viii). In Albuquerque, he feels the portable organism of history alive within him. He is 'connected' to something other than the earth which surrounds him, the 'thread' (4) of some other past which reverberates within him. 'Thousands of years ago, China sent part of her memory to the Americas and memory may sleep for thousands of years, but it will awaken.' Once he encounters the presentness of that past in China he feels 'liberated' (177), as if he has entered 'a cradle of mankind, a history stretching back in a continuous line to the early stirrings of mankind' (176).

In Albuquerque, Anaya has found remnants of Asia and wrapped them around him. But the itch of history has sent him scurrying back to China, 'a humble pilgrim' in search of 'communication' (vii) at the height of the Cold War. In his memoir, Anaya moves back in time but forward in space, travelling westward from San Francisco, like Rambo's spiritual alter ego, an adolescent 'in reverse', his 'Oriental eyes' (46) in search of symbols and 'archetypal memories of a biologic nature'. In an attempt to understand the 'other half of my nature (5), he is drawn by the power of 'collective memory', the 'thrashing' of the 'dragon' inside his body. In Bejing he senses that 'China is entering me. I am absorbing China ... The dragon settles itself in me, its eyes breathing fire through my eyes, its breath the life in my lungs, its serpentine body settled along my spine and heart and liver and stomach' (45).

On the Yangtze River, China receives him with open arms as he enters its 'stream of history' (118), he is sexually 'captured' in a 'primitive ... embrace' (124). On the Yangtze he stares at the land and drifts with the river submitting himself to a liquid 'embrace' and 'parallel streams' of 'time and history' (123). China is 'primitive', but on board the boat he discovers the origin of its sexuality. 'I enter the blood of China and, like a woman who knows she has conquered a man, China smiles, spreads her arms and thighs, her green hills, and covered with a silk mist she allows me to enter into her bloodstream her water, her history' (122). His 'identity' dissolves. He is 'no longer' (67) a Chicano on a journey of discovery but a pilgrim 'at peace ... a satisfied lover'. Lost in the 'flow' (123) he is surrounded by the 'dark' sexuality of China and the image of America's first love affair with the wilderness.

For Rudolpho Anaya, as for Mennaseh ben Israel, the first American is red and the beauty of the wilderness that flows out of Asia is the 'dragon' in the 'soul' (47). It 'sucks me back to her' like 'a jealous woman', says Anaya. The woman 'has not let go since I arrived. She holds me and makes love to me over and over again until I am exhausted' (79).

Note

1. Civic self-help groups, such as 'Dead Serious' in Fort Worth, Texas, pay $5,000 to anyone who kills a criminal in the act of committing a crime and enjoy enormous support among blue collar groups. The reason, say the organisers, is that 'most victims of crime are poor people' (Jeffreys 1995, pp. 2–3) and that law-enforcement agencies and government legislation do not protect the economically insecure. The New World Order may have opened the doors for the politically disadvantaged of Eastern Europe, but it has hardly enjoyed the confidence of the lower middle class in the United States.

6

The Spacecraft Israel: Millennial Imagining and New Age Religion

Pre-millennial tension is a popular condition for secular intellectuals seeking to explain religious fundamentalism to the uninitiated. Literary historians or 'New Hysterians', as Elaine Showalter likes to describe them (Showalter 1997, p. 7), are more than comfortable with psycho-therapies which reveal the millennium as a time of anxiety. In cultural studies secular pessimism is *de rigueur*. For Malcolm Bradbury, the pessimism is recurrent. 'The ends of millennia', he writes, 'are notorious for the rise of apocalyptic fear, and though our Einstein's monsters change, from nuclear threat to ozone depletion and global warning, the consciousness of uncertainty is with us again.' Freed from the ideological constraints of the last '50 years', says Bradbury, the veil of 'historical interpretation' which 'imprisoned' our 'imagination and intelligence' has been lifted. The political process through which we are passing is one of 'rising uncertainties', for we live 'in a world that will not stay still'. Not surprisingly, we remain anxious. The borders of our very existence are unstable. As borders fracture and re-form we become more desperate in a world where the grids of historical reference seem absent or deficient (Bradbury 1990, p. 21).

In the United States the ideological enemy may have gone but the cultural paranoia of anti-Communism remains and 'devices' for translating apocalyptic thought into new symbolic structures of anxiety tend to proliferate. As one critic puts it: 'The energy that went into finding Reds Under The Bed has undergone weird distortions' (Bygrave 1994, p. 24). In the need to resolve our pathological anxiety we require new maps and new cartographies, new definitions of state and citizenship, a visionary facility in the unfamiliar and unpatrolled territory of a New World order we are asked to live in. As the movement of history becomes more fluid and structures of authority less recognisable, we wander away from the orthodox narratives and listen to the prophets who preach from the margins: millennialists, soothsayers, shamans, futurologists, the visionaries on the internet who preach the gospel of a new religion, the anarchist phreakers who hack their way through a network of secrecy in order to penetrate the reaches of cyberspace.

Wherever we look these days the gifted Jeremiah walks in our midst. From doomsday gurus like Robert D. Kaplan and Graham Hancock to academicians like John Leslie and Paul Kennedy, *fin de siècle* historians and theorists excitedly match contemporary trends with an ominous and frenzied theory of decline. Claiming the gift of apocalyptic prophecy they switch their attention from nuclear war to natural disaster to environmental catastrophe and back again. Like Petulengros of the apocalypse they contemplate the tea leaves of an ever-darkening history, while watching their brew of dark concoctions rise to the top of the best-seller lists.

The doom-ladened approach to narrative is granted a special, millennial status by Marina Benjamin in *Living at the End of the World* (1998). Benjamin is an avid supporter of this new, priestly order of charismatics. We need our guiding lights, she argues, because in the late twentieth century we are surrounded by 'a culture of disenchantment and a climate of instability'. If 'doubt has come to characterise the terror of our age' it is because 'our senses' are 'alive to the heat given off by our failures'. The argument is glib yet grandiose. 'Primed ... for pessimism' all we are 'capable of discerning' in the future are 'signs of dreadful import', a horizon from which we 'dismiss the vistas of possibility' (4). While the ends of centuries 'are notorious for tempting fate by conjuring up apocalyptic fantasies', she continues, 'the late twentieth century' is 'different' and the 'present sense of crisis' 'justified' (6). The 1990s 'is for many people a truly frightening place' and is 'inherently more unstable, more mordant, more portentous and more climactic than its predecessors' (13). We cannot escape the 'overwhelming feeling that ... it heralds the year 2000, that mystical millennial moment which has become the focus for widespread apocalyptic belief' (14). In the act of 'constantly prospecting and speculating, hoping to catch some glimmer of how the story ends' futurologists are acceding to the view 'that our global problems are spinning out of control' (18).

In the aftermath of the Cold War, writes Benjamin, western sensibilities have proved vulnerable to the threat of the unexpected. The 1990s has been an age of 'convulsion' and 'seizure' (31, 33), its cultural paranoia, 'catastrophe theory' (Huggett 1990) and panic attacks, induced by the crash of financial markets, climate change and environmental calamity. The disasters at Bhopal, Chernobyl and the Exxon oil spill, coupled with an increase in viral epidemics gave the age a 'deeper' and 'darker' meaning and made it part of 'the apocalyptic scheme of things' (44). 'Comfort and reassurance' were 'in short supply' (25) as we came to fear both the toxic cloud that spread from Chernobyl and the hordes of migrants and rogue populations that followed in its wake once the Berlin Wall was demolished. Radioactive emission was associated in the public mind with the presence of contaminants which arrive unannounced when frameworks of containment – lead-lined structures or frontier zones – are suddenly breached. The end of containment became synonymous in the popular imagination with the removal of border controls and the uncontrollable movement of populations from Third World to First. The 'dystopic imagination' (19) which gives expression to our 'collective fears' is reflected in Ridley Scott's *Blade Runner* (1982) and James Cameron's *The Terminator* (1984), 'where cybernetically empowered forces of darkness attempt to thwart the all too human forces of light' (20). Other catastrophe stories which capture the current apocalyptic mood for Benjamin are Kim Stanley Robinson's *The Wild Shore* (1984) and Richard Preston's *The Hot Zone* (1994), a best-seller which details the outbreak of a new family of lethal airborne microbes and inspired the film *Outbreak* (1994).

Benjamin's argument is supported by a popular culture desperate to expend its Cold War energies on new external attackers. In the science-fiction cinema of the late 1980s and 1990s extraterrestrial agencies are often seen to hide behind the fragmented politics of the New World Order and take advantage of the disarray which migrant populations and airborne viruses create. Without a Strategic Defence Initiative to protect the planet, extraterrestrials work undercover to violate the bodily functions of the state and its citizens. 'A country that is founded on paranoia', says Scott Allen, must have something to be 'afraid of' and while 'the Cold War is over' Hollywood understands that in the public mind the 'anxiety' of the recent past clearly is not (Carlin 1996b, p. 13). Imprisoned for so long by the threat of Communist subversion the imagination cannot free itself from the ideological constraints of the last fifty years. In invasion narratives, the ideological imagination is remythologised by sacred fears of Communist invasion. If the process of history cannot be dispensed with, says Allen, 'that's because our two biggest fears today, terrorism and illegal immigration, tie in so closely with the film fantasy of space aliens sowing terror' and the threat to 'national identity' (13).

The search for an external source of malignancy is so great, agrees Jonathan Freedland, that a film like *Independence Day* can easily be read as 'a coded cry of panic' over the 'illegal immigrants heading for America's southern border' (Freedland 1996a, p. 7). When aliens materialise on earth, as they do in *The X-files* or *Alien Nation* (1988), the threat of abduction is dramatised by the immediate takeover of the human body. In these paranoid narratives, alien conduct resembles the behaviour of HIV, a retrovirus that smuggles itself into the body's immune system and hijacks the body's cell machinery. The body acts as host and welcomes the virus until it experiences a catastrophic breakdown in its ability to withstand the biochemical effects of infiltration. (In the *X-files* episode 'Fallen Angel', the UFO chaser, Max Fenning, is such a casualty.) In James Cameron's *Alien* (1979), and its sequel *Aliens* (1986), an alien lifeform (consisting primarily of teeth) is discovered inside an abandoned spaceship, its only function to attack and ingest animate life and to incubate its young in the body of its victims. In David Fincher's *Alien 3* (1992), incubation takes place within the body of an infected dog. Ripley (Sigourney Weaver), plays host to the alien virus, and, using a bioscanner, discovers that an alien queen is gestating inside her. As the alien's principle adversary – 'I've known you so long', she says, 'I can't remember a time when you weren't in my life' – Ripley is promised by the Company that the alien can be safely extracted and destroyed. Disbelieving the promise and realising that the Company wants the creature for its Bioweapons Division, Ripley jumps into a pit of molten metal, ending her own life and the alien threat.

For Elaine Showalter, 'alien' narratives are hysterical devices which 'clearly speak to the hidden needs and fears of a culture' (Showalter 1997, p. 203). In an insecure world, writes Showalter, malign plots and conspiracies externalise our fear of the new and are couched in narratives which terminate in scenes of sacrifice and expulsion. 'Fantasy' films which explore ideas about aliens and cover-ups, foment 'an atmosphere of conspiracy and suspicion and prevent us from claiming our full humanity as free and responsible beings'. They distract us 'from the real problems and crises of modern society' and undermine 'a respect for evidence and truth' (206).

Showalter's *Hystories* (1997) documents, in detail, the problem of hysteria, but cannot escape the malaise it exposes. *Hystories* describes how infectious hysterias are spread by narratives in the popular culture: 'self-help books, articles in newspapers and magazines, TV talk shows and series, films, the Internet, and even literary criticism' (5). It also explores the virulent paranoia 'lurking behind religious fundamentalism' (203) and the witchcraft hysteria that besets it. In the 1990s, prophetic fundamentalism, she writes, is a prime example of a discourse which attributes anxiety and distress to causes which are not medically treatable: plots, conspiracies, abduction scenarios, the presence of which confers on the patient a degree of status or chosenness. Religious zealots, she argues, are overwhelmed by 'millennial panic' (5) and rely on the presence of 'demonic scapegoats' (24) and imaginary injuries. Fundamentalism appeals to the emotionally unstable; it is a psychosomatic warning from within that the 'age of epidemics' has not, as we thought, 'passed into history' (3).

In Showalter's America, religious fundamentalism is born in the pulpit and then relayed through a 'media virus' which travels through the nation's information systems at an uncontrollable speed, inspiring the righteous with '*fin de siècle*' obsessions about 'satanic conspiracy' and 'alien infiltration' in the White House. (4) Throughout the Clinton presidency, gangsters, lesbians, the mafia and Jewish liberals were said to have invaded the White House, as had the spirits of the dead with whom Hillary Clinton communicated in her trance-like sessions with psychic advisers. The political witchhunts of the Republican Congress and the heavy breathing of its witchfinder-general, Kenneth Starr, put the virus of religious fundamentalism at the very centre of 'the hysterical hot zone' (3). Starr was one of the principle standard-bearers for 'the heroes and heroines of 1990s hysteria': the survivalist militias, the ufologists and alien abductees, the wilderness prophets and catastrophists, the purveyors of 'microtales', each of whom lie at the centre of a boiling 'crucible of virulent hysterias' (5).

Showalter's *Hystories* portrays a society burdened by fabulism and surfeited with disorders and viral contagions that interact in 'a seething mix of paranoia, anxiety, and anger' (26). Religious hysteria, as she defines it, is the right-wing answer to 'hysteresis', the term used by Jean Baudrillard in an essay which he published in the late 1980s (Baudrillard 1998, p. 115). In 'The End of US Power', Baudrillard equated 'hysteresis' with impotence and dementia, and saw little in the way of sexual resistance or 'orgy' (113) in the face of executive complacency. Reagan's America, argued Baudrillard, thrived on the basis of 'inertia' (115) and it simulated ideological power through 'the hysterical euphoria of the menopause' (117). Political energies were at the 'face-lift stage' (115) and in the post-Cold War era the motivation for new philosophies and ideological practices had been terminated. Since 'human rights had been won everywhere' and the world was almost entirely liberated', there was 'nothing left to fight for' (112). The menopausal presidency of Reagan had 'sapped the nation's energy' (117), accelerating 'the disappearance of ideologies' and the 'convalescence that grand ideas '[were] going through' (115). In a world of 'weakening ... forces' and grand contesting passions, America was damaged by its own 'fragile meta-stability' (109). As a body weakened from lack of exercise, the country was at risk from 'the disappearance of resistances and antibodies' (116) and 'the loss of immune defences in an overprotected organism' (116–17).

In *Hystories*, prophetic religions and patriarchal agendas have merged with 'more generalised paranoias' (Showalter 1997, p. 5) to cauterise the spread of impotence and ageing. The moral agendas of fundamentalism, says Showalter, are driven by a tide of new emotional energy and 'an atmosphere of conspiracy and suspicion' (206). Re-masculinisation is the dominant emotion. The male hysteria of the Christian zealots – from the Promise Keepers to the patriot militias – is a way of resisting senility and fatigue and of countering the debilitating influence of those who betray signs of womanly weakness.

Narratives fearing loss of potency can often be seen in the context of a search for political authority among those who claim the gift of intuition. Elaine Showalter is not immune to this fear and her academic authority is threatened by rival hysterians who claim to be visionary but lack her scholarly gifts and expertise. Showalter describes herself as a specialist 'in understanding and interpreting stories' about 'hysteria'. As a historian of medicine she believes she has found the way to correctly 'read' (6) and understand psychiatric illness. *Hystories* is her resistance narrative. It is designed to stem the erosion of authority from those who provide enlightened explanations for 'the appearance of disease' (14) to those who invent supernatural explanations in order to legitimise an emotional disorder. It is based, therefore, on the need for a clear understanding of the difference between 'therapeutic narratives' and the 'destructive histories' (13) of those who use an elaborate framework of plots and conspiracies to disguise their ignorance and deceive their opponents. In this sense, her work is deeply authoritarian.

Showalter understands religious fundamentalism as an episodic and irrational condition. The product of a unique alchemy, she represents it as a *fin de siècle* expression, a figment of the age in which it appears and an end-of-century apocalyptic contagion. Fundamentalism, for her, lacks the ability to sustain itself in moments of relative prosperity and mid-term calm. The right-wing attack on President Clinton is not the product of traditional Presbyterianism. It is a witchhunt conducted by the emotionally maladjusted; a deranged outburst of the sexually prurient desperate to satisfy their millennial needs. Clinton's impeachment reveals nothing to Showalter about the southern Baptist attitude to women or the expectations of a righteous patriarchy or the workings of the Antichrist in the Oval Office. The hounding of Clinton is a disease of the mind, the origin of which can be traced to the workings of a paranoid style in conservative Christianity.

Throughout *Hystories*, religious fundamentalism is referred to as an 'imaginary illness', the symptoms of which are 'new hysteria', 'psychogenic' disease, '*fin-de-siècle*' anxiety and panic (4). As one of the many 'hysterical syndromes of the 1990s' fundamentalism is on a par with multiple personality disorder, Gulf War Syndrome and chronic fatigue syndrome. Like the narratives of alien abductees, it speaks 'to the hidden needs and fears of a culture' (203) whose mind is possessed by the psychic demons that lurk within our millennial unconscious. Fundamentalists who rush to embrace the millennium, says Showalter, are driven not by a memory of Protestant history, but by mass hysteria. As an illness generated by the anxiety of death, religious fundamentalism is an apt 'metaphor for the *fin-de-siècle* sensibility' (83) of the late twentieth century.

The secular view of fundamentalism that we find in *Hystories* is a gross distortion of a Protestantism whose millennial traditions are the sober outcome of an expectant faith, and a religion which derives its inspiration from a dispensational reading of the Bible. (Richard Hofstadter stressed the importance of Bible reading as long ago as 1962 in his book, *Anti-Intellectualism in American Life*.)[1] Fundamentalism and its New Age variants, says Richard Jenkyns, are excited by the millennium, but are not reduced to a vengeful frenzy as they wait to celebrate the arrival of Armageddon. 'People now seem to be rather less anxious than they used to be', Jenkyns argues. And they are certainly not as anxious as they were thirty or forty years ago when many of them did believe 'that the world would soon come to an end' and that mankind 'had the power to destroy itself entirely' (Jenkyns 1998, p. 4).

Doom-laden narratives of hatred and despair and scenarios of hysteria are only one part of the grand narrative of fundamentalism. Beneath the fear of the Antichrist there lies, as we have seen, a fascination with creative deviance and a compelling interest in the beauty of sin. But the lure of sin can have no meaning in a world where 'the future has lost its lustre' and 'has degenerated into a land of foreboding' (Benjamin 1998, p. 1). Visionary excitement is an integral part of God's new order, sinful or not, and endtime believers who embrace the apocalypse are eager to accelerate their spiritual deliverance in the aftermath of conflict. For the millennialist, the future is an intoxicant not a depressant, a necessary challenge which occasions release but does not condemn millennial believers, irretrievably, to 'convulsion' (31) or 'seizure' (33).

In the 1990s, says Ed Vulliamy, the United States awaits the millennium 'with more zeal than any other' and its 'mystical faith remains a powerful, often frenzied propeller of everyday life' (Vulliamy 1997b, p. 2). Millennial zeal takes many forms and demonstrates phenomenal ingenuity in its desire to conclude, what Paul Boyer calls, 'God's providential oversight of history' (Boyer 1992, p. ix). In the cross-cultural atmosphere of the late twentieth century religion has acquired a less formal appearance and incorporates a huge variety of endtime narratives and 'syncretic' traditions (Bunting 1996, p. 2). In many of these narratives the 'final eschatological consummation' (Boyer

1992, p. ix) of history is achieved by blending together the church-going aspects of pre-millennialism – the Rapture, the Second Coming, the Tribulation, the apocalypse – with the prophecy traditions of visionary communities outside the church: ethnic, astrological, transcendental, neo-pagan. The ceremonial vigour of these new belief structures, together with the widespread interest in apocalyptic experience in traditional Christian communities, gives millions of Americans the opportunity, says Boyer, to 'weave Bible passages into highly imaginative end-time scenarios'. It also allows individuals and communities who are sensitive to 'world trends' and 'whose world view is ... shaped to some degree by residual or latent concepts of eschatology' (3), to construct a highly personalised faith from the fragments of Christian dispensationalism, eastern religion, neo-paganism and psychic chic.

'The apocalyptic' says Charles B. Strozier, 'is at the centre of [the] New Age' and 'the New Age apocalyptic evokes fundamentalist notions of the end times' (Strozier 1994, p. 247). Along with Catherine Albanese, Strozier believes that 'specific images from fundamentalist endtime theory – like that of Antichrist, Tribulation, even the Rapture – creep into New Age theory' (247). The idea is confirmed for us by Melanie McGrath in her brilliant account of New Age travelling in Arizona and New Mexico, *Motel Nirvana* (1995). McGrath shows us a community of 'seekers' who live on the edge of the 'enlightened desert' but remain firmly wedded to fears of psychic invasion and 'aliens feeding on human energies' (McGrath 1995, p. 19). Princess Dux's opinion that the New Age 'is coming pretty soon' and that the United States 'is programmed to become the world's first crystal matrix paradise' (22–3) cannot disguise what most travellers fear most. As McGrath puts it:

Haven't I heard? The planet is on the brink of an apocalyptic phase, during which storms and floods and earthquakes and all kinds of natural disasters will kill most of the world's population – especially the unspiritual ones – leading those remaining to a new era of peace and higher consciousness. (21)

In the rush to reconstruct millennialism at the end of the twentieth century, fringe religions and new religious practices utilise many of the traditional features of Protestant orthodoxy, including Seventh Day Adventist and Millerite belief. The failure of apocalyptic expectation in military theatres like the Gulf does little to undermine the importance of the Rapture or the advent of the apocalyptic, nor does it diminish the symbolic importance of the Jews as we approach the endtimes. Attachment to the wilderness as a sacred domain – an idea central to millennial belief since the seventeenth century – remains strong. As does an eco-theology that sees the wilderness as home to a saving remnant (the Children of Israel), who are 'hidden' but accessible in places yet to be encountered by adventurers.

Significant changes, however, have taken place in dispensationalism, particularly among those who are looking to take control of their lives and are less willing to focus their spiritual aspirations on church-directed, millennialist schemes. 'New Religious Movements', as Anthony Storr describes them (Storr 1996, p. 18), do not attach political explanations to spiritual prophecies nor are they fixated with the saving of Israel as a terrestrial site in the new millennium. In New Age religion, Israel lies outside the immediate reference of sacred territory, as do churches that pin their faith on political schemes, only to end up disappointing their followers. New Age millenarians [2] abhor the formally political (like war in the Middle East) as a route to the endtimes and are generally unwilling to mortgage their life to an external process over which they have no control. New millenarians seek a blueprint for salvation in cosmic rather than political theatres. As a basis for prophecy, they regard political events – the return of the Jews to Palestine, the coming invasion of Israel by the Arabs, the emergence of a new Russian Confederacy – as subject to unnatural, external control. Sceptical of the church's inability to disentangle itself from a Christ who never comes and a political process which promises things that never come to pass, New Religious Movements avoid the Second Coming and look for answers in cosmic deities and earthly messiahs. As a major casualty of the 1990s, Christ's chronic indecisiveness disqualifies him as a messenger of New Age redemption.

A good example is Peter Hyam's *End of Days* (1999), a millennial thriller which relies heavily on Old Testament motifs and the intervention of new charismatics with biblical aspirations. In the film Jericho Cain finds himself drawn into a world of supernatural intrigue when he discovers that the fate of mankind rests with a woman who is pursued by an evil demon. Confronted by a villain whom he cannot defeat with conventional methods, Jericho desperately searches for a way to prevail. In doing so, he must regain faith in himself, spiritually, and overcome the tragic loss of his family. Issued by Universal Studios as the definitive millennium film, *End of Days* was released to the public on the weekend of the last Thanksgiving (24 November 1999). The release date contains echoes of the Last Supper onto which is grafted an apocalyptic motif. Instead of the crucifixion we have Armageddon, a period of violence which coincides with the destruction of the Antichrist, not as a result of the Second Coming but the heroic actions of a born-again American (Arnold Schwarzenegger).

Gore Vidal's *Live from Golgotha* further illustrates the need for decisive action. Saint begins his sales pitch for Christ in Asia Minor with a message that the Day of Judgement and the Kingdom of God will 'take place just as soon as He [returns] from a few days with His father, God, in Heaven' (Vidal 1992, p. 25). Christ's prolonged absence is recognised by Timothy as 'the Great Embarrassment' of western history, something that cannot be glossed-over by Saint's on-stage dissembling. 'Despite His promise', Jesus has not only not come back, says Timothy, 'he has yet to make his return during the two thousand dismal years that separate' (31) the early Christians from the latter-day evangelists. Jesus has either abandoned 'His mission to the soon-to-be late great planet Earth' or God has refused Him permission to return, leaving the evangelists and their congregations 'on tenterhooks' (26).

If Timothy does not 'know how you can keep the Message [of the millennium] alive without an Estimated Time of Arrival' (26), charismatic leaders and cult messiahs have provided a radical answer. Where God procrastinates, the leaders of New Age movements initiate; where He appears the vicarious trickster who has allowed us to believe in His son's return, today's gurus are purposeful and intimate, designing alternative versions of the Rapture to that of 'the "sky" God of conventional Christianity' (Storr 1996, p. 5). New Age religion places 'the creative and efficacious role of human beings at the center of any possibility for transformation', says Charles B. Strozier. For the prophecy writer Douglas Grant we are all able to fulfil our own second comings by 'reviving' our 'inner Christ-selves'. Since all events, says Grant, are influenced by human thought only individual negativity and low self-esteem will stop this from happening. If we attempt to channel our God-like energies, we will 'attract energies and entities of the same Christ level of vibration and beingness' and repel 'lesser energies in our force field ... caus[ing] new levels of purification to be achieved' (quoted in Strozier 1944, pp. 240–1).

For the followers of cult leaders like Luc Jourret, Marshall H. Applewhite, David Koresh and Jim Jones, the price that worshippers pay for clairvoyance is irresistible and irreversible. Salvation through suicide is the route we take to Armageddon and the journey that enables us to encounter the supernatural on a higher level. As leader of the Order of the Solar Temple, Luc Jourret promised, in 1994, to take his followers to the planet Sirius and that their suicides would transform them into 'Christ-like' solar beings. In 1997 Marshall H. Applewhite claimed for himself God-like powers and told his followers that 'if you want to go to heaven, I can take you through that gate'. In choosing the 'wilful exit of the body' (Gledhill 1997, p. 3), the Heaven's Gate community was promised total release, physical as well as spiritual, an experience of futuristic bliss that involved the practice of Kabbala, a Zionist sexual theology that was popular in the later years of the 1990s with California's celebrities.

The fate of the 'prophet' David Koresh at the compound of the Branch Davidian's ranch in Waco, Texas, in 1993, offers conclusive proof of the appeal of terminal leadership in an expectant age. As a New Age Gnostic who considered himself, like Applewhite, co-eternal with God, Koresh preached the American right to untrammelled liberty, but did so in a monstrous way. According to Malise Ruthven, the 'boot-camp' control that Koresh exerted over his followers was absolute and his status as Messiah was such that his followers 'believed they were carrying out God's instructions' and that 'to refuse the prophet was tantamount to disobeying a divine command'. Like the Reverend Jim Jones in Jonestown, Guyana, David Koresh, 'translated Kingdom Come into Kingdom Now', says Ruthven. He was able to persuade his followers that God had made them a chosen remnant for those 'eight million Americans' who 'believe that Revelation holds the key to an imminent catastrophe in which they will be saved supernaturally while the rest of the world perishes' (Ruthven 1993a, p. 15). As a post-millennialist, Koresh translated the futuristic kingdom of heaven into a kingdom on earth, one that pre-empted Christ's unfathomable plan of return. Salvation through suicide would satisfy the needs of rapturous believers who had waited long enough for terminal departure and were more than willing to receive assistance through 'the enigmatic pulse beat of the messianic' (Steiner 1990, p. 47).

The New Age challenge to the core narrative of western civilisation and the questioning of Christ's role as a suitable messiah for the 1990s is taken up by Jim Crace in his highly acclaimed novel, *Quarantine* (1997). *Quarantine* engages in a critical reappraisal of Christ's early ministry, presenting us with a weak-bladdered dreamer, a bumpkin who undertakes his forty-day retreat into the wilderness by abstaining naively from food and drink. Whereas Norman Mailer's 'Son', in *The Gospel According to the Son* (1997), drinks copiously and purifies himself in the wilderness in training for his combat with the devil, Crace's Gally is ruined by ignorance and a lack of basic biological knowledge. Christ's sojourn in the wilderness can only be classed as a fraud, says Crace, 'because everybody knows that if you're in the desert for 40 days without food or drink you will die' (Wroe 1997, p. 3). Gally is lacking common sense and purges himself in the wrong location. His Christianity is a lie. In truth, says Crace, Gally never came out of the wilderness alive and was physically defeated by the Judean scrub. For 2,000 years he has been the author of a ministry that has survived as a hoax. Christ exists only in the marketing. Outside of that, says Vidal's Timothy, he is the 'Great Embarrassment' who refuses to return for fear of the consequences.

In Michael Tolkin's extraordinary film *The Rapture* (1991), the value of the wilderness as a place where Christian contact is made – and spiritual enlightenment found – at moments of crisis, is exposed as wilful propaganda. God is a cheat, a whimsical joker who plays with his followers. Sharon, bored by a promiscuous sex life and a dead-end job as a telesales operator, finds God through the church. Convinced that the Second Coming is imminent Sharon sees the Rapture as the final solution to her problems. Desperate to be reunited in heaven with her murdered husband, she tries to accelerate her spiritual departure by committing suicide. Fully believing she will be 'lifted up' by the Second Coming she and her six-year old daughter go into the wilderness to await the moment when He will appear to gather the pair of them. She waits, thinking she knows when, and how, God will call her. But God refuses to perform according to her timetable and does not honour His biblical prophecies. In an act of devotion and divine surrender to God, Sharon murders her daughter by shooting her in the head. God answers, rapturing her daughter into the air to live with Him in the heavens. Even though she has acted in good faith, anticipating His arrival and her bodily resurrection, Sharon is abandoned.

God's failure to act in accordance with His biblical plan (1 Thessalonians 14: 16.17) frustrates His believers who, as committed Christians, blindly put their trust in Him and sacrifice their flesh and blood in pursuit of eternal life. Those who follow the path of righteousness (as pre-tributionalists, like Sharon, do) can end up without warning in a desert of despair. If Pauline testimony is partly responsible for the delusion, God is also complicit in the failure, allowing the fantasy of vicarious pre-millennialism to continue unabated. Sharon is the casualty of God's disinterested plan and His indifferent Son, but she is also the victim of a deluded church which exists in His Name, and looks for signs of an 'any moment Rapture'.

Nancy Ammerman shows us the basis of this delusion in her study of Southside Gospel Church. 'Believers relate to God by contract: If I do this, God will do that', writes Ammerman (Ammerman 1987, p. 41). Since God is 'predictable' – which he is not – salvation becomes a matter of 'exchange' between a belief in 'right living' and 'things' guaranteed in the life 'to come'. The doctrine of a binding contract or covenant covers everything from safe travel to health. 'God's promises form a kind of rule book for explaining the way the world must work.' 'Believers are confident that God will keep his promises because their God is exact, orderly, and predictable.' The danger, as Sharon discovers to her cost, is in 'having an explanation for everything', even though this 'is a vital part of being a fundamentalist' (42). Those who see no alternative to the Lord's quick return become fixated by His promises. 'The way things are going, he's got to [return]', says one woman. 'How worse can it get? He promised it, didn't He?' (45).

Contractual relationships cannot disguise the desperation people feel about Christ's continuing absence from their lives as God's only son. Having said this, Christians have been reluctant to voice their suspicions in public about Christ's inability to arrive on cue. Doubts about His chronic indecisiveness are often the subject of New Age discussions but are rarely expressed outside the church. The one exception is Barry Downing's *The Bible and Flying Saucers* (1968), a rare example of Christian literature which attempts to engage in bridge-building between the unique Christ of 1 Thessalonians 14 and a Christ whose limited gifts have been shared out among other visiting deities.

In Downing's study, Christ is a saviour with a much-diminished status, his importance no greater than that of other cosmic presences that have appeared on earth. In Downing's reading God appears to have anticipated the problem with His Son and already decided not to employ him in a singular role. As an extraterrestrial sent among us to rid the world of sin and wickedness, Christ, says Downing, is an unexceptional visitor, one who has spent His time on earth, and, like other visitors, made His name in wilderness locations. While the wilderness is an important location in which 'contactees' can undergo a spiritual experience, it is not, in any sense, Christ's unique domain. The wilderness has long been a place where chosen individuals are able to acquaint themselves with cosmic interventionists, from Moses onwards – those who come in God's name and arrive unassisted by God's only Son.

In Downing's study spiritual visitation is a recurrent feature of the Old and New Testament and provides a valuable source of revelation and assistance to prophetic messengers. Angelic aliens, writes Downing, speak to Moses on Mount Sinai and allow him to go 'aboard the UFO' to receive the stone tablets and the specifications for 'the construction of the Tabernacle' (Downing 1968, p. 107). An Unidentified Flying Object is responsible for speaking to Elijah outside the cave. It is the source of the voice at the Transfiguration and Christ. And it is the 'bright cloud' (155) that hovers over Paul on the road to Damascus. Extraterrestrials, Downing argues, are instrumental in granting the ancient Israelites safe passage out of Egypt and in creating a hybrid diaspora which travels in parallel towards the promised land: one in outerspace, the other on a land-based journey towards the Americas.

The heart of the Old Testament religion is Exodus, says Downing. Exodus tells us 'that something resembling a space vehicle ... led the Hebrew people out of Egypt up to the "Red Sea", hovered over the sea while it parted, and then led them into the wilderness, where an "angel" proceeded to give them religious instructions' (9). Downing's theory about the arrival of an Unidentified Flying Object at a 'unique' moment in Jewish history leads him to the conclusion 'that the parting of the Red Sea was deliberately caused by intelligent beings in some sort of space vehicle' (9). A community of saints and angels then formed a sexual and spiritual partnership (in advance of Christ) with the ancient Israelites on their flight out of Egypt. They also decided to reconvene in the earth's atmosphere in order to effect a later 'resurrection', in anticipation of – or even in lieu of – His Second Coming (203).

The evacuation and salvation of good people by flying saucers and the cleansing of the world in the coming apocalypse is central to Downing's thesis. He, like other millennial visionaries, bases his predictions and endtime scenarios on traditional Christian beliefs which describe the Rapture, and the period referred to as the Tribulation, as a sign from heaven that worldly catastrophe is about to take place. Downing's speculations actively seek and assimilate 'Christian ideas' and are also a 'composite and repository' of 'other belief systems' (Wojcik 1997, pp. 184–5) including occult teachings and the popular culture of present and previous eras. Downing suggests that those who testify to alien abduction also experience a form of resurrection similar to that which occurred with the Israelites on the eastern shore of the Red Sea. The anti-gravitational, electromagnetic beam that changed the molecular composition of the sea and caused it to part is of the same forcefield that allows abductees to experience their own preliminary 'resurrection'. Like the Red Sea phenomenon, abduction is a dress rehearsal for His believers who will soon be 'caught up' and transported by angels 'to meet the Lord in the air' (Downing 1968, p. 207).

Alien abduction and 'resurrection' narratives are versions of Puritan captivity narratives in which the 'hidden' Jews of the world are no longer the unregenerate Indians in the forest but cosmic messengers who inhabit the wilderness of outer space. These cosmic Jews are already saved but pay homage to the myth of the Wandering Jew and willingly share his exiled condition. Spiritually attuned through DNA sampling to the mind and body of ancient Israel, these extraterrestrials have a spiritual link with other elect races, especially the people of the United States, where Jews have migrated in considerable numbers.

In his work Downing makes no reference to the importance of the Red Sea in Native American folklore, but he could have done. Daniel Butrick, who was appointed missionary to the Cherokees in 1817, and who worked as an anthropologist with the Indian tribes of Georgia,

North Carolina, Tennessee and Alabama, recounts a version of the Red Sea by one of his Cherokee informants named Nutsawi:

Ye ho wah told the leader of the Indians that he must go to a country which he had given to them, but they would have to pass some great water before they got there ... They were flying from their enemies. But as soon as they came to a great water, Ye ho wah told their leader to strike the water with a rod and it should divide and given them a passage through and then flow together and stop their enemies. (McLoughlin and Conser, Jun., 1987, p. 254)

The Cherokees believed they had been specifically selected by Ye ho wah (Jehovah) to inhabit the earth 'before the flood'. (In Cherokee folklore, writes William G. McLoughlin, it is claimed that 'Man was made of red earth. The first man was red' (254).) Downing's thesis suggests, but does not explain, why the Red Sea was a place of celebration in which to commemorate the peculiar destiny of the first people on earth. Perhaps Shem's colour (redness) was crucial in the election of the Jews (who were already Indian) and that 'crossing a body of water set them free from their sinful past and ... toward a new future' (Downing 1968, p. 137). If a number of Jews subsequently lost their faith on earth (or, at least, lost some of it), the extraterrestrials did not. It was they who imprinted themselves with the genetic characteristics of the Lost Tribes of Israel and, in their search for a promised land, fulfilled their needs in a cosmic wilderness.

The presence of an extraterrestrial community of saints roaming the Heavens in pursuit of a new cosmic Jerusalem inevitably diminishes the importance of Christ in the coming endtimes. If the Jews have already been instructed in the ways of religion at a time previous to Christ's ministry, then the originality of His miraculous presence is immediately subverted. According to Downing, Jesus was never more than a spokesman from another planet and even admitted he was 'not of this world' (John 8: 23). Jesus was part of a much larger plan, writes Downing:

Jesus often claimed to have come from another world; he is reported to have had contact with beings from another world, such as during his Resurrection from the dead. He accepted the teachings of Moses, and claimed to be part of a whole plan which included the Old Testament religion. After Jesus had finished his ministry on earth, the Bible reports that he was taken off into space in something which might be a space vehicle. (19)

If, as Downing claims, 'God made himself known through "angels", beings from another world', and if Jesus was one of these other 'beings', His capacity to appear in our world unassisted and to disappear back to where he came from unaided, seems unlikely. Since 'the Bible clearly claims' that '"unidentified flying objects" played a significant role in the development of the Hebrew–Christian faith' (35–6), Christ must be seen as one of a number of 'superior beings from another world' who, through their intervention, have made 'significant contributions at various times' (36) to world history.

In R. L. Dione's *God Drives a Flying Saucer* (1969) extraterrestrial visitation is a common occurrence in the prophecies and miracles of the Old and New Testament. As the manifestation of an advanced technology 'flying-saucer sightings' (Dione 1973, p. 51) allow us to connect the 'rain-producing' (84) UFO that appears in the Third Book of Kings, the 'hovering UFO' that appears in a cloud to Moses in the last chapter of Exodus and 'the whirlwind' (80) that visits Ezekiel 'as an agent of God' (79) and deposits its passengers ('four living creatures resembling men' (80)). For Dione, the uniqueness of Christ is significantly diminished by a continuing narrative of miraculous intervention, from Moses on Sinai to the vision which appeared to Our Lady of Guadalupe in Mexico in 1531.

Dione's message is more subversive than that of Downing's. His God engages our attention because he mimicks the technological Antichrist and takes on the persona of a scientific interventionist. Satan's love of control and interference – bodily interruption through microchip implantation, genetic fingerprinting and facial tattooing – is rivalled by the work of a 'master' technologist who practices abduction, miracle cures, fertility rituals and thought control. As 'leader' of the 'technologists' (15) God imposes 'divine inspiration' and signals his arrival through 'a technological device on board a nearby UFO'. God always 'refers to this device as the Holy Spirit' (77).

The most spectacular example of the power of the Holy Spirit, writes Dione, occurs during the Immaculate Conception when the angel Gabriel hypnotises Mary before injecting her with a hypodermic needle containing some of God's sperm. Artificial insemination and the birth of baby Jesus, says Dione, is one of the many ways that God employs 'the incomprehensible technology of His super society' in order 'to impress the people of earth' (100). Like the Antichrist, God makes himself 'immortal through technology' but gives His 'flying-saucer occupants' (3), such as Gabriel, responsibility 'for the scriptures, prophecies and miracles of the Christian religion' (viii). During the Transfiguration of Christ, the technology of the Holy Spirit is, once again, a resplendent force. In Matthew 17: 3–5, Jesus takes the three apostles to the top of a high mountain where His face and clothes 'shine like the sun'. Jesus and the apostles see Moses and Elias talking together until 'a bright cloud' overshadows them, and the voice of God is heard. 'Here, in one package', writes Dione, 'are all the elements of UFO technology: the luminous being, the induced hallucination, the electromagnetic voices and the luminous cloud' (77).

In UFO lore, aliens are both our ancient ancestors and a futuristic version of what human beings will become as we continue to evolve. In some millennialist narratives UFOs are our future descendants who have travelled back in time to reassure us of our future recovery at a time of threatened extinction. They are the counterpart of God and fulfil many of the traditional functions of deities. What they offer, says Harold Bloom in *Omens of Millennium* (1997), is the image of an immense, immortal figure, 'Anthropos', an angelic being that can never die and that achieves an immortality worthy of America. The alien is the essential gnosis for our age, an untrammelled libertarian who is co-eternal with God, the epiphanic source of humanity's salvation (Bloom 1997, p. 10) as we approach the millennium.

In the cosmology of the Raelians (founded in 1973 by Claude Vorilhon) human beings were created by extraterrestrials called the 'Elohim', who fashioned humankind in their own image through a synthesis of DNA in their laboratories. Raelians promote the idea that humanity will be transformed and saved not by the Second Coming of Christ but the arrival of superhuman beings. Raelians also use an earth-based messenger, Rael (Claude Vorilhon), who tells us of the return to earth of all the prophets (Jesus, Buddha, Mohammed, Joseph Smith) and the salvation that awaits us if an Elohim embassy is built in Jerusalem. The suggestion here is that the Elohim are Jews who have taken to the cosmos. They will only consider a return to earth to save us from planetary annihilation should we accept their teaching from a seat of earthly learning. Jesus, a reform Jew, is one of the many inventions whom the Elohim have created by impregnating female earthlings in order to control the religious life of the planet. His teachings must be considered not in isolation, but alongside those of other prophets and desert visionaries.

In Alison Lurie's novel *Imaginary Friends* (1967), Christ has disappeared from the cosmos and been replaced by the repro. messiah, Ro, resident of the Planet Varna and flying-saucer traveller. Ro's use of spiritual electricity and interstellar communication replicates that of the extraterrestrials on the banks of the Red Sea. Ro goes in search of the Truth-seekers, an American spiritualist community who receive cosmic messages through Verena, a sexually promiscuous teenage psychic who lives with her aunt in upstate New York. Verena's announcement that the 'teachers from Varna' are expected to arrive and minister to those 'in a fit spiritual condition' is directed at her own followers. It is also meant for the novel's Wandering Jew, Roger Zimmern, a spiritually confused college professor who '"can speak languages"' and has '"travelled to places all over the world already"' (Lurie 1967, p. 132). Zimmern may be a descendent of the Lost Tribes of Israel and (to use Downing's paradigm) already in receipt of cosmic energy from Red Sea UFOs.

Downing's study, *The Bible and Flying Saucers*, was published twelve months after Lurie's novel and employs similar motifs and symbols. Cosmic infusion, says Downing, has occurred biblically on two separate occasions: first at the Red Sea and, secondly, on Mount Sinai, when Moses 'went to the top of the mountain to converse with a being in the "cloud"'. Moses 'seems to have gone aboard the UFO' ... to receive the 'stone tablets' from 'the being' who manned it' (Downing 1968, p. 107). The 'thick cloud' he is forced to walk through on Sinai reappears over Sophis the night of 'the Coming' but prevents the Varnians from making contact with the Truth Seekers. Without the 'divine nearness' of their 'great light' the Truth Seekers are unable to receive from the Varnians the benefits of 'inflowing spiritual electricity' (179) or 'the blinding radiance of their being' (131). In Downing's book, a similar 'radiance' transforms Moses into a prophet of such luminescent power that as soon as he leaves the ambience of the spacecraft on Sinai, 'the skin on his face shone' (130). In upstate New York, this is not possible. The Varnians are thwarted by an atmosphere which is as heavy as 'mashed potatoes' and an ozone layer 'thick' and 'dirtied' (216). Verena's complaint that the 'true inner being' (135) of the world is 'congested' (134) by suburban afflictions has led her to 'expose' some of Zimmern's 'flesh surfaces' (136) so that the current can enter him and release his pent-up inhibitions. Sexual fantasies stimulate ecological fantasies as Verena encourages her followers to undress and 'rid' themselves of any 'organic fibrous materials' that are 'unclean' (156) and to burn their clothes in the house where they worship. Verena's decision to return to nature in an acrid, smoke-filled room in Sophis is tragically misguided, for it involves the use of a ceremony that creates atmospheric obstruction for the Varnians, as well as 'fatigue, discomfort, disappointment' (216) for the soot-stained communicants of Sophis. The retreat into the 'freezing' (210) air of winter is meant as a signal to the new 'messiah' (126), but does nothing to cement the old relationship between physical isolation and wilderness religion that extraterrestrials appear to cherish.

Chanellers and mediums with the best track record in receiving and transmitting inspirational messages manage to incorporate into their ministry a true appreciation of the importance of wilderness. Among the more successful, was the 'desert visionary' George Van Tassel who lived at Giant Rock, California. From 1954 to 1977 contactees under the leadership of Tassel gathered annually at the Giant Rock Spacecraft Convention in the shadow of a huge boulder in the Mojave Desert. Tassel is purported to have received messages from the Ashtar Command Pantheon, a syncretic community of gods, goddesses and spiritual masters from diverse planets, who provided warnings of imminent catastrophe and the destruction of the planet. In 1954 George King, founder of the Aetherius Society, claimed to have received similar messages about the possible threat of nuclear destruction and the salvation that was available to the planet through prayer and psychic energy discharge. In other messages the Aetherians were told to gather at certain sacred, spiritually charged mountains to await rescue. This ceremonial gathering in the wilderness, reminiscent of the enlightenment that awaited Moses on Mount Sinai, is also favoured by the Church Universal and Triumphant, a syncretic cult in California which follows instructions from Ascended Masters (including Jesus) on other planets, one of which was to purchase 1,200 acres of land in Montana to stimulate purification and enlightenment.

As the third millennium dawns, says Daniel Wojcik, the fascination with UFOs and alien beings becomes more intense. The increased frequency of 'sightings and encounters' with 'extraterrestrials' reflects the emergence of 'apocalyptic anxieties' (Wojcik 1997, p. 174), but also the inability of traditional Christianity to channel these anxieties through the orthodox routes of biblical prophecy and dispensational theology. The current 'demonisation' of UFOs and extraterrestrials by prophecy believers, like Hal Lindsey, 'illustrates the extent to which' this 'alternative mythology of creation and salvation poses a threat to Christian fundamentalist views', even though much of what it proposes is a direct plagiarism of the Second Coming of Christ and the use of the wilderness as a sacred site. In Christian fundamentalism, 'UFOs and ETs', says Wojcik, 'are devils, fallen angels, and satanic manifestations that will lead to the rise of a global religion of the Antichrist' (207), while those who promote such beliefs on earth are 'counterfeit' (97) ministers in the pay of the False Prophet.

In Robert Zemeckis's film *Contact* (1997), the UFO threat to fundamentalism is a cosmic conspiracy between maverick science and the counterfeit ministers of extraterrestrialism who, at the start of the third millennium, reach out to alien lifeforms in obscure constellations. In fundamentalism, the ufologists' route to an understanding of God's plan in the afterlife begins in a profane desert where technological contact is established with fraudulent emissaries of the Antichrist. Religious extremists sabotage a government-funded, deep-space project, inspired by a blueprint based on alien physics, but cannot prevent a privately funded probe from taking off in Japan.

This experiment is the work of a dying billionaire ufologist (John Hurt), who recruits the gifted, but wayward, astrophysicist, Ellie Arroway (Jodie Foster), to undertake a pioneering journey on his behalf. The entrepreneur is the founder of Haddon Industries and his appearance mirrors that of Marshall H. Applewhite, leader of the 1997 Heaven's Gate suicide cult in San Diego (to which reference is made in the film). While Applewhite decides to make his own contact with aliens in the tail of the comet Hale-Bopp, Haddon prefers the use of technology to launch Foster on a separate journey into the outer reaches of the cosmos. For a fraction of a second Foster is propelled into deep space and is witness to a futuristic afterlife of astonishing beauty and diversity. Fundamentalist anger is aroused by the role of President Clinton (who plays himself in the film), as a keen supporter of cosmic exploration and encounter. Clinton wants to fulfil the dreams of his mentor John F. Kennedy, and roll back the frontiers of space science. His treachery is displayed by his decision to retain, as a spiritual adviser, an ex-Jesuit priest, Father Palmer Joss, who finds himself sexually attracted to Ellie Arroway, the virgin frontierswoman.

As an astral fairytale, *Contact* is overloaded with self-conscious moments and portentous revelation, none of it helped by an over-wrought performance from Jodie Foster that includes endless foetal poses, screwed-up facial expressions, stress-induced stutters. In spite of the acting, *Contact* is a film that touches on the spirituality of the 1990s, exploring its need to believe, in what Harold Bloom refers to as 'Angels, Dreams and Resurrection' (Bloom 1997). It also celebrates, says Ed Vulliamy, a theology of the wilderness as sacred space, a belief that the search for extraterrestrial life in the desert regions taps into an old 'frontier-born distrust of authority and "official" versions of truth' (Vulliamy 1997b, p. 2).

The vulnerability of Christianity to new, experiential, post-biblical faiths has as much to do with the demand for salvation as the seething and confusing denominationalism of the age. New Age religions are unwilling to rely on a long-term plan of rescue and actively seek new ways to accelerate planetary evacuation. For conservative Christians, counterfeit ministers such as gurus and channellers, plagiarise the Rapture and offer the uninitiated the degenerate thrill of disappearance in the cosmos. The irony is that while prophecy enthusiasts accuse ufologists of entering a state of 'endtimes delusion' (202) it is they who first introduced the idea of spiritual abduction in referring to the Rapture as the 'The Big Snatch'. Even Cotton Mather found it necessary in 1690 to try 'his hand at the intriguing game of soul snatching' with a Boston Jew named Frazier in the hope that his 'trickery' (Eichorn 1978, p. 7) could bring about a Christian conversion.

Pre-millennialism is easily outdone by ufology because of its unre-lenting emphasis on Bible reading as a route to salvation. The problem with Bible study is that it promotes passive scholarly experience over physical and sensual knowledge. It offers an appreciation of signs and portents, not through personal witness, but the prophecies of those whose narratives are blessed with abstract insight. Ufology, on the other hand, encourages the righteous to abandon their books in favour of spiritual ecology and a dynamic experience of visitation in the wilderness. In ufology, nature is a place of cosmic performance where the believer can acquaint himself with the divinity of a hidden Israel, and can strive to achieve his own salvation in outer space. Here, the natural world becomes, once again, what it was for Moses; an invigorating theatre in which the spirit responds to the benevolent interventionism of a watching cosmos.

The crash of an alleged spacecraft in the desert near Roswell, New Mexico, on Independence Day, 1947, may have something to do with this. The cults that have grown up around this event believe that space aliens perished in the crash. As a result, the location in which the aliens chose to make contact with earth is of sacred significance. The crash-landing of these space gods is usually regarded as sacrificial as well as an attempt at planetary salvation.

According to Ed Vulliamy, Roswell has inspired a cult of 'pilgrimage' (Vulliamy 1997b, p. 2) to the desert. In California, Nevada and Arizona mystics pursue cosmic encounters and learn about 'celestial matters from that time-honoured tribe of sky-watchers, the Navajos' (2). '"The higher consciousness"' of these '"beings"' evokes mythic fantasies of a pilgrim race of Jews once endowed with phenomenal memories of sacred origins and of extraterrestrials blessed with the gift of cosmic insight in wilderness regions. What is fascinating, says Vulliamy, is that the terrain on which the UFO supposedly crashed has been designated by the Indians a 'Universal Sacred Site' (2). A ceremony featuring Native American dancers provides an explicit recognition of the links which connect the Old World with the New, the ancient Israelites with the extraterrestrials, and the American Indians who may well be the product of both. If 'people [in America] like the "unknown"', says Glenn Dennis, a retired undertaker at Roswell, it is because they like to think of it 'as something holy and there is nothing more holy or unknown than the desert' (3).

Desert experiences for New Age pilgrims contrast sharply with the claustrophobic fervour of the pre-millennialist faithful at their endtime conventions. The restlessness and pent-up energy of these endtime believers is revealed in David Briggs's account of a 1997 Christian 'prophecy' convention in Washington. While the year 2000 has 'heated up the endtime fever' (Briggs 1997, p. 2A), says Briggs, there is little hope for many of these delegates, some of whom are elderly and overwhelmed with post-menopausal fears and uncertainties. In the cloistered ceremonies and enclosed congregations of women believers we begin to sense the disappointed intimacy of God's believers. Those who crave, in their later years, a physical or emotional experience of God are no nearer to reaching their goal than they were in their youth, says Briggs.

God's refusal to get physical and reveal himself is compounded, agrees Paul Handley, by one of his 'more annoying attributes': his decision to remain unknowable. In Washington, God's 'endless games of patience' force the elderly 'End-Time Handmaidens' to 'pray and sway' (2A) for sixteen hours a day. They yearn for the moment when He will arrive and sweep them off their feet (in the Rapture) and give them a chance '"to dance on the streets that are golden"'. In the dance halls, those who await their celestial partner and waltz away the hours, wait in vain. If 'the old image of God as a clock-maker, winding up the world then going off to do something else' (Handley 1998), is seen in His refusal to attend to our needs, then those who yearn for an orgasm with God, are wasting their time. The elderly, 'who are clad in white and gold robes', and 'blow into rams' horns', take their sex unwillingly to the grave. Although 'their shrieks' are meant to simulate 'the Second Coming', God has stood them up. And deep down they know it. '"We're running out of time"', they tell each other. '"We're running out of time. This is God's last call"' (Briggs 1997, p. 1A).

As far as the elderly are concerned God is not much of a gentleman caller: His Son even less so. Many of those interviewed by Briggs in the privacy of the convention hall refer to Jesus almost as if he were a feckless lover who cannot be trusted. Willie Mae Johnson fears being jilted and left on her own, even if Jesus comes to take her. '"I don't want to leave anyone behind [at the Rapture], so you say yeah, and you say no ... I want Jesus to come back right now, but just wait a little while, Jesus."' A feeling of confusion exists among those who believe that '"the crisis must happen while I am alive"' and those who are prepared to 'accept delays' (2A). Jesus, once again has gained a reputation for unreliability: a lover with whom the earth does not move.

For those troubled by God's procrastination or, like Willie Mae Johnson, are scared of being left on their own, there exists the phenomenon of a halfway Rapture, one which offers interim help to millennialist believers through alien abduction. Stories of abduction privilege those who have been allowed to return to earth as mess-engers. They fuse the desire for spiritual and physical contact with a promiscuous desire for penetration and entry that has long been a source of millennial fascination. They are an ideal solution for those who yearn to enter the primordial reaches of what Harold Bloom calls 'angelology' (Bloom 1997, p. 4), but are hesitant about long-term exposure to angelic society. For abductees, the pleasure and pain of a brief flirtation – a one-night stand with an extraterrestrial – is infinitely preferrable to terminal departure.

In the film *Communion*, Whitley Streiber (Christopher Walken) is taken away in his sleep, subjected to painful examination, and returned to earth. Streiber, who is a writer (and a highly pretentious one), survives the physical distress of abduction, and in spite of disorientation, becomes convinced of the creative benefits that accrue from alien contact. The alien's rectal probes open up new psychic channels for Streiber and free the blockages that have stymied his work. As the film concludes, we see the writer in full flow, infused with sacred knowledge and able to communicate his experience with the aliens in a prose that readers can easily understand.

In *Communion*, the process of revelation runs counter to the secularised horror of abduction in *The X-files*, but is spiritually identical to that described by Louis Farrakhan, leader of the Nation of Islam. At a press conference on 24 October 1989, Farrakhan described his UFO encounter when, as he put it, he 'was carried up on this beam of light' until he entered a 'Wheel'. Inside the Wheel he met with 'the Honourable Elijah Muhammed' (Kossy 1994, p. 27), who gave him secret information about America's plan to attack Moammar Gaddafi. On his return to earth Farrakhan used his newspaper *The Final Call*, to reveal Muhammad's prophetic disclosure and to discuss the relationship between alien life and prophetic Islam as a blessing from God.

In abduction narratives alien presences are able to provide millennial exposure outside the normally hysterical channels of popular culture. In the narratives transcribed for us by John E. Mack and David M. Jacobs, the imagined entry into deep space is accompanied by 'unpleasant but necessary genetic manipulation' on board a spacecraft and an awareness of 'the necessity for alien/human hybridization' (Wojcik 1997, p. 197). As a form of virtual Rapture, abduction ceremonies are a way of fulfilling a sexual fantasy of encounter in the arms of an active and liberated lover. For the abductee, the experience of removal is far more dynamic than the passive transportation of a righteous community who fall asleep during the Rapture. As Elaine Showalter says: 'abductees often see themselves as the chosen heralds of a superior intergalactic race' and are possessed long afterwards by erotic dreams and pornographic fantasies' (Showalter 1998, p. 195).

On those rare occasions when the abductee is male, adds Showalter, an attractive female normally extracts the sperm of the experiencer. When abduction fantasies are narrated by women, their stories focus on 'the production of children', and 'begin at night when the victim is alone, either awake or asleep' (192). Conventionally, the abductees' genitalia are closely inspected and penile shafts are implanted in the body. Many female abductees refer to the 'Tall Gray Being' who bends 'over the victim, gazing deep into her eyes like an extraterrestrial Heathcliff or Fabio, filling her with love and eagerness to give herself completely' (192). In abduction narratives, 'Tall Beings are usually hypermasculine, commanding and erotic' and can 'induce rapid, intense sexual arousal and even orgasm in women'. For this reason, women experience erotic dreams after abduction and 'abduction scenarios closely resemble women's pornography'. Some abductees, says Showalter, 'belong to puritanical religious groups' and the imagery in their stories 'is a normal part of women's sexual fantasies' (196).

Extraterriestrial abduction is a way of simulating 'crisis' through penetration, a crisis born of scrupulous attention by an alien being, as opposed to the watchful and vicarious gazing of a God who never comes. In the hidden reaches of outer space, where pain and sensuality can interchange, cosmic energy is capable of many things. For Barry Downing, the sexual divinity of the extraterrestrial is that of the prophet as Wandering Jew who has cloned his identity with that of the Israelites on the eastern shore of the Red Sea. This hidden divinity which is visible and accessible in remote locations to an elect people brings to mind the 'sensuality' (Axtell 1981, pp. 152–3) of the Indian who was first encountered in the forests of New England by scholars and ministers of the Puritan faith.

Signs of divinity are still observed, as they were in New England, through the continuing imprint of an ancient Hebrew civilisation which accompanies all providential encounters. The stronger the manifestation of Israel the more inclined are those who observe it to seek a permanent departure or Rapture. In March 1997 the thirty-nine self-styled monks who committed suicide in the Rancho Sante Fe suburb of San Diego, California, explained their actions on a website and in a series of farewell videotapes which announced their departure for a 'Level Above Human in distant space' (Whittell 1997, p. 3). In this message, the monks explained their belief that a spaceship flying in the wake of the comet Hale-Bopp had been sent to seek out especially enlightened beings, beam them aboard and speed on to a cosmic destination, the star Sirius. The Heaven's Gate monks saw themselves fulfilling the role of those highly evolved beings who, after suicide, would rendezvous with the UFO. This event, they noted on their web site, corresponded with the mass suicide of 900 Jews at Masada in AD 73.

The Heaven's Gate cult and their leader, Marshall Herff Apple-white, interpreted the arrival of the Hale-Bopp comet as a sign of the earth's imminent destruction and the need for immediate evacuation.

Applewhite's astrological system derived from the Middle Ages when, says Jacque Le Goff, 'miracles took the place of social security' and 'the extraordinary' and 'supernatural' provided the vital element of 'proof' in the search for God. 'Earthquakes, comets and eclipses were the subjects worthy of admiration and study', writes Le Goff, for what they gave those who followed them was 'proof by authority' and 'proof by miracle' (Le Goff 1989, p. 329). In spite of the cosmic warning that the planet was 'about to be recycled' (Gledhill 1997, p. 3) the Heaven's Gate monks responded to the arrival of Hale-Bopp as a gesture of hope, a friendly invitation to return home to a 'Level Above Human'.

In feeding themselves a lethal dose of phenobarbital mixed with apple sauce and vodka, Applewhite's followers believed they were embarking on a journey in which their souls would be gathered up by the UFO concealed within the tail of the Hale-Bopp comet. Theirs was an act of 'complete severance between the dying old world and the paradisiacal new', one which interpreted the dispensationalist doctrine of the Rapture as an extraterrestrial summons from beyond. In this way the Heaven's Gate community were not only escaping the threat of 'global destruction', they were hurling themselves directly into 'the lap of God', using their suicide as a way of 'bridging the chasm' between an earthly world which had no future and 'a thousand years of unmitigated peace'. Death provided them with an opportunity to look forward 'happily' 'to the restoration of a primordial paradise – the millennium that is described in the Book of Revelation'. It was a pursuit of 'purity and truth' rather than 'a will to nothingness'. It belonged not on the 'apocalyptic fringes of religious culture where madmen and extroverts are wont to make their home' but to a central place in 'the millenarian enclaves of mainstream fundamentalist Christianity'. Their suicide was 'emblematic'; it extended the 'fantastic hermeneutic' of colonial New England into 'the physical leap' required by the Rapture. This 'sloughing off of the body' allowed the righteous to be 'hurled into paradise' (Benjamin 1998, p. xvi).

For New Religious Movements that attempt to penetrate the outer reaches of space through the Viagra of suicide, death holds no fear and space no adversaries. If there is hysteria it is an hysteria of the sublime in pursuit of the transcendent. Expectant suicide eschews the need for the conflict and conspiracy that Elaine Showalter associates with the 'obsessional disorders' (Showalter 1997, p. 17) of fundamentalism. This rationale was expounded by Luc Jourret, leader of the Order of the Solar Temple in 1994. Before staging the death of his followers, Jourret announced that 'it is with unfathomable love, ineffable joy, and without any regret that we leave this world. Men, cry not over our fate, but rather cry for your own. Ours is more enviable than yours' (quoted in Benjamin 1998, p. xv). Jourret's message was endorsed by Applewhite. To read the website of the Heaven's Gate sect is to enter a world of eternal promise. Among those who are going home for good, there is only 'joy', 'the rapture of the saved', the blissful prophecy of the 'Talmudic sages' (Carlin 1997b, p. 12).

The decision by the Heaven's Gate community to seek their salvation in suicide appears on the web site to have been requested by a higher being who, from time to time, returns his exiled communities on earth back to 'their World in the literal Heavens' (Katz 1997, p. 3). The suggestion that Jews, or their descendants throughout history, are regularly intercepted by an ancient starfleet and carried back to the promised land of Sirius, invests the Heaven's Gate community with all the ancient spiritual attributes of the Ten Lost Tribes. Their suicide transforms the exodus myth into a starfleet mythology in which spaceships lurk in the tail of meteorites whenever they enter earth's atmosphere. In the Bible, says Barry Downing, the appearance of cloud formation – 'spacecloud' (Downing 1968, p. 152) or 'bright cloud' (148) – as cover for divine messengers testifies to the continual presence of a technological divinity in outer space. It is this which reveals itself, at crisis moments, to elect societies in the Old and New Testament.

The Heaven's Gate website noted the imminence of crisis. 'Planet about to be recycled', it said, but added the coda: 'Your only chance to survive – leave with us' (Gledhill 1997, p. 3). Hale-Bopp provided revelations in accordance with the standard dispensationalist belief, that the story of human existence in the endtimes is characterised by dramatic preordained events. For those who believe that the history of salvation, as Barry Downing claims, is written in 'clouds', meteorite showers – such as Haley's Comet or Shoemaker-Levy – have long been regarded as signs of catastrophe and planetary decline. Hale-Bopp was a logical omen of prophetic or mystical significance: a comet in the form of a Talmudic sage or immigrant-tsadik who, like the prophet Elijah, 'wanders over the earth in many and varied guises as a celestial messenger, a warner and an adviser' (Nahmad 1970, p. 24).

The medium through which Hale-Bopp channelled its cosmic vision of rescue was the space theologian Marshall H. Applewhite, a doomsday prophet determined to make a name for himself selling cutout versions of the apocalypse to the bored and lonely. For California's emigrés, tired of their lives and disappointed with their bodies, Applewhite proposed a 'final exit', a New Age version of the Rapture in which the living are spirited away on a spacecraft to be 'with the Lord' in Heaven (Thessalonians 4: 14–17). Applewhite presented himself as a kind of Jim Casey, the spiritual guide of the Joads in John Steinbeck's *The Grapes of Wrath*, a driven and idealistic wanderer leading the Heaven's Gate community across the desert of space to the Sirius of California. Disengaged from the church (in which they were both trained as evangelical ministers), but not from the belief in a redemptive mission, both Applewhite and Casy abandon the negative aspects of religion to endorse its spirit, exchanging the metaphysics of Christianity for the transcendentalism of the Over Soul. In their movement from Bible-Belt evangelism to social prophecy, Casey and Applewhite slough off the past and the doctrines associated with the parched Presbyterianism of their youth in the southwest. Escape or flight is not an act of cowardice; it is an act of courage or 'nerve', as the Needles gas station attendant calls it, referring to the foolishness of the Joads' decision to cross a hundred miles of desert in an ancient Hudson.

Like many of those who went to California to escape the depression in the 1930s, the Heaven's Gate community found itself a stranger in the state. Its members 'had left the corn states, the southwest desert and the east coast cities to make their stand on the continent's edge', says Peter King. 'In this they were following a great tradition.' As the refrigerated trucks carrying the dead left the Solina Norte mansion for the mortuaries of San Diego, the question was asked: 'How could anyone want to kill themselves in such a beautiful place?' (King 1997, p. 17). As the myth of open frontier proves fraudulent so the reality of confinement is too overwhelming to endure. The tragedy of Jody's grandfather in Steinbeck's 'The Leader of the People' is that westering 'didn't last long enough'. Like his ageing compatriots the old pioneer discovers that, '"There's no place to go. There's the ocean to stop you. There's a line of old men along the shore hating the ocean because it stopped them"' (Steinbeck 1959, p. 254). It is this scene of the American westerner with nowhere left to go, with the frontier closed, with only California at his feet, with shores and waves but no passage to India, that the pioneer can never accept.

As Israelites who were attempting to renew America's earliest dream of adventure, the Heaven's Gate community were engaged on a spiritually uplifting quest. With escape cut off and their lifelong dreams further and further ahead of their limitations, the only serious philosophical problem, becomes suicide. In *To a God Unknown*, Steinbeck introduces 'the last man in the western world to see the sun go down'. Each evening he makes ritual observances to the western sky and prepares to 'go over the edge of the world with the sun' (Steinbeck 1969, p. 175). The threat is no fiction. In an essay entitled 'The Jumping-Off Place', written in 1932, Edmand Wilson noted that:

The Americans still tend to move westward and many drift southward toward the sun. San Diego is the extreme southwest of the United States; and since our real westward expansion has come to a standstill, it has become a veritable jumping-off place. On the west coast today the suicide rate is twice that of the Middle Atlantic coast, and since 1911 the suicide rate of San Diego has been the highest in the United States ... Since the depression the rate seems to have increased. (Wilson 1968, pp. 257, 259)

The closed frontier becomes an eschatological matter; the American is both consumed and consummated by fire. Pursuit of the sun initiates, says Charles Sanford, a 'journey toward light', an act of illumination, a 'fulfilment of self through self-destruction' (Sanford 1955, p. vi). Jumping-off into the west is an extension of Huck Finn's urge to light out for new territory, a way of pursuing the magic space and sky light, of what Ole Rölvaag terms 'hilder' (Rölvaag 1931, p. 234).

Notes

1. In his essay 'The Revolt against Modernity' Richard Hofstadter emphasises the importance of Bible reading in the 1960s to southern fundamentalists. He quotes a Georgia assemblyman who uses the Bible to justify both his literary and his anti-intellectual stance: 'Read the Bible. It teaches you how to act. Read the hymn-book. It contains the finest poetry ever written. Read the almanac. It shows you how to figure out what the weather will be. There isn't another book that it is necessary for anyone to read, and therefore I am opposed to all libraries' (Hofstadter 1965, p. 125).
2. Here, I have accepted Daniel Wojcik's distinction between millennialism and millenarianism. Millennialism, argues Wojcik, is more commonly used to characterise Christian beliefs; millenarianism is frequently employed to designate any belief system or movement that includes expectations of a future age of perfection or salvation. (Wojcik 1997, p. 218 n.).

References

Abelman, Robert (ed.) (1990) *Religious Television: Controversies and Conclusions*, Norwood, NJ: Ablex.

Aho, J. A. (1994) *This Thing of Darkness: A Sociology of the Enemy*, Seattle: University of Washington Press.

Aho, J. (1990) *The Politics of Righteousness: Idaho Christian Patriotism*, Seattle: University of Washington Press.

Ammerman, N. A. (1987) *Bible Believers: Fundamentalists in the Modern World*. New Brunswick: Rutgers University Press.

Anaya, R. A. (1986) *A Chicano in China*, Albuquerque: University of New Mexico Press.

Anon. (1983) 'Signs and wonders today', *Christian Life Magazine*, pp. 31–6.

Appleby, R. S. (1993) 'Fundamentalism's modern origins', *Foreign Affairs*, Summer, 72 (3), 217–18.

Ariel, Y. (1991), *On Behalf of Israel: American Fundamentalist Attitudes toward Jews, Judaism and Zionism, 1865–1945*, New York: Caeloon.

Austin, A. J. (1990) 'Blessed adversity: Henry W. Frost and the China Inland Mission', in Carpenter, J. A. and Shank, W. R., *Earthen Vessels in American Evangelicals and Foreign Missions. 1880–1980*. Grand Rapids, MI: William B. Eerdmans, pp. 50–78.

Axtell, J. (1981), *The European and the Indian: Essays in the Ethnohistory of Colonial North America*, Oxford: Oxford University Press.

Axtell, J. (1997) 'Paddling their own canoes', *Times Literary Supplement*, 6 June, pp. 4–5.

Bakke, R. J. (1983) 'The urban church', in Noll, M. A., Hatch, N. O., Marsden, G. M., Wells, D. F. and Woodbridge, J. D. (eds), *Christianity in America*, Grand Rapids, MI: William B. Eerdmans, pp. 452–62.

Balaban, J. (1991) *Remembering Heaven's Face: A Moral Witness in Vietnam*, New York: Simon and Schuster.

Balmer, Randall (1988) 'Apocalypticism in America: the argot of premillennialism in popular culture', *Prospects*, 13, pp. 417–33.

Barber, T. (1995) 'It could have been different', *The Independent on Sunday*, 20 August, p. 19.

Barkun, M. (1974) *Disaster and the Millennium*, New Haven: Yale University Press.

Barkun, M. (1997) *Religion and the Racist Right: The Origins of the Christian Identity Movement*, Chapel Hill: University of North Carolina.

Baudrillard, J. (1988) *America*, London: Verso.

Baudrillard, J. (1994) *The Illusion of the End*, trans. C. Turner, Stanford: Stanford University Press.

Begley, S. (1994) 'In search of the sacred', *Newsweek*, 28 November, pp. 39–41.

Bell, D. (1988) 'The predicament of liberalism: a symposium', *Dialogue* (80), 2, pp. 2–8.

Benjamin, M. (1998) *Living at the End of the World*, London: Picador.

Berman, R. (1984) 'From counter culture to contra', *Telos*, Summer, pp. 143–7.

Bernières, L. de (1998) 'The impatience of Job', *The Guardian Weekend*, 19 September, pp. 20–1.

Bercovitch, S. (1978) *The American Jeremiad*, London: University of Wisconsin Press.

Bhatia, S. (1995) 'Bombay's McCarthyite terror', *The Observer*, 23 April, p. 16.

Bigsby, C. W. E. (1975) *Superculture: American Popular Culture and Europe*, London: Elek.

Bilik, D. S. (1981) *Immigrant Survivors: Post–Holocaust Consciousness in Recent Jewish-American Fiction*, Middletown, CT: Wesleyan University Press.

Block, R. (1994) 'The tragedy of Rwanda', *The New York Review*, 20 October, pp. 3–8.

Bloom, H. (1992) *The American Religion: The Emergence of the Lost Christian Nation*, New York: Simon and Schuster.

Bloom, H. (1997) *Omens of Millennium: The Gnosis of Angels, Dreams, and Resurrection*, Fourth Estate: London.

Boorstin, D. (1965) *The Americans: The Colonial Experience*, New York: Random House.

Boyer, P. (1992) *When Time Shall Be No More: Prophecy Belief in Modern American Culture*, Cambridge, MA: Harvard University Press.

Bradbury, M. (1990) 'Frontiers of imagination', *The Guardian*, 15 February, p. 21.

Bradbury, M. (1995) 'Let's do the Popomo a-go-go', *The Guardian*, 9 December, p. 29.

Briggs, D. (1997) 'The start of a millennium or the end of time?', *Tallahasee Democrat*, 27 October, pp. 1A–2A.

Brittain, V. (1991) 'Under the horizons of hope', *The Guardian*, 14 June, p. 21.

Brouwer, S., Gifford, P. and Rose, S. D. (1996) *Exporting the American Gospel: Global Christian Fundamentalism*, New York: Routledge.

Browne, R. B. (1987) 'The rape of the vulnerable', in Fishwick, M. and Browne, R. B. (eds), *The God Pumpers: Religions in the Electronic Age*, Bowling Green, OH: Bowling Green State University Press.

Bunting, M. (1996) 'Shopping for God', *The Guardian*, 16 December, pp. 34–41.

Burkett, L. (1991) *The Illuminati*, Nashville: Thomas Nelson.

[Burnham, W. D.] (1988) 'The predicament of liberalism: a symposium', *Dialogue*, 8, 2/88, pp. 2–9.

Bush, G. (1992) 'State of the Union Address', *United States Information Service*, January, pp. 1–3.

Butler, J. (1990) *AWASH in a Sea of Faith: Christianizing the American People*, Cambridge, MA: Harvard University Press.

Bygrave, M. (1994) 'The dream that's dying', *The Guardian, Weekend*, 26 November, pp. 21–32.

Caldwell, P. (1983) *The Puritan Conversion Narrative: The Beginnings of American Expression*, Cambridge: Cambridge University Press.

Campion, N. (1994) *The Great Year: Astrology, Millenarianism and History in the Western Tradition*, Arkansas: Harmondsworth.

Canup, J. (1990) *Out of the Wilderness: The Emergence of an American*

Identity in Colonial New England, Middleton, CT: Wesleyan University Press.

Carlin J. (1995) 'Once upon a time in the West', *The Independent on Sunday*, 9 March, pp. 9–11.

Carlin, J. (1996a) 'The Clintons: America's top-rated soap', *The Independent on Sunday*, 30 June, p. 12.

Carlin, J. (1996b) 'America falls to an invasion of aliens', *The Independent on Sunday*, 14 July, p. 13.

Carlin, J. (1997a) 'Clinton cloned: a dastardly deed that duped the world', *The Independent on Sunday*, 2 March, p. 12.

Carlin, J. (1997b) 'Who's next through Heaven's Gate?', *The Independent on Sunday*, 30 March, p. 12.

Carlin, J. (1997c) 'Something nasty in the backyard', *The Independent on Sunday*, 4 May, p. 12.

Carlin, J. (1998) 'The great conspiracy', *The Independent on Sunday*, 1 February, p. 20.

Carroll, P. N. (1969) *Puritanism and the Wilderness: The Intellectual Significance of the New England Frontier, 1629–1700*, New York: Columbia University Press.

Castells, M. (1997) 'Hauling in the future', *The Guardian*, 13 December, p. 31.

Chamberlain, E. R. (1975) *Antichrist and the Millennium I*, New York: Dutton.

Chidester, D. (1988) *Salvation and Suicide: An Interpretation of Jim Jones, the Peoples Temple, and Jonestown*, Bloomington: Indiana University Press.

Coates, J. (1987) *Armed and Dangerous: The Rise of the Survivalist Right*, New York: Noonday Press.

Cohn, N. (1970) *The Pursuit of the Millennium: Revolutionary Millenarians and Mystical Anarchists of the Middle Ages*, rev. and exp. edn, New York: Oxford University Press.

Coles, J. (1998) 'Church tells wives who's boss', *The Guardian*, 11 June, p. 3.

Conrad, C. (ed.) (1971) *God's New Israel: Religious Interpretations of American Destiny*, Eaglewood Cliffs, NJ: Prentice-Hall.

Cosgrove, S. (1995) 'Truth be damned', *The Independent*, 30 June, p. 9.

Cox, H. (1987) 'Fundamentalism as an ideology', in Neuhaus, R. J. and Cromartie, M. (eds), *Piety and Politics: Evangelicals and Fundamentalists Confront the World*, Lanhan, MD: University Press of America, pp. 287–303.

Crace, J. (1997) *Quarantine*, London: Viking.

Cummings, B. (1992) 'The wicked witch of the west is dead. Long live the wicked witch of the east', in Hogan, M. J. (ed.), *The End of the Cold War: Its Meaning and Implications*. Cambridge: Cambridge University Press.

Curran, Douglas (1985) *In Advance of the Landing: Folk Concepts of Outer Space*, New York: Abbeville Press.

Dalrymple, J. (1995) 'Nightmare USA', *The Sunday Times Magazine*, 3 September, pp. 28–41.

Daniels, T. (1992) *Millennialism: An International Bibliography*, New York: Garland.

Davis, D. B. (ed.) (1971), *The Fear of Conspiracy: Images of Unamerican Subversion from the Revolution to the Present*, Ithaca, NY: Cornell University Press.

Davis, D. B. (1994) 'The slave trade and the Jews', *The New York Review*, 22 December, pp. 14–16.

Dejevsky, M. (1996) 'US Culture: the latest bogey for Le Pen's Front', *The Guardian*, 14 September, p. 21.

Delbanco, A. (1989) *The Puritan Ordeal*, Cambridge, MA: Harvard University Press.

Dexter, P. (1989) *Paris Trout*, London: Flamingo.

Diamond, S. (1989) *Spiritual Warfare: The Politics of the Christian Right*, London: Pluto Press.

Didion, J, (1981) (1979) *The White Album*, Harmondsworth: Penguin.

Didion, J. (1998) 'Vanities of madness', *The New York Review*, 23 April, pp. 17–21.

Dione, R. L. (1973) *God Drives a Flying Saucer*, New York: Bantam.

Downing, Barry H. (1968) *The Bible and Flying Saucers*, Philadelphia: J. B. Lippincott Co.

Dunn, K. and Redden, J. (1995) 'Fear and loathing', *Los Angeles Times Book Review*, 2 June, p. 11.

Dyer, C. H. (ed.) (1991) *The Rise of Babylon: Sign of the End Times*, Wheaton, IL: Tyndale House.

Easterman, D. (1995) *The Judas Testament*, London: Harper Collins.

Eastlake, W. (1969) *The Bamboo Bed*, New York: Simon and Schuster.

Eco, U. (1995) 'Pointing a finger at the fascists', *The Guardian*, 19 August, p. 27.

Edsall, T. B. (1994) 'America's sweetheart', *The New York Review*, 6 October, pp. 6–10.

Eichorn, D. M. (1978) *Evangelising the American Jew*, New York: Jonathan David.

Englehardt, T. (1995) *The End of Victory Culture: Cold War America and the Disillusioning of a Generation*, London: Harper Collins.

Enroth, R. M. (1983) 'The Christian counterculture', in Noll, M. A., Hatch, N. O., Marsden, G. M., Wells, D. F., and Woodbridge, J. D. (eds), *Christianity in America*, Grand Rapids, MI: William B. Eerdmans, pp. 469–73.

Epstein, J. (1996) 'White mischief', *The New York Review*, 17 October, pp. 30–2.

Faid, R. W. (1988) *Gorbachev! Has the Real Antichrist Come?*, Tulsa: Victory House.

Ferraro, T. J. (1993) *Ethnic Passages: Literary Immigrants in Twentieth Century America*, Chicago: University of Chicago Press.

Festinger, L., Riecken, H. W., and Schocter, S. (1956) *When Prophecy Fails: A Social and Psychological Study of a Modern Group that Predicted the Destruction of the World*, New York: Harper and Row.

Fisk, R. (1995) 'Scenes from an unholy war', *The Independent on Sunday*, (April), pp. 4–10.

Fitzgerald, F. (1986) *Cities on a Hill: A Journey through Contemporary American Culture*, London: Picador.

Fitzgerald, F. S. (1953) *The Great Gatsby*, New York: Charles Scribner's Sons.

Flamini, R. (1994) *Thalberg: The Last Tycoon and the World of M. G. M.*, New York: Crown.

Foege, A. (1996) *The Empire God Built: Inside Pat Robertson's Media Machine*, New York: John Wiley & Sons.

Freedland, J. (1994) 'Republicans join to attack Clinton foreign policy', *The Guardian*, 29 July, p. 9.

Freedland, J. (1996a) 'Aliens are coming home', *The Guardian*, 11 July, p. 7.

Freedland, J. (1996b) 'Politics for sceptics', *The Guardian*, 26 October, pp. 1–2.

Freedland, J. (1996c) 'America's dirty war', *The Guardian*, 2 April, pp. 2–3.

Freedland, J. (1998) 'Empathy vote', *The Guardian*, 2 November, pp. 2–3.

Fukuyama, F. (1989) 'The end of history?' *The National Interest*, 16, Summer, pp. 3–18.

Fukuyama, F. (1990) 'Forget Iraq – history is dead', *The Guardian*, 7 September, p. 23.

Fukuyama, F. (1992) *The End of History and The Last Man*, Toronto: The Free Press.

Fuller, J. (1984) *Fragments*, Sevenoaks: Coronet.

Gabler, N. (1989) *An Empire of their Own: How the Jews Invented Hollywood*, London: W. H. Allen.

Gelb, L. and Betts, R. (1979) *The Irony of Vietnam: The System Worked*, Washington, DC: Brookings Institution.

Gelderman, C. (1989) *A Life*, London: Sidgwick and Jackson.

Ghosh, A. (1994) *In an Antique Land*, New York: Random House.

Gibson, J. W. (1986) *The Perfect War: Technowar in Vietnam*, Boston: Atlantic Monthly Press.

Gibson, J. W. (1991) 'The return of Rambo: war and culture in the post-Vietnam era', in Alan Wolfe (ed.), *America at Century's End*, Berkley: University of California Press, pp. 376–95.

Gibson, J. W. (1994) *Warrior Dreams: Paramilitary Culture in Post-Vietnam America*, New York: Hill and Wang.

Gibson, J. W. (1998) 'American paramilitary culture and the reconciliation of the Vietnam war', in Walsh, J. and Aulich, J. (eds), *Vietnam Images: War and Representation*, Basingstoke: Macmillan, pp. 10–43.

Gledhill, R. (1997) 'Preacher's son spreads gospel on the Internet', *The Times*, 29 March, p. 3.

Glenny, M. (1992), *The Fall of Yugoslavia: The Third Balkan War*, Harmondsworth: Penguin.

Gliona, J. (1995) 'A religious renaissance sweeps through US jails', *The Guardian*, 30 May, p. 7.

Gold, M. (1984) *Jews Without Money*, New York: Carroll and Graf.

Goldman, A. (1975) 'A remnant to escape: the American writer and the minority group', in Cunliffe, M. (ed.), *American Literature since 1900*, London: Sphere.

Goodwin, C. (1995) 'Militia holds provisions for long guerrilla war', *The Sunday Times*, 30 April, p. 17.

Gott, R. (1989) 'The bear turns bullish', *The Guardian*, 20 November, p. 23.

Gott, R. (1995) 'The Latin conversion', *The Guardian Weekend*, 10 June, pp. 14–27.

Gott, R. (1996) 'Reason blinks in the light of faith', *The Guardian*, 20 April, p. 31.

Gourevitch, P. (1996) 'The poisoned country', *The New York Review*, 6 June, pp. 58–64.

Grass, G. (1987) 'What shall we tell our children?', *On Writing and Politics*, Harmondsworth, Middlesex: Penguin, p. 79.

Gray, J. (1994) 'The great Atlantic drift', *The Guardian*, 12 December, p. 18.

Grenz, Stanley G. (1992) *The Millennial Maze: Sorting out Evangelical Options*, Downer's Groves, IL: Inter Varsity Press.

Gumble, A. (1999), 'Sleaze deluge dooms tabloid sales all over the US', *The Independent on Sunday*, p. 17.

Gumpert, L. (1983) *The End of the World: Contemporary Visions of the Apocalypse*, New York: New Museum of Contemporary Art.

Gunn, G. (1979) *The Inspiration of Otherness: Literature, Religion and the American Inspiration*, New York: Oxford University Press.

Hamm, M. S. (1997) *Apocalypse in Oklahoma: Waco and Ruby Ridge Revenged*, Boston: Northeastern University Press.

Handley, P. (1998) 'God – a curriculum vitae', *The Independent on Sunday*, 4 January, pp. 6–7.

Harding, S. (1993) 'Contesting rhetorics in the PTL scandal', in Silberstein, L. J. (ed.), *Jewish Fundamentalism in Co-operative Perspective: Ideology and the Crisis of Modernity*, London: New York University Press, pp. 56–73.

Harris, N. (1996) *The New Untouchables: Immigration and the New World Order*, Oxford: Oxford University Press.

Harris, R. (1998) 'America lost to its witch-hunt insanity', *The Sunday Times*, 13 September, p. 15.

Hawthorne, N. (1987) *Selected Tales and Sketches*, Harmondsworth: Penguin.

Hayden, J. D. (ed.) 1981, 'A Jewish Family', in *William Wordsworth: The Poems*, 2 vols, 11, 43, 46–7, pp. 650–1, New Haven, CT: Yale University Press.

Heimert, A. and Delbanco, A. (1985), *The Puritans in America: A Narrative Anthology*, New Haven, CT: Harvard University Press.

Henry, F. (1990) *The Middle East – Destined*, Monroe, LA: Word of Prophecy Inc.

Hertzberg, A. (1993) 'Is anti semitism dying out?' *The New York Review*, 24 June, pp. 51–57.

Hindson, Ed (1996) *Find Signs: Amazing Prophecies of the Endtimes*, Eugene, OR: Harvest House.

Hinson, K. (1997) 'Calvinism resurging among S. B. C.'s Young Elites', *Christianity Today* 41 (11), 6, October.

Hirst, D. (1994) 'The second liberation', *The Guardian*, 29 January, pp. 19–21.

Hirst, D. (1995) 'Mullahjustice', *The Observer*, 19 January, p. 13.

Hitchens, C. (1995) 'Look over your shoulder', *London Review of Books* (17) 10, 25 May, p. 12.

Hitchens, C. (1998) 'What Clinton and Lewinsky really got down to', *The Independent on Sunday*, 16 August, p. 28.

Hobsbawm, E. (1993) 'The new threat to history', *The New York Review*, 16 December, pp. 62–4.

Hofstadter, R. (1964) *Anti-Intellectualism in American Life*, London: Jonathan Cape.

Hofstadter, R. (1965) 'The paranoid style in American politics and other essays', New York: Knopf.

Holdsworth, N. (1996) 'Rare masonic books stolen to order', *Times Higher Education Supplement*, 25 October.

Holstun, J. (1987) *A Rational Millennium: Puritan Utopias of Seventeenth Century England and America*, New York: Oxford University Press.

Horton, R. (1995) 'Infection: the global threat', *The New York Review*, 6 April, pp. 24–8.

Huddlestone, L. E. (1967) *Origins of the American Indians: European Concepts, 1492–1729*, Austin: University of Texas Press.

Huggett, R. (1990) *Catastrophism: System of Earth History*, London: Edward Arnold.

Hunter, J. D. (1987) 'The evangelical worldview since 1980', in Neuhaus, R. J. and Cromartie, M. (eds), *Piety and Politics: Evangelicals and Fundamentalists Confront the World*, Lanhan, MD: University Press of America, pp. 19–55.

Huntington, S. P. (1993), 'The clash of civilisation', *Foreign Affairs*, Summer, pp. 22–49.

Huntington, S. P. (1996a) 'The west v. the rest', *The Guardian*, 23 November, p. 23.

Huntington, S. P. (1996b) *The Clash of Civilizations and the Remaking of World Order*, New York: Simon and Schuster.

Ignatieff, M. (1993) 'The Balkan tragedy', *The New York Review*, 13 May, pp. 3–5.

Jacques, M. (1998) 'Politics? Let's get personal', *The Observer*, 8 February, pp. 22–3.

Jeffrey, G. R. (1994) *Prince of Darkness: Antichrist and the New World Order*, New York: Bantam Books.

Jeffreys, D. (1995) '$5,000: the price of a life', *The Independent*, 5 July, pp. 2–3.

Jenkins, K. (1991) *Re-thinking History*, London: Routledge.

Jenkyns, R. (1998) '2001', *The New York Review*, 28 May, pp. 4–7.

Jones, T. (1995) *Cold Snap*, London: Faber & Faber.

Jorstad, E. (1970) *The Politics of Doomsday: Fundamentalists of the Far Right*, Nashville: Adingdon Press.

Judt, T. (1996) 'Europe: the grand illusion', *The New York Review*, 11 July, pp. 6–7.

Julius, A. (1996) 'Whose line is it anyway?', *The Guardian*, 30 November, p. 5.

Kane, J. (1993) 'Letter from the Amazon: with spears from all sides', *The New Yorker*, 27 September, pp. 54–79.

Kane, P. (1995) 'In thrall to New Age thrills', *The Guardian*, 4 June, pp. 12–13.

Karacs, I. (1998) 'Race rears shaven head at the polls', *The Independent on Sunday*, p. 19.

Katz, I. (1997) '"Nerds" seek gateway to heaven', *The Guardian*, 28 March, p. 3.

Kelly, M. (1995) 'The road to paranoia', *New Yorker*, 19 June, pp. 61–5.

Kepel, Gilles (1994) *The Revenge of God*, London: Policy Press.

Kermode, F. (1966) *The Sense of an Ending: Studies in the Theory of Fiction*, New York: Oxford University Press.

Kettle, M. (1998a) 'Lynch-mob usurps sense and mercy', *The Guardian*, 21 September, p. 2.

Kettle, M. (1998b) 'Republican sympathisers desert Clinton', *The Guardian*, 16 December, p. 3.

King, P. (1997) 'Beyond sanity on the continent's edge', *The Guardian*, 29 March, p. 17.

Kirban, S. (1970)(1973) (Pictorial Format) *666 and 1000*, AMG Publishers, unlocated.

Kohn, M. (1997) 'Bones of contention', *The Independent on Sunday*, 7 December, p. 45.

Kornfeld, E. (1995) 'Encountering "the Other"', American intellectuals and Indians in the 1790s, *The William and Mary Quarterly*, 3rd series, VII (2), April, pp. 286–314.

Kossy, D. (1994) *Kooks*, Portland: Feral House.

Krauthammer, C. (1991) 'The unipolar movement', *Foreign Affairs*, 7 (1), pp. 23–33.

Krzeminski, A. (1994) 'Back to the future', *The New York Review I*, 17 November, pp. 41–7.

Kuran, T. (1993) 'The economic impact of Islamic fundamentalism', in Marty, M. E. and Appleby, R. S. (eds), *Fundamentalism and the State: Remaking Politics, Economies and Militance*, Chicago, IL: University of Chicago Press, pp. 302–42.

Lal, D. (1995) 'Eco-fundamentalism', *International Affairs*, 71 (3), July, pp. 515–26.

Lalonde, P. and Lalonde P. (1994) *The March of the Beast*, Eugene, OR: Harvest House.

Lamont, W. (1996) *Puritanism and Historical Controversy*, London: UCL Press.

LaPierre, W. R. (1994) *Guns, Crime and Freedom*, Washington, DC: Regnery Publishings Inc.

Lawrence, B. B. (1989) *Defenders of God: The Fundamentalist Revolt against the Modern Age*, San Francisco: Harper and Row.

Lazenby, M. E. (1940) *Herman Husband: A Story of His Life*, Washington, DC.

Lebeson, A. L. (1931) *Jewish Pioneers in America*, New London: Coward-McCann.

Le Goff, J. (1989) *Medieval Civilisation: 400–1500*, trans. Julia Barrow, London: Blackwell.

Lewis, James R. (ed.) (1995) *The Gods Have Landed: New Religions from Other Worlds*, Albany: SUNY Press.

Lewis, S. (1926) *Babbitt*, London: Jonathan Cape.

Lichfield, J. (1992) 'Dream of an aged child', *The Independent on Sunday*, 1 November, p. 19.

Lieb, M. (1998), *Children of Ezekiel: Alien UFOs, the Crisis of Race and the Advent of End Time*, Durham: Duke University Press.

Lieberman, T. (1996) 'The Vince Foster factory', *Columbia Journalism Review*, March/April, pp. 8–9.

Lieven, A. (1993) *The Baltic Revolution: Estonia, Latvia, Lithuania and the Path to Independence*, New Haven, CT: Yale University Press.

Limerick, P. N. (1997) 'Where the oats don't grow to perfection', *Times Literary Supplement*, 28 February 28, pp. 6–7.

Lind, M. (1995) 'Rev. Robertson's grand international conspiracy theory', *The New York Review*, 2 February pp. 21–5.

Lindsey, H. (1970), *The Late Great Planet Earth*, New York: Bantam.

Lindsey, H. (1981) *The 1980s: Countdown to Armageddon*, New York: Bantam.

Lindsey, H. (1984) (1973) *There's a New World Coming*, Eugene Oreg.: Harvest House.

Lindsey, H. (1990) *The Road to Holocaust*, New York: Bantam.

Lindsey, H. (1995) *The Final Battle*, Western Front, California: Palos Verdes.

Lindsey, H. and Carlson, C. C. (1992) *Satan is Alive and Well on Planet Earth*, Grand Rapids, MI: Zonderevan.

Lurie, A. (1967) *Imaginary Friends*, Minerva: London.

Macdonald, A. (1994) *Hunter*, Hillsboro, WV: National Vanguard Books.

Macdonald, A. (1996) *The Turner Diaries*, New York: Barricade Books.

Mailer, N. (1998) 'Clinton for Pres. No, not for you, Bill', *The Observer*, 8 February, p. 1.

Marable, M. (1995) 'A black tie occasion', *The Guardian*, 16 October, p. 13.

Marsden, G. (1990) *Religion and American Culture*, New York: Harcourt Brace Jovanovich.

Marshall, A. (1998a) 'No place like home', *The Independent on Sunday*, 27 September, p. 27.

Marshall, A. (1998b) 'Hillary's role is crucial', *The Independent on Sunday*, 13 September, p. 3.

Marty, M. E. (1992) 'Fundamentals of fundamentalism', in Kaplan, L. (ed.), *Fundamentalism in Comparative Perspective*, Amherst: The University of Massachusetts Press, pp. 15–24.

Marty, M. E. and Appleby, R. S. (1993) 'Introduction' and 'Making the state:

the limits of the fundamentalist imagination', in Marty, M. E. and Appleby, R. S. (eds), *Fundamentalism and the State: Remaking Politics, Economics and Militance*, Chicago, IL: University of Chicago Press. pp. 1–13, 620–45.

Mather, Increase (1669) *The Mystery of Israel's Salvation Explained and Applyed*, London: Printed for John Allen.

Matthiessen, P. (1987) *At Play in the Fields of the Lord*, New York: Vintage, 2nd edn.

McCarthy, M. (1968) *Hanoi*, London: Weidenfeld & Nicholson.

McClay, E. T. (1989) *Images of Latin America in Contemporary US Literature* (Ph.D. 1987), Ann Arbor, MI: The George Washington University, University Microfilms International.

McCrystal, C. (1993) 'The world at war', *The Independent on Sunday*, 14 March, p. 39.

McDowell, J. and Stewart, D. (1992) *The Occult: The Authority of the Believer Over the Powers of Darkness*, San Bernadino, CA: Here's Lite Publishers.

McGrath, M. (1995) *Motel Nirvana: Dreaming of the New Age in the American Desert*, New York: Picador.

McKeever, J. (1987) *The Rapture Book: Victory in the End Times*, Medford, OR: Omega.

McLoughlin, W. G. and Conser, Jun., W. H. (1987) '"The first man was red" – Cherokee Response to the Debate over Indian origins, 1760–1860', *American Quarterly*, 41 (2), June, pp. 243–64.

McNeill, W. H. (1997) 'Decline of the west?', *The New York Review*, 9 January, pp. 18–22.

McWilliams, C. (1964) 'Aimee Semple McPherson: sunlight in my soul', in Leighton, I. (ed.), *The Aspirin Age: 1919–1941*, Harmondsworth, Middlesex: Penguin, pp. 60–91.

Miller, A. (1998) 'Behind the Lewinsky affair, some may discern the work of the Devil', *The Guardian*, 16 October, p. 20.

Montefiore, S. S. (1995) 'Warlords come to America', *The Sunday Times*, 30 April, p. 7.

Morgan, R. (1989) *The Demon Lover: On the Sexuality of Terrorism*, New York: W. W. Norton & Co.

Morgenthau, T. (1993) 'America: still a melting pot?' *Newsweek*, 9 August, pp. 5–15.

Mottram, E. (1989) 'Out of sight, but never out of mind: fears of invasion in American culture', in *Blood on the Nash Ambassador: Investigations in American Culture*, London: Hutchinson, pp. 138–81.

Nahmad, N. M. (1970) *A Portion in Paradise and Other Jewish Folk Tales*, New York: Schocken.

Neustatter, A. (1996) 'Occult status', *The Guardian*, 17 September, pp. 6–7.

Nye, Jun., J. S. (1992) 'What new world order?', *Foreign Affairs*, 71, Spring, pp. 83–96.

Oelschlaeger, M. (1991), *The Idea of Wilderness: From Prehistory to the Age of Ecology*, New Haven, CT: Yale University Press.

O'Hagan, A. (1997) 'The martyrdom of Mailer', *The Guardian Weekend*, 30 August, pp. 11–21.

O'Leary, S. D. (1994) *Arguing the Apocalypse: A Theory of Millennial Rhetoric*, New York: Oxford University Press.

Paglia, C. (1996) 'Bookworm that turned' *The Guardian*, 2 February, p. 2.

Parker, I. (1994) 'The reporter as poet', *The Independent on Sunday*, 18 September, pp. 4–8.

Peck, J. (1993) *The Gods of Televangelism: The Crisis of Meaning and the Appeal of Religious Television*, Cresskill, NJ: Hampton Press.

Pitcavage, M. (1996), 'Bo Gritz and Almost Heaven', 'Patriot' Profile no. 2, http://www/militia-watchdog.org/gritz.htm.

Poole, T. (1998) 'Last days for China's forgotten Jews', *The Independent on Sunday*, 8 November, p. 17.

Popkin, R. H. (1980) 'Jewish messianism and Christian millennialism,' in *Culture and Politics: From Puritanism to the Enlightenment*, Berkeley: UCLA Press, pp. 67–91.

Potok, C. (1981) 'Culture confrontation in urban America: a writer's beginnings', in Jaye, M. C., and Watts, A. C. (eds), *Literature and the American Urban Experience: Essays in the City and Literature*, Manchester: Manchester University Press, pp. 161–9.

Preston, R. (1994) *The Hot Zone*, New York: Random House.

Raban, J. (1996) *Bad Land: An American Romance*, London: Picador.

Race, J. (1972) *War Comes to Long An*, Berkeley: University of California Press.

Redfield, J. and Adrienne, C. (1995), *The Celestine Prophecy: An Experiential Guide*, London: Bantam.

Reed, R. 'The quotable Pat Robertson', http:www.geocities.com/Capitol Hill/7027/quotes.html.

Reed, C. (1997) 'Prosecution "hid Unabomber huts"', *The Guardian*, 27 January, p. 2.

Reeves, P. (1996) 'The park-keepers in combat boots and black shirts', *The Independent on Sunday*, 13 October, p. 15.

Reeves, P. (1996) 'Lebed plans Russia's moral salvation', *The Independent on Sunday*, 30 June, p. 14.

Reichley, A. J. (1987) 'The evangelical and fundamentalist revolt', in Neuhaus, R. J. and Cromartie, M. (eds), *Piety and Politics: Evangelicals and Fundamentalists Confront the World*, Lanham, MD: University Press of America, pp. 69–99.

Reston Jun, J. (1984) *Sherman's March and Vietnam*, New York: Macmillan, p. 244.

Richmond, A. H. (1996) *Global Apartheid: Refugees, Racism and the New World Order*, New York: Oxford University Press.

Riesbrodt, M. (1990) *Pious Passions: The Emergence of Modern Fundamentalism in the United States and Iran*, Los Angeles: UCLA Press.

Robertson, P. (1991) *The New World Order*, Dallas: World Publishing.

Robertson, P. (1993) *The Turning Tide: The Fall of Liberalism and the Rise of Common Sense*, Dallas: World Publishing.

Robinson, D. (1985) *American Apocalypses: The Image of the End of the World in American Literature*, Baltimore: Johns Hopkins University Press.

Rölvaag, O. (1931) *Their Fathers' God*, trans. Trygve M. Ager, New York: Harper and Row.

Rose, S. and Schultze, Q. (1993) 'The evangelical awakening in Guatemala: fundamentalist impact on education and media', in Marty, M. E. and Appleby, R. S. (eds), *Fundamentalisms and Society: Reclaiming the Sciences, The Family, and Education*, Chicago, IL: University of Chicago Press.

Rushkoff, D. (1996), *Media Virus: Hidden Agendas in Popular Culture*, New York: Ballantyre.

Russo, S. (1994) *The Devil's Playground: Playing With Fire Can Get You Burned*, Eugene, OR: Harvest House.

Ruthven, M. (1989) *The Divine Supermarket: Shopping for God in America*, London: Vintage.

Ruthven, M. (1993a) 'The audio vision of God', *The Guardian*, 1 May, p. 31.

Ruthven, M. (1993b) *Rambo and Revelation*, London Review of Books, 9 September, pp. 14–15.

Ruthven, M. (1997) 'Made in the USA: the social practice and strange doctrine of the Nation of Islam', *Times Literary Supplement*, 30 May, pp. 6–7.

Samuel, R. (1995) 'The people with stars in their eyes', *The Guardian*, 23 November, p. 27.

Sandeen, E. R. (1970) *The Roots of Fundamentalism: British and American Millenarianism, 1800–1930*, Chicago: University of Chicago Press.

Sanford, C. L. (1955) 'An American pilgrim's progress', *American Quarterly*, V, Winter, pp. 297–310.

Schlesinger, A., Jun. (1993) *The Disuniting of America*, New York: W. W. Norton and Co.

Schultze, Q. J. (1991) *Televangelism and American Culture: The Business of Popular Religion*, Grand Rapids: Baker Book House.

Schwartz, H. (1990) *Century's End: A Cultural History of the Fin de Siècle from the 90s through the 1990s*, New York: Doubleday.

Schwartz, R. M. (1997) *The Curse of Cain: The Violent Legacy of Monotheism*, Chicago: University of Chicago Press.

Sherry, M. (1995) *In the Shadow of War: The United States Since the 1930s*, New Haven: Yale University Press.

Showalter, E. (1997) *Hystories: Hysterical Epidemics and Modern Culture*, London: Picador.

Simmons, W. S. (1979) 'Conversion from Indian to Puritan', *The New England Quarterly*, 52, pp. 197–218.

Slotkin, R. (1973) *Regeneration through Violence: The Mythology of the American Frontier: 1600–1860*, Middletown, CT: Wesleyan University Press.

Smith, C. (1998) *American Evangelicalism: Embattled and Thriving*, Chicago, IL: Chicago University Press.

Soyinka, W. (1994) 'Bloodsoaked quilt of Africa', *The Guardian*, 17 May, p. 20.

Stanniard, D. (1992) *American Holocaust: The Conquest of The New World*, New York: Oxford University Press.

Steele, J. (1996) 'Tyranny of the Taliban', *The Guardian*, 9 October, pp. 2, 3, 17.

Steinbeck, J. (1959) 'The leader of the people', *The Long Valley*, London: Heinemann, pp. 236–54.

Steinbeck, J. (1969) *To a God Unknown*, London: Corgi.

Steiner, G. (1990) 'Shadows at the heart of the carnival', *The Observer*, 20 February, p. 47.

Stern, K. S. (1997) *At One Upon the Plain: The America Militia Movement and the Politics of Hate*, Norman: University of Oklahoma Press.

Stoll, D. (1990) *Is Latin America Turning Protestant? The Politics of Evangelical Growth*, Berkeley: University of California Press.

Stone, N. (1994) 'And in Africa?', *The Sunday Times*, 17 April, p. 9.

Stone, O. (1998) 'It really is all a conspiracy', *The Sunday Times*, 8 November, p. 4.

Stone, R. (1973) *Dog Soldiers*, New York: Ballantine.

Storr, A. (1996) *Feet of Clay: A Study of Gurus*, London: Harper Collins.

Streiber, W. (1987) *Communion: A True Story*, New York: Morrow.

Strozier, C. B. (1994) *Apocalypse: On the Psychology of Fundamentalism in America*, Boston: Beacon Press.

Tarantino, Q. (1994) *Pulp Fiction: Three Stories About One Story*, London: Faber & Faber.

Tehranian, M. (1993) 'Fundamentalist impact on education and the media', *Fundamentalisms and Society*, pp. 313–40.

Theroux, L. (1998) *Louis Theroux's Weird Weekends*, BBC TV, 5 February.

Thompson, R. (1989) 'Attitudes towards homosexuality in the seventeenth-century New England colonies', *Journal of American Studies*, 23 (1), April, pp. 277–41.

Thomson, D. (1998) 'It's been a long, Lewinsky summer', *The Independent on Sunday*, 9 August pp. 1–2.

Traynor, I. (1998) 'Neo-Nazi tide sweeps through East Germany' and 'Neo-Nazis rule the east', *The Guardian*, 21 January, pp. 1 and 10.

Trilling, L. (1951) *The Liberal Imagination: Essays on Literature and Society*, Secker and Warburg.

Usborne, D. (1994) 'Yellow dogs have had their day', *The Independent on Sunday*, 20 November, p. 15.

Verdun, K. (1983) 'Our cursed natures: sexuality and the puritan conscience', *New England Quarterly*, 56, pp. 220–37.

Vidal, G. (1992), *Live from Golgotha*, London: Quality Paperbacks Direct.

Vulliamy, E. (1995) 'Cults 2', *Life*, 21 May, pp. 21–31.

Vulliamy, E. (1997a) 'Not kissing but telling', *The Guardian*, 20 October, pp. 6–7.

Vulliamy, E. (1997b) 'Uforia', *The Guardian*, 5 August, p. 2–3.

Wagar, W. W. (1982) *Terminal Visions: The Literature of Last Things*, Bloomington: Indiana University Press.

Walker, M. (1995) 'It all fits', *The Guardian*, 13 July, pp. 1–2.

Walker, M. (1994) 'America's reverse-gear revolution', *The Guardian*, 26 November, p. 14.

Walker, M. (1995) 'America's sullen gun culture made by angry white males', *The Guardian*, 26 April, p. 24.

Wavell, S. (1998), 'White mischief', *The Sunday Times*, 15 November, p. 7.

Webster, P. (1996) 'France turns to Internet to display looted artwork', *The Guardian*, 13 November, p. 15.

Whitfield, S. J. (1991) *The Culture of the Cold War*, Baltimore: Johns Hopkins.

Whittell, G. (1997) 'Why we beamed up, by middle-aged UFO fans', *The Times*, 29 March, p. 3.

Wiesel, E. (1991) 'Welcome stranger', *The Guardian*, 14 June, p. 3.

Wills, G. (1996) 'The Clinton scandals', *The New York Review*, 18 April, pp. 59–67.

Wills, G. (1995) 'The new revolutionaries', *The New York Review*, 10 August, pp. 50–5.

Wilson, C. R. (1980) *Baptized in Blood: The Religion of the Lost Cause, 1865–1920*, Athens: University of Georgia Press.

Wilson, C. R. (1992) 'The religion of the lost cause: ritual and organisation of the southern civil religion, 1865–1920', in Marty, M. (ed.), *Modern American Protestantism and Its World*, New York: K. G. Saur, pp. 42–62.

Wilson, E. (1968) 'The jumping-off place', *The American Jitters: A Year of the Slump*, New York: Farrar, Straus, pp. 249–60.

Wimmer, A. (1989) 'Rambo: American Adam, anarchist and archetypal frontier hero', in Walsh, J. and Aulich J. (eds), *Vietnam Images: War and Representation*, London: MacMillan, pp. 69–86.

Winerip, M. (1998) 'Judge dread', *The Guardian*, 9 September, pp. 2–3.

Wojcik, D. (1997) *The End of the World as We Know it: Faith, Fatalism and Apocalypse in America*, New York: New York University Press.

Wolf, E. (1982) *Europe and the People Without History*, Berkeley: UCLA Press.

Wollacott, M. (1994) 'A mad world of Rambos', *The Guardian*, 14 November, p. 20.

Wollacott, M. (1995a) 'Living in the age of terror', *The Guardian*, 22 April, p. 22.

Wollacott, M. (1995b) 'Keeping our faith in belief', *The Guardian*, 23 December, p. 20.

Wordsworth, W. 'A Jewish Family', in Hayden, J. O. (ed.), *The Poems*, 2 vols, New Haven: Yale University Press, 1981.

Wroe, N. (1997) 'Messiah in the wilderness', *The Guardian*, 19 June, p. 15.

Young, H. (1994) 'The rot will stop on the shores of the Atlantic', *The Guardian*, 10 November, p. 24.

Index

FUNDAMENTALISM IN AMERICA